D1417542

ETF
STRATEGIES
AND TACTICS

HEDGE YOUR PORTFOLIO
IN A CHANGING MARKET

LAURENCE M. ROSENBERG
NEAL T. WEINTRAUB
ANDREW S. HYMAN

New York   Chicago   San Francisco   Lisbon   London   Madrid   Mexico City
Milan   New Delhi   San Juan   Seoul   Singapore   Sydney   Toronto

The McGraw·Hill Companies

1 2 3 4 5 6 7 8 9 0   DOC/DOC   0 9 8

ISBN 978-0-07-149734-3
MHID 0-07-149734-X

This publication is designed to provide accurate and authoritative information in regard to the subject matter covered. It is sold with the understanding that neither the authors nor the publisher is engaged in rendering legal, accounting, futures/securities trading, or other professional service. If legal advice or other expert assistance is required, the services of a competent professional person should be sought.

> —*From a Declaration of Principles jointly adopted by a Committee*
> *of the American Bar Association and a Committee of Publishers*

McGraw-Hill books are available at special quantity discounts to use as premiums and sales promotions, or for use in corporate training programs. To contact a representative please visit the Contact Us pages at www.mhprofessional.com.

This book is printed on acid-free paper.

Library of Congress Cataloging-in-Publication Data

Rosenberg, Laurence M.
  ETF strategies and tactics / by Laurence M. Rosenberg, Neal T. Weintraub, and Andrew S. Hyman.
    p. cm.
  Includes bibliographical references and index.
  ISBN-13: 978-0-07-149734-3
  ISBN-10: 0-07-149734-X
  1. Exchange traded funds. 2. Hedge funds. 3. Portfolio management. I. Weintraub, Neal. II. Hyman, Andrew S. III. Title.
  HG6043.R67   2008
  332.63'27—dc22

2007046250

In memory of Joni Rosenberg;
To my children David, Danny, Michael, and Emma;
And to Jan, my wife,
your support and love mean everything.

Laurence M. Rosenberg

I dedicate this book to the Maggini family of Roviano, Italy. Their fortuitous courage and generosity helped my father survive a harrowing bail-out from his crippled bomber, as he returned from the famously troubled August 1943 raid on Regensburg. Without their bravery and commitment to humanity, my dad may not have survived the war.

Neal T. Weintraub

This book is dedicated to my lovely wife, Adiel, and my daughter, Julia—for their forbearance during the writing of this book.

It is also dedicated to my in-laws, Juana and Candido,
And to my parents, Judy and Leonard,
For helping take care of Julia (so this book could get finished.)

Andrew S. Hyman

CONTENTS

ACKNOWLEDGMENTS

I want to acknowledge my father, Buddy, who died too soon while I was still in school. Dad always encouraged me to be my own person and respect others, no matter who they were or where they stood on the societal ladder. My mother, Lorraine, gave me the support and encouragement to go into the futures business when almost everyone else told me I was crazy.

My thanks to Lee Stern who introduced me to the futures markets and brought me to the Chicago Board of Trade for my first job in the industry. And the members of the Chicago Mercantile Exchange who elected me to the board and ultimately to chairman. By their action the members of the CME allowed me the privilege of being a part in the development of this great financial institution.

To Neal and Andrew, I want to say that it is great working with both of you.

And finally my wife, Jan, and my children who encouraged me to do this project.

Laurence M. Rosenberg

Two outstanding schools are responsible for any competence or success I have enjoyed as an author who specializes in the discussion, explanation, and formation of futures and options trading strategies. To my undergraduate alma mater, Michigan State University, I owe the critical development of skills in sequential analysis which permit observation of trading strategies as logically interrelated consequences of macroeconomic, political, and social trends rather than as isolated serendipitous events. Subsequent graduate study at the Ohio State University, in journalism, forms the bulwark of a statistical analysis skill set which has proven to be invaluable in relating news and events in trading.

In the ever-changing world of exchange-traded funds (ETFs), the assistance of Mookesh Patel, who owns Chapter 14, "Design, Maintain, and Manipulate Your ETF Portfolio"; Michael Noonan; Mary Ambrose; and Charles Cottle made this book relevant and "tied to the market." Thanks also to Barrett Fiske for his market comments.

Several fine people stand out among the many good folks I encountered during my years at the Chicago Mercantile Exchange. Deborah Lenchard hired me as a CME instructor. Cyril Smith, an independent trader, further honed my computer skills in back-testing, and Wayne Church spotted trends a year before the public did.

In addition, an author in this discipline can be no better than his or her research sources; fortunately for me I can acknowledge some of the finest. The Globex Center of the Chicago Mercantile Exchange has been a gold mine of statistical information. In addition, three outstanding local libraries loom large in the composition of this book: the University of Chicago Library, and the public libraries of Evanston and Skokie, Illinois. A special thanks goes to the director of the Skokie Library, Carolyn Anthony.

The Everyday Thai Restaurant in the Rogers Park neighborhood of Chicago, Pick a Cup Coffee House in southwest Evanston, and the

Noodle Garden Restaurant also in Evanston must be acknowledged as homes away from home for this harried author, given that they provided safe, quiet havens where I could compose myself and my thoughts. But truly the best trading ideas are hatched out of the egg foo young at Tsing Tao on Green Bay Road in Wilmette. They taught me a valuable thing about trading: everybody's a client until they run out of money.

A special thanks goes to Jody Rosenbaum. This book would not have been possible without her kindness, patience, and word processing skills. She helped to keep me focused. And finally, to our editors Dianne Wheeler, Jeanne Glasser, and Jane Palmieri, who kept the troops in line as we marched toward our final objective.

Neal T. Weintraub

This book could not have been written without help from many people. First, I would like to thank Gary Walter, my colleague, who got me involved with this book and the world of ETFs, by referring me to his friend, Neal Weintraub—who was looking for a coauthor. Next, I need to thank my father, Leonard Hyman, who assisted by editing and critiquing much that I have written for this book.

A special thank you to all those ETF managers who were willing to give up their time to be interviewed for this book, as well as the hardworking marketing and PR people who helped make the interviews happen. Thanks to the following people:

iShares Germany: Andreas Fehrenbach, managing director of iShares Germany; Thomas Pohlmann, marketing director; and Mark Bubeck, principal in media relations at Barclays Global Investors.

XShares Advisors LLC and HealthShares: Jeffrey Feldman, chairman and founder of XShares; Marsha Zapson, the fund's communications director; and Patricia Sturms, senior vice president of financial communications at Edelman Worldwide.

American Stock Exchange: Scott Ebner, senior vice president of the ETF Marketplace at the American Stock Exchange; Bari Trontz, director of media relations at the American Stock Exchange; and Mary Chung, senior vice president of corporate communications at the American Stock Exchange.

Van Eck Global: Adam Phillips, director of ETF sales at Van Eck Securities Corporation; Adam Schiff of MacMillan Communications.

Dow Jones: John Prestbo, editor and executive director, Dow Jones Indexes and the chairman of Dow Jones Index Oversight Committee; Naomi Kim and Sybille Reitz of Dow Jones. Special thanks to William Wolff and Ralph Marish of First Manhattan Corporation for providing facilities and assistance that made this interview possible.

Keefe, Bruyette, and Woods (KBW): John Howard, director of research at KBW, and Siddharth Jain, vice president of equity research at KBW; Neil Shapiro, executive vice president of Intermarket Communications.

WisdomTree: Luciano Siracusano, III, director of research at WisdomTree, and Julie Silcox, director of marketing at WisdomTree; Nevin Reilly, of Sloane Public Relations.

MSCI: Dimitris Melas, executive director and head of EMEA equity and applied research at MSCI; Ann Taylor Reed, senior account executive, at the Abernathy MacGregor Group.

New York Stock Exchange: Lisa Dallmer, senior vice president of NYSE Euronext Group's ETF Listing and Trading Services; Mirtha Medina and Stephanie Scotto of the NYSE's Media Relations and Communications Department.

Thanks to Greg Newton, the editor of the NakedShorts Blog (nakedshorts.typepad.com), who provided great insight into both the ETF market and why many ETF look-alikes have considerable tracking error. Greg covers major financial stories before they hit the front pages of the major newspapers, and reading his blog should be a must for those in the business.

As cochairman, in 2006, of the Chicago Steering Committee of the Professional Risk Managers International Association, I have benefited from the advice of Timur Gök, professor at Northern Illinois University; Hilary Till, of Premia Capital (www.premiacap.com); and David Carman, former CBOE options trader and director of Business Network Chicago (www.bnchicago.org).

In addition, Ed Grebeck, head of PRMIA (Professional Risk Managers International Association) Stamford has been most informative in his comments on markets, credits, and investment bankers, which have helped shape my approach to this book.

I am also grateful for the advice I received from both David Koenig, PRMIA executive director, and Mark Abbott, a PRMIA board member and the managing director of investments at The Guardian Life Insurance Company of America.

Thanks to Dan Gary, a good friend and fellow PRMIA member, who has provided wise counsel on where this book should go and the issues facing foundations in making and managing investments, as well as the mechanics of retirement funds.

Thanks to David Sgorbati, CFP, vice president, financial advisor, and wealth management advisor at Merrill Lynch, and his able assistant, Ann Fredlin. Chris Cooper of Chris Cooper & Company convinced me of the need for this book during the Ninth Annual Financial Advisor Symposium in October 2006 in Chicago.

Thanks also to Robert Allen Daugherty, the circulation librarian, and Thomas Mantzakides, the friendly services supervisor, of the Richard J. Daley Library at the University of Illinois at Chicago for allowing me to make the best use of my alumnus membership.

A note of thanks is due to Curt Zuckert, associate director of the CME Group's Globex Learning Center, for allowing the authors to use the center's splendid library and research facilities.

Thanks to the following people at optionsXpress for allowing us to use their screen shots in Chapter 16: Philip Bennett, executive vice president and head of customer service; Dan O'Neil, executive vice president, futures; and Hillary Victor, corporate counsel.

Finally, this book could not have been written without the determination and effort of our editors at McGraw-Hill—Dianne Wheeler, Jeanne Glasser, and Jane Palmieri—who effectively brought together the efforts of three authors to create a coherent whole. I am very thankful for their involvement with this project. Jeanne's assistant, Morgan Ertel, was very helpful in handling the administrative matters related to publishing.

Andrew S. Hyman

INTRODUCTION

With many mutual funds having fallen into disrepute resulting from malfeasance, poor performance, or more importantly high expenses, there is a need for cost-effective, diversified, tax-efficient investment products. Exchange-traded funds (ETFs) can fill this role. An ETF is made up of a basket of securities that, unlike a mutual fund, trades continuously throughout the day. From one fund in 1993, the number is now approaching 700. The market has grown from a one billion dollar market in 1995 to over half a trillion dollars in October 2007. This book explains how to use ETFs in a systematic investment plan.

Chapter 1 provides an overview of the ETF market: what ETFs are, their rationale for existence, their origins, the growth of the market, and why investors use them to execute investment strategies.

When readers first encounter ETFs, they may wonder: why not invest in mutual funds—are ETFs all that special? Chapter 2 explains the differences. There are a number of similarities and, more importantly, differences between ETFs and mutual funds, one highly important aspect being that ETFs are continuously traded throughout the day, whereas mutual funds are valued only at the end of the day.

In order to make effective trading decisions, it is necessary to understand how ETFs are developed, what types of indexes are used, and, most importantly, the costs that determine returns. This material is covered in Chapter 3. Chapter 4 examines key aspects of ETF regulation and how the investor can use knowledge of regulation to spot red flags in funds and avoid tax problems. Chapter 5 helps the investor understand the tools that underlie every ETF and provides insight into how to apply that knowledge to trade effectively and minimize costs and taxes. Chapter 6 discusses ETFs and ETF look-alikes, giving an overview of the different fund categories.

Chapter 7 explains how to use the technical indicator of pivot points in trading ETFs. The most important parts of money management are covered in Chapter 8. Proper use of ETFs in a portfolio is based on the understanding of investment goals and the investor's ability to manage risk. Chapter 9 explains how to short ETFs as well as trade inverse ETFs for portfolio insurance and to mitigate volatility in a down market.

Chapter 10 discusses the considerable profit possibilities that are currently used by very few large investors. Options are very popular trading instruments. Chapter 11 explains the basic principles of options and options strategies and how to use ETF options. Chapter 12 encourages the analysis of the top stocks of any ETF that is being considered for investment purposes. It explains specific tools that can be used to determine an ETF's acceptability to the investor.

Chapter 13 requires that the investor come to terms with a realistic assessment of the markets and their volatility. Then create a portfolio of ETFs using Yahoo! Finance in Chapter 14. Chapter 15 shows investors how to trade European markets through ETFs and gain diversification for individual portfolios. In Chapter 16 we pull all our information together and show you how to actually use the information in a practical situation. Finally, a section consisting of one-on-one interviews with professionals from some of the major ETFs rounds out the general content of the book.

The book concludes with three appendixes that will serve as a ready reference for the ETF investor. Endnotes and a bibliography complete this new ETF title.

1

WHAT ARE ETFs, AND WHAT MAKES THEM GOOD INVESTMENTS?

I nvesting is challenging. Individual stocks and bonds go up and down, often rapidly and unpredictably. Trading commodities requires expertise most people don't have, not to mention a commodity trading account with a futures broker. Investors attempt to reduce risk by diversifying, not putting all their eggs into one basket: spreading risk over many investments. Investors usually turn to mutual funds for diversification, but mutual funds come with high costs—management fees, transaction costs, and unnecessary taxes— that devour profits. An investor who wants to buy commodities can't do it through a mutual fund at all. Finally, in the mid-1990s, Wall Street developed a way for investors to diversify their holdings into stocks, bonds, and commodities, in a low-cost, tax-efficient manner, with the creation of the exchange-traded fund (ETF), a basket of securities or commodities that trades as simply and inexpensively as shares in IBM, Procter & Gamble, or McDonald's.

What Is an ETF?

An ETF is usually made up of a fixed list of securities or commodities, with changes made to the list only in special circumstances. The ETF, unlike a mutual fund, trades (as a stock) continuously through-out the day—on an exchange. This contrasts with an open-ended mutual fund, where, at the close of the day, the shares are bought from, and sold to, the fund, itself.[1]

Origins of ETFs

ETFs sprang from the development of indexed mutual funds. In the late 1960s and early 1970s, academics and financial professionals realized that few investment managers outperformed the market. In 1969, pension fund managers at Wells Fargo Bank set up a pension fund that contained all the stocks in the New York Stock Exchange index in equal amounts. Since the fund's assets were fixed, no active management was needed, and the cost of running the fund was low. In 1974, another bank created an index fund based on the stocks in the S&P 500 Index, with holdings weighted by the market value of the stocks in the index, which turned out to be the successful model for index investing, because the S&P 500 is representative of the market as a whole. The index fund has one other advantage for investors. Because it rarely buys, or sells, the stocks held by the fund, it minimizes the taxes that its investors have to pay.

The index fund makes sense for investors in light of the factors that govern investment success: risk, returns, time, and costs. Investors cannot control risk, which means the only way to avoid the impacts of revolutions, crooked CEOs, or earthquakes is to not invest—at all. For that matter, the fund manager won't be able to come up with a portfolio of companies whose earnings always go up more than expected. Regarding returns, even if the investment manager can predict events, the manager can't predict how the market will react to those events—notably the returns that will be earned.

Time presents another problem for investors. Their time frames are determined by their age, whether they are just starting to work or about to retire. Every time the investor changes investment policies to meet life goals, the costs of the change reduce the returns. But, more importantly, small annual costs, over time, pile up and significantly reduce returns. What investors can choose is the cost of an investment policy. Cutting costs and compounding those savings over time can significantly improve an investor's chances of meeting investment goals.

For instance, Figure 1-1 contrasts returns after deducting expenses. Beginning with an investment of $10,000, Fund A is an

	Fund A	Fund B
Initial Rate of Return	8.00%	8.00%
Expense Ratio	0.20%	2.00%
Rate of Return after Expenses	7.80%	6.00%
Return after 25 Years	$65,384	$42,919

Figure 1-1   Investments and Returns after Expenses

index fund that tracks the S&P 500 that charges for expenses at the rate of 0.2 percent of assets per year. Fund B, an actively managed fund investing in S&P 500 companies, has an expense ratio of 2.0 percent of assets per year. (These are representative numbers.)

Over 25 years, the low-cost index fund will return $22,465 more than the expensive fund, while taking the same risks in the same market. These cost efficiencies have made index funds the standard by which funds are measured.

Few active managers can beat these numbers because of:

1. **Investment management fees:** It costs more to hire a manager and staff to find investment opportunities than it does to buy an index.

2. **Transaction costs:** Actively managed funds tend to engage in frequent trading. This creates higher transaction costs than those created by an index fund, which infrequently trades its holdings.

3. **Taxes:** The tendency of managers to turn over portfolios very quickly produces taxable events which are passed on to the fund's shareholders, when items are in taxable accounts. This denies fund holders the benefits of deferring taxes and taking taxable events when it suits their financial needs. In addition, if the volume of shares redeemed by current shareholders exceeds the volume of new fund purchases, the fund will have to sell shares in order to pay departing fund holders, which creates more tax obligations for long-term holders of portfolios. Therefore, remaining fund holders are penalized in terms of taxes for the decisions that others

made—mutual fund holders in this case do not have control over their fund-related taxes.

4. **Cash drag:** Money managers tend to hold cash when markets perform well, creating a drag on performance. They often seem short of cash to make bargain-priced purchases when markets fall.

5. **Sales charges/loads:** Fund holders often have to pay high fees to buy and redeem their shares in funds. In addition, fund shareholders pay distribution fees, which are used to help the fund sell its shares to new shareholders. Distribution fees, along with other fees, are explained in Chapter 2. Shareholders receive no benefit from the fund's expansion, though. The benefits accrue to fund managers who receive more investment management fees as the size of the fund grows.

Although indexing was derided at first, this concept, implemented successfully by the Vanguard Group, has made the Vanguard Index Trust the largest mutual fund in the United States. In addition, indexing, and its emphasis on low-cost, tax-efficient products, encouraged the development of ETFs.

Growth of the ETF Market

The success of index investing and passive investment strategies led to the development, in the early 1990s, of the first exchange-traded fund—the Standard & Poor's depository receipt or SPDR (pronounced "Spider"). The SPDR was structured as a unit investment trust, which is a mutual fund form that does not require a board of directors.[2] In addition, it didn't need an investment advisor, because the trustee built a mechanism into the trust so that its holdings would always match those of the S&P 500 Index.

The ETF market has grown rapidly since the launch of the SPDR. From 2 ETFs in 1995, with just over $1 billion in assets, to nearly 600 ETFs, with over half a trillion dollars in assets, in the United States alone in late 2007, the growth of the market has been explosive.[3] Over that same time ETFs have evolved from an instrument mainly used by stock market professionals to one widely used by retail investors. Cliff Weber, senior vice president for the ETF Marketplace at the American Stock Exchange, described the growth of ETF markets since the birth of the SPDR:

> The initial growth in the product line extended to more domestic products and international products both country-based funds, regions, sectors, etc. The U.S. market has been sliced and diced fairly well: large-cap, mid-cap, small-cap, growth/value, blend, various sectors. It is really getting down finer and finer in terms of the slicing and dicing of the indexes. Even internationally, there are individual countries, regions, sectors. There's fixed income, too.[4]

Product Varieties

Growth and innovation have continued. New ETFs now invest in gold mines, biotech companies, alternate energy firms, and commodities such as gold, silver, and oil and even commodity price indexes. In addition, new ETFs employ quantitative screening in an attempt to capture performance opportunities. As an example, financial experts, such as Robert Arnott, have put together indexes weighted not by market capitalization (the most common weighting method), but by fundamental factors, such as asset size. These new indexes may, in some cases, outperform the market capitalization weighted indexes over selected time frames.[5] (See Chapter 5 for more details.) More time is needed to see whether these quantitative funds will actually outperform in the marketplace, as opposed to in the laboratory. Sometimes, once a fund starts trading an index using quantitative rules, the outperformance of an index disappears, because the trading by the fund affects the marketplace.

Why Investors Are Embracing ETFs

Investors are flocking to ETFs for a number of reasons:

1. **Diversification:** ETFs allow investors to easily diversify portfolios and gain exposure to specific regions of the world, investment styles, or themes.

2. **Trading is like trading for stock:** ETFs provide diversification while they are traded like a share of stock. Investors can buy or sell shares in a mutual fund only once a day, after the markets have closed. In contrast, ETFs trade continuously throughout the day, allowing

investors to get in, and out, rapidly when the market makes large moves.

3. **Low cost:** ETFs are more cost-effective than mutual funds for a number of reasons. The first is that they tend to be index products, so they don't require active management. In addition, ETFs are bought and sold through brokers, so there is less need for marketing directly to investors, which is not the case with mutual funds. In general, brokerage fees for buying or selling an ETF will be smaller than those for mutual fund purchases and sales, unless the investor has very large mutual fund holdings. Another reason for the cost efficiency is that record keeping and customer service are handled by the broker, not the ETF developer—all securities are book entry—and no certificates are issued. Compare this to a mutual fund, which needs extensive infrastructure to handle record keeping and customer support.

4. **Tax efficiency:** Investors can control when they will pay capital gains taxes, or take tax losses, with ETFs. They incur the taxes only when they sell the shares. This contrasts with the situation of the mutual fund holder, whose tax position is determined by the actions of the mutual fund manager. First, when the manager faces a high level of redemptions by its shareholders, it sells shares held by the fund in order to pay back the investors. Selling those shares leads to capital gains taxes that the remaining shareholders must pay. Second, mutual fund managers like to sell shares to pay

capital gains dividends to investors each year, which creates taxes for investors. Third, when a new manager comes in to run the fund, that new manager may sell the old holdings to create a new portfolio, leading to capital gains taxes for the owners of the fund. With ETFs, small investors incur taxes only for their trading decisions and don't suffer from the actions of others.

5. **Hedging for the average investor:** ETFs allow investors to hedge portfolios (unlike mutual funds) because investors can short ETFs (which can't be done with mutual funds). This can allow them to protect portfolios from falling prices.[6] Federal law prohibits mutual fund managers from shorting stocks thereby denying investors the opportunity to profit from falling prices.[7] The concept of shorting ETFs is discussed in Chapter 9.

6. **Hedge fund strategies:** ETFs allow investors to imitate many hedge fund strategies, without the high costs imposed on hedge fund investors. ETFs allow investors to implement common hedge fund strategies such as market-neutral strategies, long-short equity, and other spreading strategies. (Market-neutral and spreading strategies are discussed in Chapter 10.)

7. **Investor protection:** Since ETFs trade on regulated exchanges, under the jurisdiction of the Securities and Exchange Commission (SEC), they provide investors with more protection than does investing in hedge funds.

8. **Liquid markets:** ETFs also benefit from liquid markets, which means that investors can buy, or sell, whenever they want to, without pushing the stock up or down. Of course, this doesn't mean that liquidity can't dry up and be missing in action when it's needed.

ETF Strategy

ETFs provide a low-cost, tax-efficient, diversified (risk-reducing) way to invest. They have changed the investment industry for the better, by allowing investors to keep more of their money because they pay fewer expenses to intermediaries (such as mutual fund management companies) and reduce tax payments, while at the same time creating diversified portfolios that meet the investors' needs.

2

ETFs COMPARED TO MUTUAL FUNDS

Today's investors can buy securities in two varieties: the individual securities (stocks or bonds) themselves or an investment fund that owns the securities for the investors. The real problem, though, has been figuring out how to buy a diversified, tax-efficient, liquid investment at a low cost. Or in simple language, how the investor can find an easily traded security that represents ownership of many stocks and bonds without spending a lot of money to do so and without paying unnecessary taxes. Investors who want to buy a diversified investment product, nowadays, have a choice: they can buy mutual funds or exchange-traded funds (ETFs).

Although mutual funds have been around far longer than ETFs, this does not mean that they are the better choice. Many mutual funds—especially actively managed funds with high cost structures—produce poorer returns for investors, after subtracting expenses and taxes. Investors can make an informed choice between investment vehicles only after examining the differences between ETFs and mutual funds. Investors who want low-cost, diversified, tax-efficient investments that they can buy, and sell, in the same way as ordinary stocks and bonds might discover that a well-structured ETF beats a similar mutual fund hands down, especially net of all the expenses that nobody likes to talk about.

The Investment Universe

Figure 2-1 illustrates the choices that investors in marketable securities can make that fit into two basic categories: debt (bonds) and equities(stocks).[1] Within each of the two categories, they can buy individual securities (such as a Treasury bond or 100 shares of AT&T), or they can buy shares in a registered investment company, which aggregates investors' funds in order to buy a portfolio of securities and then passes on to the investors any income or capital

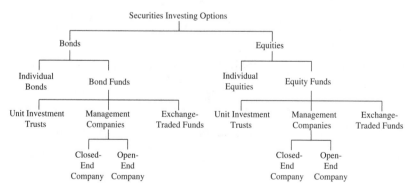

Figure 2-1 Securities Investing Options

gains earned in proportion to the investors' holdings in the fund. Investors should choose an investment instrument based on individual circumstances, such as willingness to incur or avoid risk, age before retirement, need for immediate income, and knowledge of the markets.

The Case for Individual Investing

One advantage of individual investing is that it allows investors to control their realization of capital gains that require payment of taxes. Individual investors decide when to buy, or sell, securities and can therefore choose if, and when, to incur capital gains taxes. This is in contrast to the situation of mutual fund share owners, who have to pay capital gains taxes whenever the fund sells one of its holdings at a profit. The individual investor can choose to defer the incidence of capital gains taxes, which is almost like getting a loan from Uncle Sam.

Another advantage of individual investing is that investors can buy and sell thinly traded securities. Most funds, because of their size, cannot, or will not, trade in less liquid securities, because they are unable to purchase the shares in meaningful amounts, or at advantageous prices, given that their actions may move the market.

Mutual fund managers are also limited in the types of investments they can make; for example, they can't short stocks, while the individual investor is able to go short on equities in a bear market and incorporate all sorts of derivatives into portfolio development.

In addition, the costs of individual investing tend to be lower than those of investment companies because an individual does not pay for:

- An investment manager to make investment decisions—the investor makes those decisions, perhaps in consultation with a broker

> **Trader's Notebook**
>
> Before discount brokers, individual investors might have had a hard time doing business at a lower cost than a mutual fund. Not so today.

- Mutual fund advertising designed to attract new fund subscribers
- Mutual fund service infrastructure
- Many other fees that a mutual fund charges its investors

Drawbacks of Individual Investing

Individual investment does have its drawbacks. Not having an investment advisor means that the investor has to put time, and effort, into choosing investments. Many people do not have the inclination, talent, or time to do so. They prefer to delegate the task to an investment manager. Yet choosing a manager requires time, and effort, as well.

Investment Companies

ETFs and mutual finds are investment companies. In both cases, many investors combine their resources, entrusting their money to a manager who chooses the investments for the fund. Managers come in two types: active and passive. The former buys and sells securities in order to realize investment objectives spelled out by the fund prospectus (such as investing in a combination of conservative stocks and bonds to produce above-average income or investing entirely in energy stocks or bonds of foreign countries). The latter does nothing more than make sure that the portfolio of securities in the fund tracks some prescribed index (such as ensuring that the fund owns all the stocks in the S&P 500 Index in the same proportion as they make up the index). Passive management requires less work and costs far less to support.

The Case for Investment Companies

Investment companies have raised hundreds of billions of dollars from millions of investors. Clearly they must have something to offer. And they do, although perhaps less now than in the past.

Record keeping

Investment companies do provide the information and record keeping necessary for income tax filings, at a cost, of course. Nowadays however, a full-service broker that provides good statements and tax information at year-end may serve the same purpose as the record-keeping function of a mutual fund. The irony, though, is that the investor has to pay many of these capital gains taxes resulting from the manager's actions, which may often lead to an unnecessary tax burden.

Professional management

Another supposed advantage of investment companies is their professional management of investments. In recent years, this ability of professional investment managers to consistently deliver superior risk-adjusted results has been called into question. While fund managers may beat their benchmarks periodically, only a small number of them consistently beat the index against which they are measured. In fact, they are more likely to underperform an index fund, such as an ETF, especially after expenses and taxes are subtracted from the returns.

Diversification at lower cost

Mutual funds provide a cost-effective way to buy a broad index of stocks at a reasonable price, especially for small investors who would incur odd-lot charges. For instance, it would take a lot of work for an individual investor to buy the companies that make up the S&P 500 Index, especially in the same proportion as they appear in the index. Still, while funds make it easy to buy the equivalent of a broad list of stocks and bonds, ETFs do it at a lower cost.

Lower transaction costs for large blocks of stock

Theoretically, investment companies should have lower transaction costs than individual investors. They buy in bulk, after all. This ability, however, contains a double-edged sword. In order to get those low transaction costs by transacting in large blocks, investment funds may shun less liquid, or less widely traded, investments, which reduces the chance of obtaining the outperformance possible from the pricing inefficiencies that may exist in less traded securities. In addition, the low transaction costs may encourage managers to overtrade and run up capital gains and related taxes for the fund holders.

Drawbacks of Investment Companies

Investment companies have some major drawbacks, the main one being expenses. The often high expenses of investment companies can reduce, or even eliminate, investment returns. They may even cause investors to lose money in rising markets. Investment managers are not compensated based on their performance, but rather for the size of assets under their management and their ability to generate fees. The topic of fees and taxes is covered later in this chapter.

Types of Investment Companies

Figure 2-2 shows the classification of registered investment companies according to the 1940 Investment Company Act (the primary

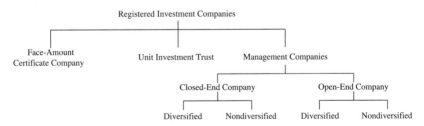

Figure 2-2 Registered Investment Companies

law regulating investment companies in the United States). Figure 2-3 shows the legal definitions of the different types of companies, as provided by the act. Figure 2-4 lists key characteristics and terms that are necessary for understanding the differences between the various types of mutual funds and ETFs.

Type of Investment Company	Description of the Company under the Investment Company Act of 1940
Face-Amount Certificate Company	An investment company that is engaged or proposes to engage in the business of issuing face-amount certificates of the installment type, or which has been engaged in such business and has any such certificate outstanding.*
Unit Investment Trust	An investment company that (1) is organized under a trust indenture, contract of custodianship or agency, or similar instrument; (2) does not have a board of directors, and, (3) issues only redeemable securities, each of which represents an undivided interest in a unit of unspecified securities, but does not include a voting trust.
Management Company	Any investment company other than a face amount certificate company or a unit investment trust. (1) Open-end company refers to a management company that is offering for sale or has outstanding any redeemable security of which it is the issuer. (2) Closed-end company refers to any management company other than an open-end company. Management companies are divided into diversified and nondiversified companies. (a) Diversified company refers to a management company which meets the following requirements: at least 75 percent of the value of its total assets is represented by cash and cash items (including receivables), government securities, securities of other investment companies, and other securities for the purposes of this calculation limited in respect of any one issuer to an amount not greater in value than 5 percent of the value of the total assets of such management company and to not more than 10 percent of the outstanding voting securities of such issuer. (b) Nondiversified company refers to any management company other than a diversified company.

*Rarely used today.

Figure 2-3   Types of Investment Companies under the Investment Company Act of 1940

Source: Investment Act 1940 Title 1. Sections 4 and 5.

Closed-End Fund: An *investment company*, legally known as a "closed-end company," that sells a fixed number of shares at one time in an initial public offering, which then trade on a secondary exchange, such as the New York Stock Exchange. The price of a closed-end fund is based on supply of, and demand for, the fund's shares, which may not correlate with the value of the securities it holds. Closed-end funds may trade at premiums, or discounts, to the values of their portfolios. A closed-end fund does not continuously offer its shares for sale, nor is it required to redeem them or have a managed portfolio.

Exchange-Traded Fund (ETF): An *investment company*, set up either as an *open-end company* or a *unit investment trust (UIT)*. Its shares (underlain by a basket of securities) trade intraday on a stock exchange at prices determined in the market. ETFs are bought or sold through brokers the same way that publicly traded companies are.

ETFs differ from other *open-end companies* and *unit investment trusts* because their shares trade only on regulated exchanges, and the shares can be redeemed only from the fund in large blocks (such as 50,000 shares).

Investment Company: A company (corporation, business trust, partnership, or limited liability company) that pools investors' funds and invests those funds in securities designed to meet the company's stated objectives.

Mutual Fund: The common name for an *open-end* investment company. It pools money from investors and invests those funds in a portfolio of securities (such as stocks, bonds, and money-market instruments) in a way designed to meet the fund's financial goals, such as growth, or income, capital preservation, or other targets. A mutual fund issues redeemable shares that investors buy either directly from the fund or through a broker. Each mutual fund share provides fractional ownership of the fund's portfolio. Each share can be redeemed from the fund at its net asset value (NAV), which is the total value of the fund's assets minus its liabilities, divided by the number of shares of the fund outstanding:

$$\text{Net asset value (NAV)} = \frac{\text{Assets} - \text{Liabilities}}{\text{Shares outstanding}}$$

For example, say a mutual fund has assets of $20,000, liabilities of $1,000, and 1,000 shares outstanding. The net asset value is:

$$\text{Net asset value} = \frac{\$20,000 - \$1,000}{1,000 \text{ shares}}$$

$$= \frac{\$19,000}{1,000 \text{ shares}}$$

$$= \$19 \text{ per share}$$

Open-End Company: Legal name for a *mutual fund*. Type of investment company that will buy back (redeem) its shares from investors on any business day.

Unit Investment Trust (UIT): A type of investment company that buys and holds a fixed number of shares until the trust terminates. A UIT typically makes a one-time public offering of a fixed number of units.

A UIT terminates and dissolves on a date established when the UIT is set up. When the trust dissolves, the proceeds are paid to shareholders. UITs do not trade their portfolios. UIT shares can be redeemed, as can those of a mutual fund, on any business day.

Figure 2-4 Investment Company Terminology

Sources: U.S. Securities and Exchange Commission, "Invest Wisely: An Introduction to Mutual Funds," modified October 12, 2006, www.sec.gov/investor/pubs/inwsmf.htm; Investment Company Institute, "A Guide to Understanding Mutual Funds" (Washington, D.C.: Investment Company Institute, 2006), www.ici.org.

Following is a brief classification of the types of companies and their characteristics (see Figure 2-4). (This list excludes the *face-amount certificate company* which is not widely found today.)

Unit investment trust (UIT)

An investment company that buys and holds a fixed number of shares until the trust terminates is a *unit investment trust* (UIT). A UIT typically makes a one-time public offering of a fixed number of units, and it terminates and dissolves on a date established when the UIT is set up. When the trust dissolves, the proceeds are paid to shareholders. The trust provides the sponsor with a convenient vehicle to package a group of easily marketed stocks, often with a theme, such as electric utilities or telecommunication manufacturers. UITs do not trade their portfolios, although the trust agreement may permit changes in the portfolio for unusual circumstances. UIT shares can be redeemed, as can those of a mutual fund, on any business day. The trusts offer rigid portfolios, low costs, and a limited life span. The purchaser of a trust who holds the trust shares to date of dissolution will incur taxes on profit or loss at the time of dissolution.

Management company

By process of elimination, a management company is an investment company that is neither a face-amount certificate company nor a unit investment trust. Given the lack of face-amount certificate companies, today, management companies are investment companies that are not unit investment trusts. Management companies fall into two basic categories: closed-end and open-end, which are further subclassified as diversified and nondiversified companies.

These categories of management companies are explained below and with the aid of Figure 2-5, which provides a graphic depiction of the management company universe.

- **Closed-end company (fund):** Sells a fixed number of shares at one time in an initial public offering. The shares trade on a stock exchange afterwards, in the same manner as any other stock. The closed-end fund may raise additional money, in the future, by making another offering of its stock to its shareholders or to the public at large. The fund might have the power to raise money by selling senior securities, such as preferred stock, too, which mutual funds cannot do. The price of a closed-end company's shares is based on

	Open-End	Closed-End
Diversified	Commonly known as a mutual fund.	Closed-end fund.
Nondiversified	Subject to double taxation. (Taxation at fund level and at shareholder level.)	Subject to double taxation. (Taxation at fund level and at shareholder level.)

Figure 2-5 Types of Management Companies

supply of, and demand for, *its* shares, which may not depend on the value of the securities it holds.

Closed-end companies may trade at premiums, or discounts, to the values of their portfolios. This means that shareholders cannot be assured that the price they pay or receive when buying or selling the stock in the fund equals the market value of the investments underlying the shares. A closed-end company does not continuously offer its shares for sale, nor is it required to redeem them or to have a managed portfolio. Because it is not required to redeem shares at the request of its owners, the closed-end fund has greater latitude in its investment policy than does an open-end fund.

It can, prudently, own less liquid investments (because it does not have to worry about how to sell them at a moment's notice when shareholders want their money out of the fund) and it can take a longer view (because it need not fear losing assets to redemption if the investment policy does not work well in the short term). Against these advantages, there is the drawback that the market price of the fund's shares may reflect any current investor dissatisfaction with investment policy.

• **Open-end company:** Legal name for a *mutual fund*, the most popular investment fund vehicle for individual investors. This type of investment company will buy back (redeem) its shares from investors during any business day. Generally, open-end funds offer new shares continuously, but a few funds close the fund to new shareholders because the funds have become too big to manage effectively.

- **Diversified company:** Has at least 75 percent of the value of its assets in cash, cash items (including receivables), government securities, securities of other investment companies, and other securities. No one security can constitute more than 5 percent of the total assets under management, and the fund cannot own more than 10 percent of the outstanding voting securities of one issuer. Being diversified, however, does not mean that the fund has a portfolio that resembles the market as a whole. The fund might concentrate a large part of its investments in sectors that the managers consider attractive. The biggest mutual funds—such as Magellan and Investment Company of America—are open-end and diversified.

- **Nondiversified company:** If a management company isn't diversified, then it is a nondiversified company; at least that is the way the rules read. Such a company (fund) may specialize in one industry or one region of the world and may have large holdings in a few securities. Some look more like holding companies or business development enterprises masquerading as investment funds. The classification may mislead investors because a fund that meets the legal definition of "diversified" may have a portfolio of investments that makes a concentrated bet on certain industries or market developments. In that sense, it has not diversified risk for its owners, even if it does not fit into the legal definition of nondiversified.

Figure 2-5 categorizes management companies into four groups. The lower range of the grid, shaded in gray, highlights those structures that are not diversified. Investors must pay attention to this classification because nondiversified funds are subject to taxation at *both* the fund *and* the individual investor level, if the fund does not follow Internal Revenue Service (IRS) requirements. These same comments apply to ETFs and their taxation. Some investors think that if their funds are in a nontaxable account that taxes don't matter, but they are wrong. While they may not pay taxes at the individual level, the fact is that a nondiversified fund can incur taxes at the corporate level, which means that less money will flow to investors.

For this reason, it is very important to determine whether investments are in diversified or nondiversified funds. This may require the advice of a tax professional or, at the very least, a perusal of IRS regulations relating to the definition of diversified investment companies in order to avoid investing in a product whose profit will be eaten away by avoidable taxes.[2] Admittedly, an experienced and well-run management company will not subject its shareholders to avoidable taxation, but with the proliferation of funds nowadays, some management companies may not qualify as experienced, or well run. (The importance of this diversification and its effect on taxes is discussed in more depth in Chapter 4.)

How Do Exchange-Traded Funds Fit into the Picture?

An exchange-traded fund (ETF) is an investment company, set up either as an open-end company or a unit investment trust (UIT). It has shares (underlain by a basket of securities) that trade intraday on a stock exchange at prices determined in the market. ETFs are bought or sold through stockbrokers the same way that the shares of publicly traded companies are.

ETFs differ from other open-end companies and unit investment trusts, because the shares trade only on regulated exchanges, and the shares can be redeemed from the fund only in large blocks (such as 50,000 shares). (More details about the creation and mechanics of exchange-traded funds are addressed in Chapter 3.)

One form of ETF structure, but not a registered investment company, is the exchange-traded *grantor trust*. An investor in a grantor trust buys a basket of securities and receives all the voting rights and dividends associated with those securities.

The most commonly traded grantor trust is the *HOLDR* (holding company depository receipt) developed by Merrill Lynch. The shares of a HOLDR represent an interest in a portfolio of stocks that is focused on a particular industry or economic sector. They must be purchased in 100-share units. If a stock disappears from the market (as in a cash buyout), it is not replaced in the HOLDR. The shareholder can redeem the HOLDR for a modest fee and receive possession of all the individual components of the trust. The tax treatment of a grantor trust is the same as the individual shares, in that taxes are incurred only because of sale of the HOLDR or sale or buyout of a component, not because of the actions of an investment manager, as may occur with a mutual fund. The HOLDR provides transparency, liquidity, and easy diversification.

Expenses

Probably the most important difference between mutual funds (whether actively managed or passive) and ETFs is cost. In short, investors seeking low-cost, diversified investments should choose ETFs in most cases. If the investor can choose between two investments in comparable products, for example an actively managed mutual fund and an ETF that both specialize in ownership of large capitalization stocks, there is a strong likelihood that their investment performances will be similar but that the actively managed mutual fund's costs will be so much higher that even if it beats the investment performance of the ETF, its net profit for shareholders, after fees and taxes, will most likely fall short of that of the ETF.

To understand how costs can be a decisive factor in investing, consider Figure 2-6, which compares costs of mutual fund investments with those of ETFs, based on the fees described in detail in Figure 2-7. (Read Figure 2-6 from left to right to see how expenses reduce the returns for investors.)

The investor who decides to buy shares in a mutual fund first has to pay the *front-end load*, a commission to the person who sells the fund, which can be up to 8.75 percent of the initial investment, and a *purchase fee*, which a fund company can charge in addition to a front-end load. The investor who decides to buy an ETF pays

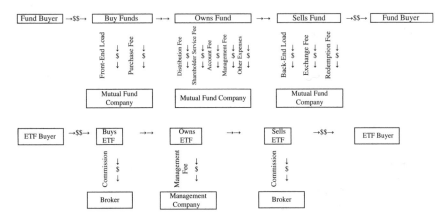

Figure 2-6 Mutual Funds Have More Ways of Reducing Investors' Returns Than Do ETFs

12b-1 Fees: Mutual fund fees, named after the SEC rule that spawned them, that investors pay to cover the costs of marketing and selling their fund's shares to *new* fund buyers, and sometimes to cover the cost of providing shareholder services. 12b-1 fees consist of *distribution fees* and *shareholder service fees*. If a fund has a 12b-1 fee, it will be disclosed in the fund's prospectus in the fee table. Although the SEC does not regulate 12b-1 fees, the National Association of Securities Dealers (NASD) limits 12b-1 fees to no more than 1 percent of a fund's assets.

Account Fee: Fee that some funds require investors to pay to keep an account with that fund. Investors usually pay account fees when the balance in their account falls below a certain level.

Back-End Load: *Sales charge* (also known as a *deferred sales charge*) that investors pay when they redeem (sell) their mutual fund shares. The fund uses the amount paid to compensate brokers. (See *sales charge.*)

Commission: Fee that an investor pays to a stock broker to buy or sell securities.

Contingent Deferred Sales Load: Type of *back-end load*. Investors pay this charge when they redeem (sell) their shares. These charges may decline over time. (See *sales charge.*)

Deferred Sales Charge: See *back-end load*.

Distribution Fees: Fees that the fund's current investors pay to the fund to market the fund to *new* investors. These fees cover expenses for marketing and selling the shares of the fund, which may include advertising costs, compensation to brokers and others who sell shares in the fund, as well as the cost of printing and mailing prospectuses and sales literature to new investors. These are one form of *12b-1 fees*. Although the SEC does not regulate the size of distribution fees, the NASD limits distribution fees to 0.75 percent of a fund's assets. (See *12b-1 fees.*)

(Continues)

Figure 2-7 Types of Investment Company Expenses

Exchange Fee: A charge that investors may pay when they transfer from one fund to another within the same family of funds.

Front-End Load: A *sales charge* that investors pay to the fund when they buy a fund's shares. The fund uses the money received to compensate brokers who sell the fund's shares. Front-end loads reduce the amount of money that the investor has to purchase fund shares. For example, consider an investor who has $1,000 to invest in a fund with a 5 percent front-end load. After paying the load of 5 percent ($50), the investor has only $950 to buy fund shares. (See also *sales charge*.)

Load: See *sales charge*.

Management Fee: The amount investors pay to the investment advisor of the fund to manage the fund's portfolio.

Operating Expenses: The amount it costs to run a fund, including *management fees, 12b-1 fees,* and *other expenses*.

Other Expenses: These are shareholder service expenses that are not covered by *management fees* or *12b-1 fees,* such as custodial expenses, legal expenses, accounting expenses (such as the independent audit), transfer agent expenses, and other administrative expenses.

Purchase Fee: The amount that some funds charge investors to buy shares. This is not the same as, and may be in addition to, a *front-end load*.

Redemption Fee: The amount that some funds charge shareholders to redeem (sell) their shares. These fees, which are paid to the fund, are not the same, and may be in addition to, a *back-end load*, which is used to compensate a broker. The SEC limits redemption fees to 2 percent.

Sales Charge (or "**Load**"): The amount that investors pay when they buy or redeem (sell) shares in a mutual fund. A *front-end load* is paid when purchasing a fund, and a *back-end* load is paid when an investor redeems shares. SEC rules do not limit the sizes of sales loads, but the NASD's rules prohibit sales loads from exceeding 8.5 percent and mandate that they must be lower depending on other fees and charges that the fund imposes on investors.

Shareholder Service Fees: Fees that investors pay to the fund to respond to their inquiries and provide them with information about their investments. These fall under the category of *12b-1 fees*. Although the SEC does not regulate *12b-1 fees*, the NASD limits shareholder service fees to 0.25 percent of a fund's assets. (See *12b-1 fees*.)

Figure 2-7   Types of Investment Company Expenses (*Continued*)

only a brokerage commission, which can be very low at a discount broker.

Next comes the ongoing expense of fund ownership. The mutual fund owner may have to pay up to five different fees simply to own the fund. The *distribution fee* is the most difficult to justify. The current owner of the fund has to pay a fee to the fund so that the fund can market itself to new investors. These expenditures in no way benefit the current shareholder, because bringing in new shareholders will not create higher returns, and in many ways they may make the fund more unwieldy, which may keep it from making advantageous investments.

Shareholder service fees compensate the fund for servicing its investors, including answering phone calls and mailing out documentation, such as annual reports. *Account fees* are usually leveled on accounts with small balances, because these small accounts may have costs that are disproportionate to their size. *Other expenses* typically cover such items as paying for the annual audit and other record keeping.

With an ETF, the only charge is a *management fee*. ETF management fees for indexed products can be less than 0.10 percent of assets, a fraction of what mutual funds charge. One reason that ETFs can charge so little is that they have little infrastructure compared to the conventional mutual fund. Because the shares are held in book entry, an electronic record, by the broker, the broker is the point of contact with the investor, and the broker's infrastructure services the investor. Given that ETFs (to date) have been index funds, or some sort of tracking fund, an ETF does not bear the costs associated with actively managed mutual funds. The ETF is a very lean structure, which shows up in low costs.

The mutual fund investor who sells shares in the fund faces a whole raft of fees. The *back-end load* is a sales charge imposed when the investor sells shares. The mutual fund company uses it to compensate brokers and others who sell the company's products. Some funds assess an *exchange fee* when investors exchange one fund for another within the same mutual fund family. In addition, mutual funds may charge *redemption fees* of up to 2 percent when investors redeem their shares—on top of any other fees the fund charges.

Figure 2-8 summarizes the fees that could be assessed on mutual fund shareholders in comparison to ETF holders. There are nine potential fees for a mutual fund investor and two for the ETF investor. With all those expenses, compared to ETFs, mutual funds have to perform extraordinarily well in order to produce better profits than ETFs.

> **Trader's Notebook**
>
> Exchanges within the same mutual fund family, essentially selling one fund and buying another, are subject to income or capital gains taxes. The amount of these taxes depends on the length of the holding of the initial investment.

Think of it this way. The investor buys a mutual fund, keeps it for 10 years, and pays for expenses that add up to about 17 percent of the original investment over that time period, or an average of 1.7 percent per year. The value of the investment (dividends plus capital gains) goes up by about 9 percent per year, the same as the market as a whole, before expenses are deducted. That leaves the investor with a return of 7.3 percent per year before taxes. Instead, the investor could buy an ETF, and pay brokerage and management fees that add up to maybe 4 percent, or 0.4 percent per year. If the ETF's portfolio produces the same 9 percent per year before expenses, the investor nets 8.6 percent per year. In order for the mutual fund shareholder to come out ahead, the mutual fund manager would have to produce performance of 1.2 percent over that of the market, on a steady basis. Not an easy thing to do.

The example in Figure 2-9 starts with the case of an investor who has $10,000 to invest and four choices: (1) a mutual fund with a

Fee Type	Mutual Fund	Exchange-Traded Fund
Distribution Fees	 ☹	
Account Fee	 ☹	
Commissions		 ☹
Exchange Fee	 ☹	
Management Fee	 ☹	 ☹
Other Expenses	 ☹	
Purchase Fee (Not a Front-End Load)	 ☹	
Redemption Fee	 ☹	
Sales Charge (Load) Including Front-End Loads, Contingent Deferred Sales Charges, and Back-End Loads	 ☹	
Shareholder Service Fees	 ☹	
Number of Potential Fees	9	2

Figure 2-8 Funds and Their Fees

Case 1: 0% Return

	Mutual Fund with Front-End Load	Mutual Fund with Back-End Load	No-Load Fund	Exchange-Traded Fund
1 Initial Investment	$10,000.00	$10,000.00	$10,000.00	$10,000.00
2 Front-End Load (5.75%)	$575.00	$0.00	$0.00	$0.00
3 Commission ($20)	$0.00	$0.00	$0.00	$20.00
4 Total Purchasing Costs: (2) + (3)	$575.00	$0.00	$0.00	$20.00
5 Net Equity: (1) − (4)	$9,425.00	$10,000.00	$10,000.00	$9,980.00
6 Rate of Return Necessary to Recoup Initial Investment: (4)/(5)	6.10%	0.00%	0.00%	0.20%
7 Rate of Return on Net Equity (0.0%)	0.00%	0.00%	0.00%	0.00%
8 Dollar Value of Return on Net Equity: (7) × (5)	$0.00	$0.00	$0.00	$0.00
9 Value of Investment after Return: (5) + (8)	$9,425.00	$10,000.00	$10,000.00	$9,980.00
10 Rate of Return on Initial Investment: [(9) − (1)]/(1)	−5.75%	0.00%	0.00%	−0.20%
11 Rate of Return Necessary to Recoup Initial Investment: [(1) − (9)]/9	6.10%	0.00%	0.00%	0.20%
12 Distribution Fees (12b-1) (0.75%): 0.75% × (9)	$70.69	$75.00	$75.00	$0.00
13 Shareholder Service Fees (12b-1) (0.25%): 0.25% × (9)	$23.56	$25.00	$25.00	$0.00
14 Mutual Fund Management Fee (1.0%): 1.0% × (9)	$94.25	$100.00	$100.00	$0.00
15 ETF Management Fee (0.15%): 0.15% × (9)	$0.00	$0.00	$0.00	$14.97
16 Other Expenses (0.50%): 0.50% × (9)	$47.13	$50.00	$50.00	$0.00
17 Total Expenses: (12) + (13) + (14) + (15) + (16)	$235.63	250	250	14.97
18 Available Equity after Expenses: (9) − (17)	$9,189.37	$9,750.00	$9,750.00	$9,965.03
19 Rate of Return on Initial Investment: [(18) − (1)]/(1)	−8.11%	−2.50%	−2.50%	−0.35%
20 Rate of Return Necessary to Recoup Initial Investment: [(1) − (18)]/18	8.82%	2.56%	2.56%	0.35%
21 Back-End Load (5.0%): 5.0% × (18)	$0.00	$487.50	$0.00	$0.00
22 Redemption Fee (2.0%): 2.0% × (18)	$183.79	$195.00	$195.00	$0.00
23 Commission ($20)	$0.00	$0.00	$0.00	$20.00

32

	Mutual Fund with Front-End Load	Mutual Fund with Back-End Load	No-Load Fund	Exchange-Traded Fund
24 Total Sales Costs: (21) + (22) + (23)	$183.79	$682.50	$195.00	$20.00
25 Amount Available after Sale: (18) − (24)	$9,005.58	$9,067.50	$9,555.00	$9,945.03
26 Final Return on Initial Investment: [(25) − (1)]/(1)	−9.94%	−9.33%	−4.45%	−0.55%
27 Rate of Return Necessary to Recoup Initial Investment: [(1) − (25)]/25	11.04%	10.28%	4.66%	0.55%

Case 2: 10% Return

	Mutual Fund with Front-End Load	Mutual Fund with Back-End Load	No-Load Fund	Exchange-Traded Fund
1 Initial Investment	$10,000.00	$10,000.00	$10,000.00	$10,000.00
2 Front-End Load (5.75%)	$575.00	$0.00	$0.00	$0.00
3 Commission ($20)	$0.00	$0.00	$0.00	$20.00
4 Total Purchasing Costs: (2) + (3)	$575.00	$0.00	$0.00	$20.00
5 Net Equity: (1) − (4)	$9,425.00	$10,000.00	$10,000.00	$9,980.00
6 Rate of Return Necessary to Recoup Initial Investment: (4)/(5)	6.10%	0.00%	0.00%	0.20%
7 Rate of Return on Net Equity (10.0%)	10.00%	10.00%	10.00%	10.00%
8 Dollar Value of Return on Net Equity: (7) × (5)	$942.50	$1,000.00	$1,000.00	$998.00
9 Value of Investment after Return: (5) + (8)	$10,367.50	$11,000.00	$11,000.00	$10,978.00
10 Rate of Return on Initial Investment: [(9) − (1)]/(1)	3.68%	10.00%	10.00%	9.78%
11 Rate of Return Necessary to Recoup Initial Investment: [(1) − (9)]/9	N/A	N/A	N/A	N/A
12 Distribution Fees (12b-1) (0.75%): 0.75% × (9)	$77.76	$82.50	$82.50	$0.00
13 Shareholder Service Fees (12b-1) (0.25%): 0.25% × (9)	$25.92	$27.50	$27.50	$0.00
14 Mutual Fund Management Fee (1.0%): 1.0% × (9)	$103.68	$110.00	$110.00	$0.00

(Continues)

Figure 2-9 Impact of Expense Funds on Returns

Case 2: 10% Return

	Mutual Fund with Front-End Load	Mutual Fund with Back-End Load	No-Load Fund	Exchange-Traded Fund
15 ETF Management Fee (0.15%): 0.15% × (9)	$0.00	$0.00	$0.00	$16.47
16 Other Expenses (0.50%): 0.50% × (9)	$51.84	$55.00	$55.00	$0.00
17 Total Expenses: (12) + (13) + (14) + (15) + (16)	$259.20	$275.00	$275.00	$16.47
18 Available Equity after Expenses: (9) − (17)	$10,108.30	$10,725.00	$10,725.00	$10,961.53
19 Rate of Return on Initial Investment: [(18) − (1)]/(1)	1.08%	7.25%	7.25%	9.62%
20 Rate of Return Necessary to Recoup Initial Investment: [(1) − (18)]/18	N/A	N/A	N/A	N/A
21 Back-End Load (5.0%): 5.0% × (18)	0	536.25	0	0
22 Redemption Fee (2.0%): 2.0% × (18)	$202.17	$214.50	$214.50	$0.00
23 Commission ($20)	$0.00	$0.00	$0.00	$20.00
24 Total Sales Costs: (21) + (22) + (23)	$202.17	$750.75	$214.50	$20.00
25 Amount Available after Sale: (18) − (24)	$9,906.13	$9,974.25	$10,510.50	$10,941.53
26 Final Return on Initial Investment: [(25) − (1)]/(1)	−0.94%	−0.26%	5.11%	9.42%
27 Rate of Return Necessary to Recoup Initial Investment: [(1) − (25)]/25	0.95%	0.26%	N/A	N/A

Case 3: 10% Loss

	Mutual Fund with Front-End Load	Mutual Fund with Back-End Load	No-Load Fund	Exchange-Traded Fund
1 Initial Investment	$10,000.00	$10,000.00	$10,000.00	$10,000.00
2 Front-End Load (5.75%)	$575.00	$0.00	$0.00	$0.00
3 Commission ($20)	$0.00	$0.00	$0.00	$20.00
4 Total Purchasing Costs: (2) + (3)	$575.00	$0.00	$0.00	$20.00

5	Net Equity: (1) − (4)	$9,425.00	$10,000.00	$10,000.00	$9,980.00
6	Rate of Return Necessary to Recoup Initial Investment: (4)/(5)	6.10%	0.00%	0.00%	0.20%
7	Rate of Return on Net Equity (−10.0%)	−10.00%	−10.00%	−10.00%	−10.00%
8	Dollar Value of Return on Net Equity: (7) × (5)	−$942.50	−$1,000.00	−$1,000.00	−$998.00
9	Value of Investment after Return: (5) + (8)	$8,482.50	$9,000.00	$9,000.00	$8,982.00
10	Rate of Return on Initial Investment: [(9) − (1)]/(1)	−15.18%	−10.00%	−10.00%	−10.18%
11	Rate of Return Necessary to Recoup Initial Investment: [(1) − (9)]/9	17.89%	11.11%	11.11%	11.33%
12	Distribution Fees (12b-1) (0.75%): 0.75% × (9)	$63.62	$67.50	$67.50	$0.00
13	Shareholder Service Fees (12b-1) (0.25%): 0.25% × (9)	$21.21	$22.50	$22.50	$0.00
14	Mutual Fund Management Fee (1.0%): 1.0% × (9)	$84.83	$90.00	$90.00	$0.00
15	ETF Management Fee (0.15%): 0.15% × (9)	$0.00	$0.00	$0.00	$13.47
16	Other Expenses (0.50%): 0.50% × (9)	$42.41	$45.00	$45.00	$0.00
17	Total Expenses: (12) + (13) + (14) + (15) + (16)	$212.07	$225.00	$225.00	$13.47
18	Available Equity after Expenses: (9) − (17)	$8,270.43	$8,775.00	$8,775.00	$8,968.53
19	Rate of Return on Initial Investment: [(18) − (1)]/(1)	−17.30%	−12.25%	−12.25%	−10.31%
20	Rate of Return Necessary to Recoup Initial Investment: [(1) − (18)]/18	20.91%	13.96%	13.96%	11.50%
21	Back-End Load (5.0%): 5.0% × (18)	$0.00	$438.75	$0.00	$0.00
22	Redemption Fee (2.0%): 2.0% × (18)	$165.41	$175.50	$175.50	$0.00
23	Commission ($20)	$0.00	$0.00	$0.00	$20.00
24	Total Sales Costs: (21) + (22) + (23)	$165.41	$614.25	$175.50	$20.00
25	Amount Available after Sale: (18) − (24)	$8,105.02	$8,160.75	$8,599.50	$8,948.53
26	Final Return on Initial Investment: [(25) − (1)]/(1)	−18.95%	−18.39%	−14.01%	−10.51%
27	Rate of Return Necessary to Recoup Initial Investment: [(1) − (25)]/25	23.38%	22.54%	16.29%	11.75%

Figure 2-9 Impact of Expense Funds on Returns (*Continued*)

front-end load, (2) a mutual fund with a back-end load, (3) a no-load mutual fund, and (4) an exchange-traded fund. The expenses that are listed are typical for each type of fund. The analysis covers three cases: the market does not move, the market goes up by 10 percent, and the market goes down by 10 percent.

Certain conclusions can be drawn. First, any front-end load leaves the investor at a disadvantage from the beginning. With a 5.75 percent front-end load, the fund will have to return 6.1 percent to break even. The second major point is that even in a rising market, fees can keep investors from profiting on their investments. Consider the mutual funds with front-end and

> **Trader's Notebook**
>
> The ultimate message: low-cost index ETFs are much more cost-effective than mutual funds, and more likely, in the long run, to provide superior returns for their investors because their costs are lower than those of mutual funds.

back-end loads. Even when the market goes up by 10 percent, their investors are down because of the fees. In addition, the fees magnify downward market moves. Where the market declines by 10 percent, the fees make a bad situation worse, by around 100 percent—a 10 percent decline becomes a 20 percent decrease in assets.

Tax Efficiency

One of the major disadvantages of actively managed mutual funds is their inherent tax inefficiency. The practices of mutual fund managers, as well as the fundamental structure of mutual funds, result in mutual fund investors tending to pay more taxes than do ETF investors. In addition, exchange-traded funds allow investors to control if and when they incur capital gains taxes.

Short-Term versus Long-Term Gains

Capital gains are lower in portfolios held for more than one year. However, when a fund manager turns the fund's portfolio over in less than a year, it is distinctly possible that the investor may be saddled with unfavorable tax burdens.

Tax Deferral

As mentioned earlier, one advantage of individual investing is deferral of capital gains taxes, which decreases the present value of the taxes. Should the investor pay a tax of $100 now or 10 years in the future? The answer is 10 years in the future. First of all, that money will be worth less in 10 years; second, the investor can make use of the $100 to earn more money during the 10-year period. Unfortunately, because most mutual funds tend to turn over their portfolios fairly quickly, they prevent their owners from being able to take advantage of that deferred tax benefit.

Redemptions

Mutual funds have an inherent structural flaw related to taxes that ETFs do not possess. When a large number of mutual fund holders decide to sell, or redeem, their investments, the fund may not have enough cash on hand to pay them, especially if the volume of redemptions exceeds the volume of cash flowing into the fund.

To meet this cash shortfall, the mutual fund must sell securities in its portfolio. Selling shares, most likely those with the largest capital gains, means that the fund's remaining owners incur capital gains taxes by receiving a capital gains distribution. They have no say in whether or not they want the distribution—or the resulting tax burden. In fact, they could wind up paying capital gains taxes even when their holdings have decreased in value, because the fund had to sell shares to meet the redemptions. This aspect of mutual fund operation is also inequitable, because the costs for current investors are the result of the actions of others.

In contrast, the ETF does not have this weakness. When ETF holders sell their shares, they simply sell them on the open market—the fund has no involvement with the transaction. In this way, the ETF structure is far more equitable than that of mutual funds at distributing costs, because those who choose to hold onto their shares are in no way burdened by the actions of others who sell, in contrast to the mutual fund. The ETF is a clear winner in this area.

New Managers and Other Portfolio Turnover

When actively managed mutual funds bring in new managers, the new managers often sell the old portfolio and replace it with their own selections. This behavior can be very costly for investors with their holdings in taxable accounts. Essentially, the portfolio manager clears the whole portfolio, which means incurring capital gains, and uses the proceeds to buy new securities. Consider a portfolio with $1,000 worth of stock. The new manager sells the portfolio for $1,000 and uses that $1,000 to buy a totally new portfolio. However, let us consider that the portfolio had $500 of capital gains in it. The shareholders reinvest the $500 capital gains dividend. That $500 of capital gains is taxed at a rate of 15 percent, or $75. The holders of the fund now have to pay $75 in taxes, even though the portfolio's value has not changed. The investor retains the same amount of money in the fund, but has had to lay out $75 from other sources to pay the taxes.

Even if there isn't a new manager, high portfolio turnover may, or may not, generate profits, and it will definitely generate taxes. Say a portfolio manager turns the portfolio over twice a year. Even though the portfolio may not change in value, the value of each investor's total assets is diminished by the taxes that must be paid.

Choice of When to Pay Taxes

Another inherent failing of mutual funds is that they deny investors the ability to choose when to pay taxes. When a manager clears the portfolio or makes major changes, or when the fund has to sell shares to pay for redemptions, investors in the fund have to pay taxes, even though they may not wish to. While, admittedly, investors probably would like to never pay taxes, the reality is that they would rather incur capital gains when they choose to, such as to neutralize a tax loss and reduce their overall tax bills, than incur capital gains distributions in a year when they are also selling large blocks of stock. Random capital gains distributions eliminate that element of control.

Buying into a Tax Liability

A new buyer of shares in a mutual fund pays a price for the shares that represent the market value of the portfolio. That market value includes any unrealized capital gains in the portfolio. Thus, when the fund decides to sell investments at a profit, it will create a tax liability for the new fund share owner, even if the share owner sees no increase in the value of the investment. In effect, the new buyer takes on a tax obligation without any profit. For example, the buyer purchases a fund share at $10. The investment behind the shares cost the fund $8. The fund decides to sell the investment, producing a $2 capital gain, which it pays to the shareholder. The shareholder has to pay a 15 percent tax on the gain, or $0.30. The share owner now has a fund share worth $8, and $1.70 in cash after paying the tax. Anyone buying shares of a successful mutual fund almost certainly will incur taxes without having made a profit on the investment. Investors in ETFs, in contrast, never incur taxes based on past share price movements. The basis for the tax they pay is the purchase price of the ETF share, not the original purchase price of the underlying investments in the ETF.

Stepped-Up Basis at Death

For heirs to an estate, the base value of the securities held in the estate for the purpose of calculating capital gains taxes for future sales of those securities is the value of the securities when they are inherited. This means that the heirs will calculate the capital gains on the securities from when they receive them, not when they were originally purchased, which could greatly reduce capital gains taxes, if, and when, those securities are sold by the heirs. Frequent turnover of that portfolio before the death of the parent creates capital gains that require tax payments, which eats into an estate in a way that is as insidious as estate taxes.

Index funds can be compared with index ETFs, and in most cases the index ETF will probably be cheaper. However, it is important that the index fund and the ETF be in the same investing category. An S&P 500 Index fund may be cheaper than an ETF that invests in Spain, but the comparison is like the one between apples and oranges. On taxes, index funds are less likely to incur taxes than are actively managed funds because of portfolio turnover, but investors still face capital gains if a fund needs to sell shares when redemptions of the fund's shares exceed new money flowing into the fund. Thus an index fund can have the same structural flaw as an actively managed fund—a large number of redemptions can create capital gains that lead to taxes, which the investor cannot control or prevent. This structural flaw points in favor of ETFs, even when they are compared with index funds.

Similarities and Differences between Mutual Funds and ETFs

In addition to fees and taxes, there are other significant differences between mutual funds and ETFs, which are shown in Figure 2-10.

Purchasing

Mutual funds can be bought in a number of ways: through brokers and directly from funds and other financial institutions. Mutual funds constantly create shares to sell to new investors. ETFs are bought and sold only through a stockbroker. There are no stock certificates; all holdings are book entry with the broker, which makes for a low-cost management operation.

Pricing

Mutual funds are priced at net asset value (NAV) plus any sales charges. They are priced only at the end of the day, which is the only price at which an investor can purchase or redeem shares. In contrast, ETFs trade continuously, with continuous revaluation throughout the trading day.

Price is based on supply and demand for shares.

Shorting

Mutual fund managers cannot go short on their holdings, and individual investors cannot go short on mutual funds. In contrast, investors can short ETFs at any time.

Characteristic	Mutual Funds	ETF
Method of Purchase	Buy from brokers, directly from funds, and other financial institutions. Mutual funds generally create and sell new shares to accommodate new investors.	Trades like a stock. Can buy only through a broker.
Pricing	Price = net asset value (NAV) + any sales charges. Only priced at end of day based on NAV of portfolio. Can buy only at this price.	Continuous pricing and trading throughout the day.
Short	Cannot go short.	Can go short.
Tax Efficiency	Actively managed funds are tax inefficient (see discussion)	Potential for high efficiency.
Redemption	Investors buy directly from the mutual fund and redeem (sell) their shares back to the mutual fund.	Retail investors cannot redeem their shares. They must sell them in the open market. Redemption available for holders of large baskets of stock.
Costs	Variable	Low
Liquidity	Can't enter or exit during the day.	Can trade throughout day.
Invest outside of Securities	No	Yes
Options	No	Yes
Transparency	Modest	High
Management	Active and passive	Passive to date.
Leverage	No	Yes
Strategic Applications	No	Yes. Replicate hedge fund strategies. Capability of taking market-neutral positions. Create synthetic positions.

Figure 2-10   Key Differences between Mutual Funds and ETFs

Tax Efficiency

Actively managed mutual funds are not tax efficient. Index ETFs, on the other hand, are highly efficient.

Redemption

Investors in funds buy their shares from the fund and redeem their shares to the fund. In the ETF world, retail investors cannot redeem their shares; they need to sell them in the open market. Redemption is available only for holders of large baskets of shares (usually 50,000).

Costs

As discussed above, actively managed mutual funds tend to have many costs that eat into returns, whereas ETFs have few with a small bite.

Liquidity

A mutual fund holder can buy or sell only at the end of the trading day when the NAV is determined. If there is an adverse market move during the day and the fund goes down, the investor can't get out until the NAV is calculated at the end of the day. In contrast, ETF holders can get in and out throughout the day.

Invest Outside of Securities

Mutual funds are limited in what they can invest in—they can't participate in futures or commodities markets. ETFs have more flexibility so they can participate in other markets.

Options

There are no options on mutual funds. ETFs can have options (and futures).

Transparency

Mutual funds may not have transparent portfolios. Managers are required to report their holdings only twice a year. ETFs all track some sort of index, so their composition is always known.

Management

Mutual funds have active and passive management. To date, ETFs have had passive management, because they are index funds, but applications for actively managed ETFs are in process at the SEC (as this book is written, fall 2007).

Leverage

Investors cannot buy mutual funds on margin (that is, borrow money to make the purchase). ETFs trade like stock—margining is possible, depending on the broker.

Strategic Applications

ETFs can be used to replicate hedge fund strategies, take market-neutral positions, and create synthetic positions using derivatives. Investors cannot use mutual funds to pursue those investment strategies.

Trader's Notebook

The beauty of ETFs is that they allow an investor to have the advantages of trading an individual stock (notably control over taxes), combined with instant diversification, without the high fees.

ETF Strategy

Effectively choosing to use ETFs, mutual funds, a combination, or none at all requires an understanding of the instruments and their strengths and weaknesses. For some investors, ETFs may be the better bet, and for others, mutual funds, or combination thereof, might be better. When making the decision, the investor should focus on the efficiency of the investment, after subtracting costs. What ultimately matters to an investor is not the gross return that a fund or ETF reports, but what the investor *receives* after paying fees, expenses, and taxes. Unless the investor has chosen an exceptionally well-run fund, the ETF will always win hands down.

3

HOW ETFs WORK

Most investors just buy or sell ETFs in the market. They neither know nor care about how the ETF functions or how the ETF structure differs from other investments. Yet they should care, because the structure makes the ETF a compelling investment.

The ETF comes in two forms: the unit investment trust (UIT) and the open-end company. To date, all ETFs launched in the United States have been passive; that is, they are designed to track an index. The Securities and Exchange Commission (SEC) has not yet approved actively managed ETFs. The grantor investment trust looks like, but is not, an ETF. (Grantor trusts are not registered investment companies and are regulated in a manner different from that of ETFs.)

Buying and Selling ETFs: An Illustration

Figure 3-1 shows a simplified version of how the typical ETF investor buys, or sells, an ETF. The buyer in the upper left-hand

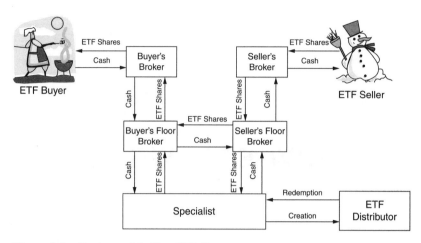

Figure 3-1 Buying and Selling ETF Shares

corner of the diagram, Mrs. Barbecue, starts the process by placing an order with her broker to buy 100 shares of the SPDR (Standard & Poor's depository receipts), one of the most popular ETFs.[1] (Remember, investors can buy ETFs only through a licensed stockbroker.)

Next, the broker transmits the order to the firm's broker on the floor of the exchange, who executes the order. The broker has two ways to execute the order at the best possible price for the customer. First, he may find another floor broker with shares to sell. Or he may buy them from a specialist, an independent market maker who helps ensure liquidity in the shares of certain securities, such as ETFs.

The specialist, or market maker, makes money by purchasing shares at a low price and selling them at a higher price, or by selling shares at a higher price and buying an equivalent number back at a lower price.

Simultaneously, the seller, Mr. Snowman in the upper right-hand corner, wishes to sell his 100 shares of the SPDR. His broker phones in his order to the floor of the exchange to its respective floor broker. That floor broker may sell directly to Mrs. Barbecue's broker or to the designated market maker (who may in turn sell 100 SPDR shares to Mrs. Barbecue's floor broker).

Either way, the buyers and sellers make the trade on the market, without dealing directly with the ETF's manager. That contrasts with the purchase, or sale, of conventional mutual fund shares, which requires the participation of the fund manager, who extracts hefty fees from the transaction. The ETF management company collects most of its income, instead, from a small annual management fee from the owner of the ETF shares.

ETF Mechanism

ETF shares require a mechanism to bring them to market.

Figure 3-2 shows how ETF shares are created, traded, and redeemed. The ETF sponsor (fund manager) starts by selecting an index, such as the Dow Jones Industrial Average or the S&P 500, and attempts to replicate it in managing the ETF. The sponsor pays the index developer for the rights to use this index. The sponsor then transmits those index specifications, such as the securities making up the index and their weights, to the ETF distributor. The distributor makes this information available, prior to the start of the day's trading, to authorized participants intending to create (through a portfolio deposit) or redeem ETFs.

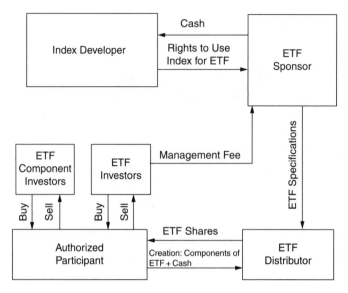

Figure 3-2   ETF Creation and Redemption

A portfolio deposit for the SPDR comprises the shares required to create 50,000 SPDR shares plus a cash component to account for the difference between the value of the shares and the net asset value (NAV) of the ETF, as well as processing fees. An authorized participant is a broker-dealer or other organization that is either a member of the Continuous Net Settlement System of the National Securities Clearing Corporation or a Depository Trust Company (DTC) participant.

An authorized participant that wishes to create ETF shares deposits the underlying components needed to produce a creation unit (usually 50,000 shares or more) of the ETF. In return for the shares, and a cash component that goes toward handling transaction costs and accounts for any accrued dividends, the authorized participant receives a block of shares known as a *creation unit* that it can break up and sell in the secondary markets to individual investors, or hold in toto.

If an authorized participant wishes to redeem its ETF shares, it does so by exchanging a creation unit for the component securities that are underlying the redemption basket and that are identified by the fund manager prior to the start of the trading day. The redemption basket, the mirror image of the creation unit, consists of a basket of securities and cash, because the value of the redemption basket equals the NAV of the ETF share in the creation unit. This limited redemption feature of ETFs, in contrast to the open-ended nature of mutual funds, means that the SEC prohibits ETFs from calling themselves mutual funds. Since most individual investors do not have enough ETF shares (50,000 or more) to redeem them, most ETF investors exit their holdings by selling their shares in the market.

Arbitrage and ETFs

Arbitrage keeps the ETFs closely aligned with the NAV of their components, unlike closed-end funds that can trade at significant premiums, or discounts, to the NAV of their underlying shares. If ETF shares start to trade at a discount to the NAV of their underlying shares, arbitrageurs can buy enough ETF shares to put together a redemption basket and then redeem the ETF to get the more valuable securities in the redemption basket. That buying pressure raises the price of the ETF to create a market price closer to the NAV. On the other hand, if ETF shares trade at a premium (with a price greater than the NAV) to the component shares, an arbitrageur can buy the securities making up the portfolio deposit (creation basket) and use that deposit to obtain the more valuable creation units and then sell the ETF shares in the market for a profit. The increase in supply of ETF shares on the market tends to drive down ETF prices so that they are more in line with their NAV.

Differences between Unit Investment Trusts and Open-End Companies

While the above mechanisms apply to both unit investment trusts and open-end companies, there are some differences in the operations of the two types of companies that relate primarily to the replication of the index.

Unit Investment Trust

A unit investment trust (UIT) needs to fully replicate the index it tracks—the components deposited with the trustee in a creation unit must include all the members of the index in the weights specified by the index developer. For example a unit investment trust based on the S&P 500 would have to include each of the 500 components of the index in the trust. If the index is adjusted—or *reconstituted* as it is referred to in the industry—the trustee adjusts the makeup of the creation and redemption baskets. When Standard

& Poor's makes a change to the S&P 500, substituting one company for another, the SPDR trustee must sell the securities that have been removed and buy the ones that have been added within three business days before or after the day the change takes effect.

Open-End Company

In contrast to UITs, open-end companies do not need to fully replicate the index. They can replicate the index through a technique called *representative sampling* that the SEC has approved for use in open-end companies to track the performance of an index, provided that the tracking error, or difference between the index's performance and the fund's performance, is no greater than 5 percent on an annual basis. Representative sampling involves investing in a representative sample of the securities in the underlying index in an effort to track that underlying index. In addition, the fund's advisor may also acquire securities for the ETF portfolio that are not part of the underlying index. The resulting sample should have investment characteristics similar to those of the underlying index, notably market capitalization, industry weightings, return variability, valuation of earnings, and liquidity.

A fund matching its index perfectly—a 100 percent correlation—exhibits no tracking error. A fund with a correlation of less than 100 percent exhibits a tracking error; for example, a fund with a 95 percent correlation with its index exhibits a 5 percent tracking error (100 percent – 95 percent = 5 percent), the maximum allowed on an annual basis by the SEC for open-end funds engaging in representative sampling of an index.

Another difference between UITs and open-end funds is that open-end ETFs are able to lend out securities, and use futures and options, in meeting their investment objectives, while UITs are forbidden from doing so. Revenue generated by these activities may help an ETF offset expenses that could cause the ETF's performance to fall short of its benchmark index. Although securities lending and using futures and options may create the appearance of an actively managed fund, this is not the case because funds use these tools simply to track an index.

Grantor Trusts/HOLDRs

As mentioned in Chapter 2, another form of security somewhat similar to an ETF, and often mistaken for an ETF, is the grantor trust, such as the HOLDR (holding company depository receipt) developed by Merrill Lynch. In addition, many of the new funds tracking commodities, such as streetTRACKS Gold Trust, which holds a basket of gold in trust, are grantor trusts. They are not ETFs and cannot (and should not) advertise themselves as ETFs. Because grantor trusts are not registered investment companies, they do not fall under the jurisdiction of the Investment Company Act of 1940. They fall under the jurisdiction of the SEC's Division of Corporation Finance, not the Division of Investment Management, which regulates ETFs and mutual funds.

Figure 3-3 shows the operation of a grantor trust for HOLDRs, but the same principle applies to other grantor trusts, including commodity and currency trusts.

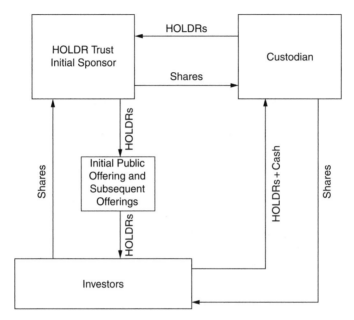

Figure 3-3 HOLDR Creation and Distribution

The *HOLDR trust initial sponsor* (Merrill Lynch) selects an industry, say utilities, and determines the companies to include and their weights within the HOLDR, based on criteria such as market capitalization and liquidity. It purchases the shares in those proportions and deposits them with a custodian. The custodian then issues HOLDRs to the HOLDR trust initial sponsor, which offers them in an initial public offering and later in subsequent continuous offerings to investors. Investors can either sell their HOLDRs in the open market or redeem them, for a small fee, with the custodian. In addition, investors can also deposit the component shares of the HOLDR in specified proportions and redeem them for HOLDRs.

The currency and commodity trusts function in a similar manner. For streetTRACKS Gold Trust, the sponsor deposits gold with the trustee, and the shares of the trust are then offered to the public. The fund also allows continuous creation of shares. Creating or redeeming shares requires that

Trader's Notebook

Unlike ETFs, HOLDRs' investors retain voting rights on stocks in the portfolio, even though they don't own the shares outright. In contrast to a management fee for an ETF, HOLDR owners pay a small custodial fee.

the investor be a licensed broker-dealer and a participant in the Depository Trust Company. In addition, the investor must set up various accounts in which gold can be deposited.[2] To create a basket, the investor deposits 10,000 ounces of gold and pays transaction fees. To redeem a basket, the investor deposits 100,000 shares and pays the necessary transaction fees and receives 10,000 ounces of gold. The streetTRACKS Gold Trust pays trustee expenses by selling some of the gold it holds in trust.

The HOLDRs have a number of limitations compared to ETFs:

- If trading halts in one or more of the constituent securities, trading in the HOLDRs can be halted, even if trading continues in the other securities. This could make it difficult to exit a position in the HOLDR.

- HOLDRs are not necessarily diversified. Say that a HOLDR starts out with 20 companies, and 10 are bought out by other businesses and cease to trade in the market. Those that are bought out leave the trust, and the shareholders are left with only 10 components, which reduces diversification.

- HOLDRs are not necessarily representative of an industry. Say that a holding company had a utility component and a TV station, but the utility part was the major business, so the company was classified as a utility. Say that it sells the utility to a private equity group. It will still remain part of a utility HOLDR even though it is no longer in the utility business.

- When a stock within a HOLDR merges, or goes out of business, it is not replaced, nor is the HOLDR rebalanced, which means that the positions become concentrated, and more volatile.

- HOLDRs' performance compared to ETF counterparts seems inferior, based on recent experience.

Actively Managed ETFs in the Future

To date, the SEC has not approved actively managed ETFs. Wall Street likes the idea of active management because actively traded ETFs would create a new source of revenues. The question for investors is whether they really need actively traded ETFs. Given that mutual fund managers do not consistently beat their benchmarks, why would ETF managers be any different? The only advantages an actively traded ETF *might* have over an actively traded mutual fund, are: (1) it *might* have lower costs resulting from the fact that the manager would not have to maintain a service infrastructure, given that the shares would probably be held in

book-entry form (basically a computerized record) at a broker, and
(2) investors would not face capital gains taxes when large numbers of investors redeem their shares, given that the shares would
be sold in the secondary market. Another advantage of an actively
traded ETF over an actively managed mutual fund is that the
investors could get in and out during the day and short the fund.

The SEC, in its concept release,
"Actively Managed Exchange-Traded
Funds," described key forms an
actively managed ETF would have.
First, since the ETF would be actively
managed, it would have to take the
form of an open-end company because
the management would be changing
the constitution of the ETF; this is
impossible with the unit investment
trust form. In addition, actively managed ETFs would keep many of the
same features as the current generation
of passive ETFs. They could differ in certain areas, however.

Trader's Notebook
Unlike the index-based ETFs described above, an actively managed ETF would not passively track an index through replication, or sampling, of its compo- nents. Instead, the managers of an actively managed ETF would select securities consistent with the objec- tives and policies their fund selects—much like a mutual fund.

One area of potential difference is in the transparency of the fund.
Currently, the content of an index fund is made public daily for the
purpose of creating and redeeming shares. It is not yet clear whether,
and how, an actively managed ETF would communicate changes in
its portfolio throughout the trading day. This could reduce the transparency of the fund and the efficiency of the arbitrage mechanism
that keeps the prices of ETFs closely in line with the value of the
underlying shares, in contrast to the premiums and discounts often

associated with closed-end funds. Still, some transparency would be required for market makers and specialists; they must be provided with the information they need so that they can put together creation and redemption baskets and the knowledge they need to hedge their portfolios between ETFs and their components. The ETF sponsor needs to keep market makers and specialists informed if the ETF sponsor wants a liquid product.

Another related question is: When would a fund need to announce its trades? It certainly would not wish to announce its trades before making them so as to avoid the possibility of other traders taking advantage of that knowledge—which happens now with passively indexed ETFs. When a change to an index is announced, the players in the market know index funds need to buy and sell shares, so other traders "front run" those trades and try to take advantage of that knowledge, a process that makes it more expensive for index funds to adjust their portfolios. The prices of the shares they wish to buy rise, and the prices of the shares they wish to sell decline, because other traders anticipate the actions of the index funds. Because of this phenomenon, reconstitution of indexes such as the Russell 2000, which can have over 25 percent annual turnover in its portfolio, can be very expensive for index funds.

Index number providers need to be independent of the fund sponsors, according to SEC regulations, and changes in an index need to be publicly announced. As noted above, this transparency can create significant transaction costs for an exchange-traded fund when an index is reconstituted. Some financial experts have proposed allowing funds to track certain "silent indexes" or even base an index on a particular managed portfolio and announce the changes after the fund has traded in order to avoid the transaction costs associated with front running. Alternatively, a fund manager could set up its own index for the purpose of running its fund and then announce changes after the fund has made the transactions necessary to keep it in compliance with the index.

ETF Strategy

The exemplary features of the ETF—low cost, diversified, and tax efficient—are a function of its structure. Understanding that structure and its strengths can help guide investors toward better investments, especially in terms of looking at how funds adjust their portfolios when indexes are reconstituted and how well they track their indexes through the quality of their sampling procedures. While average investors may not create or redeem an ETF, they benefit because those features exist.

4

ETF REGULATION

Although understanding regulations won't necessarily make it possible for investors to make money, understanding regulations will certainly show them ways to avoid losing money or paying unnecessary taxes, so investors can keep more of their profits.

ETF regulations exist for a reason. They help protect investors from harmful practices, such as conflicts of interest between investment companies and investors. ETF look-alikes do not have these protections, which unfortunately some investors have found out after the fact. Regulations affect the investor's bottom line. The wise investor will apply knowledge of regulations when formulating investment strategies and then putting those strategies into action. Understanding regulations may provide an edge or help keep investors from losing money on a poorly structured investment product.

ETFs and ETF Look-Alikes

When investing in ETFs, know the difference between ETFs and ETF look-alikes. ETFs are "investment companies that are registered under the Investment Company Act of 1940 as open-end funds or UITs."[1]

Any other investment product that does not fit that definition is not an ETF. This is not semantic quibbling. ETF look-alikes do not have the investor protections of ETFs, may create tax problems, and may suffer from tracking error. (Tracking error occurs when a fund's performance does not exactly match that of the index it tracks. Tracking error can come from obvious items, such as fees and expenses, which an index does not have, or from sampling problems, changes to an index (but not to the fund), poor fund construction, and even simple items such as rounding off prices.) Unfortunately, the media covering ETFs do not usually distinguish correctly between these instruments, labeling most products that track some sort of index as ETFs.

The Investment Company Act of 1940, often known as the "40 Act," regulates ETFs and provides important protection for ETF investors. This law differs considerably from other securities laws, which emphasize disclosure. The 40 Act, instead, tends to prohibit certain actions, and imposes strong criminal penalties, under the theory

> **Trader's Notebook**
>
> Investors need to know that when they invest outside the umbrella of the 40 Act, they receive fewer protections, notably from fund managers who have conflicts of interest, who engage in self-dealing, or who put their interests ahead of those of the investors.

that the less sophisticated investors who may be clients of investment companies (mutual funds and ETFs, for example) require greater protection than the presumably more sophisticated investors who buy and sell individual securities that come under the jurisdiction of the 1933 and 1934 securities acts.

When Congress passed the 40 Act, it stated in its introduction that the purpose of the act was to "mitigate and, so far as is feasible, to eliminate the conditions . . . which adversely affect the national public interest and the interest of investors." Among those conditions were:

- Inadequate, unfairly presented information about the financial status of investment companies.

- Investment companies that were run for the interests of the investment company managers and affiliated parties, as opposed to the interests of investors.

- Investment companies that were managed by irresponsible people.

- Investment companies engaged in questionable accounting in calculating the earnings and value of the securities they owned, without adequate scrutiny.[2]

Under the aegis of the 40 Act, SEC rules:

- Regulate who can be affiliated with a registered investment company. This keeps out people who have been convicted of securities fraud or other similar crimes.

- Regulate the composition of a fund's board of directors.

- Regulate the conduct of industry participants.

- Regulate the methodologies for calculating net asset value of a fund.

- Regulate the fund's expenses and how to disclose and display them.

- Prohibit a fund from changing its investment policies without the consent of the investors.

Although ETFs did not exist at the time the 40 Act was written, mutual funds (the predecessors of ETFs) fell under its jurisdiction. As such, the form and structure of SEC regulation still applies to ETFs, with these major exemptions from SEC rules:

- ETFs redeem shares only in creation units, in contrast with mutual funds where the mutual fund company must redeem shares for all owners, regardless of size.

- ETFs are traded on secondary markets rather than being bought and sold at the end of the day based on the net asset value of a share in a fund. This differs from the way mutual funds are traded.

- ETFs need not deliver prospectuses to investors who buy and sell ETFs in the secondary market, although they are required to do so for those who create and redeem creation units.

Illustration of an ETF Look-Alike

Let's take a look at the prospectus and disclosure of the United States Oil Fund, LP (limited partnership), as an illustration of potential land mines in the ETF look-alike field.

Tracking Error

When an ETF chooses to replicate an index by representative sampling, by SEC regulations it needs to stay within 5 percent of the index. A grantor trust does not need to meet these same requirements. This tracking error phenomenon has shown itself most recently with a number of ETF look-alikes whose actual performances have not matched those of the indexes they are supposed to track. One notable example is the United States Oil Fund (USOF) launched in 2006 to great fanfare as a way for individual investors to track the oil markets without having to open a futures account. The fund was supposed to track oil price movements. However, in the time since its inception in 2006 through April 2007, oil prices fell by 10 percent, yet the shares of USOF fell by 25 percent. While the potential for these variances may have been disclosed in the prospectus, an ETF would not be permitted to have such a large tracking error.[3]

Conflicts of Interest

The USOF states in its prospectus that it may have conflicts of interest between the general partner of the fund and the investors:

> The structure and operation of USOF may involve conflicts of interest. For example, a conflict may arise because the General Partner and its principal and affiliates may trade for themselves. In addition, the General Partner has sole current authority to manage the investments and operations, which may create a conflict with the unitholders' best interests. The General Partner may also have a conflict to the extent that its trading decisions may be influenced

by the effect they would have on any other commodity pool the General Partner may form in the future.[4]

USOF and the General Partner may have conflicts of interest, which may permit them to favor their own interests to your detriment.[5]

So the fund's general partner may not only trade for the fund's investors, but also for itself. The partner states outright that it may favor its own interests over those of the investor. Does that inspire confidence? Could the partner use the knowledge of the fund's trading strategy to its own benefit? Who knows? But who wants to find out? Note these sorts of conflicts of interest are prohibited for registered investment companies.

Personnel Issues

Unlike ETFs, which operate almost mechanically, the USOF depends highly on the actions of a few people.

The General Partner is leanly staffed and relies heavily on key personnel to manage trading activities. In managing and directing the day-to-day activities and affairs of USOF, the General Partner relies heavily on Mr. Nicholas Gerber, Mr. John Love and Mr. John Hyland . . . If Mr. Gerber, Mr. Love or Mr. Hyland were to leave or be unable to carry out their present responsibilities, it may have an adverse effect on the management of USOF. Furthermore, it is anticipated that Mr. Gerber, Mr. Love and Mr. Hyland will be involved in the management of United States Natural Gas Fund, LP ("USNG").[6]

ETFs are passive investments once they are put together, aside from the initial selection of indexes and representative sampling, and should not depend on the expertise of one or two people. ETFs are simple, relatively automatically operating investments. The USOF is not. Investors have a choice: to go with a simple, relatively automatic investment or a highly complex one that is dependent on a few people who may not stay with the organization.

Managers Are Not Full Time

Another fascinating fact about the USOF is that the managers do not work for the fund full time. Some of them have another employer and other responsibilities — including some that may conflict with their responsibilities to USOF's investors.

> Mr. Gerber and Mr. Love are also employed by Ameristock Corporation, a registered investment adviser that manages a public mutual fund. USOF estimates that Mr. Gerber will spend approximately 50% of his time on USOF and USNG matters, Mr. Love will spend approximately 30% of his time on USOF and USNG matters and Mr. Hyland will spend approximately 50% of his time on USOF and USNG matters.[7]
>
> The General Partner's officers, directors and employees do not devote their time exclusively to USOF. These persons are directors, officers or employees of other entities which may compete with USOF for their services. They could have a conflict between their responsibilities to USOF and to those other entities.[8]

Investors need to think carefully about ETF look-alikes that depend highly on the ability of managers — and the fact that managers may not be on the job full time. ETFs are kind of "dumb" investments that manage themselves with replication of an index; they do not depend on significant management intervention. ETFs, given their requirements to closely follow an index, may require considerable planning in their development, but they should require relatively little active management once they are in operation.

Tax Matters

Investors also need to know that ETF look-alikes do not always have the same tax benefits of ETFs.

> We could be treated as a corporation for federal income tax purposes, which may substantially reduce the value of your units.[9]

This means double taxation for fund investors—taxation at the corporate level and taxation at the individual investor level. This results in less income for investors, which would not happen with a regulated investment company.

May Get Too Big for the Good of Our Investors

While growth in assets does not usually hurt ETF investors, growth in a look-alike can be problematic.

> The General Partner may manage a large amount of assets and this could affect USOF's ability to trade profitably. Increases in assets under management may affect trading decisions. In general, the General Partner does not intend to limit the amount of assets of USOF that it may manage. The more assets the General Partner manages, the more difficult it may be for it to trade profitably because of the difficulty of trading larger positions without adversely affecting prices and performance and of managing risk associated with larger positions.[10]

With an ETF based on an index, this is not an issue. ETFs are not supposed to be about "trading decisions" but about tracking an index. This fund has trading decisions that may affect it as it grows. (The fund makes trading decisions to purchase oil futures and other products that it uses to track the price of oil.) However, the fund manager is compensated by assets under management, so it may have an incentive to increase fund assets, because it will mean a larger management fee, even if fund investors may suffer.

Read the Prospectus

Read the ETF look-alike's prospectus and be on the lookout for red flags before you decide to use it as part of your investment strategy. The real question is, with all the places you can put your money, why would you want to invest with a fund:

- Whose managers have a conflict of interest—and have announced that they will put their interests ahead of yours?
- Whose managers don't care if their funds grow to a point where their ability to trade effectively on your behalf will be affected?
- Whose managers don't work full time—is that whom you want managing your money?

Taxes

Benjamin Franklin once said, "A penny saved is a penny earned." Actually when you take taxes into account, a penny saved is better than a penny earned, because after taxes are taken into account, a penny earned is less than a penny saved.

Investors in ETFs need to pay attention to the tax status of any ETFs, or ETF look-alikes, in which they invest. ETF look-alikes may not have the benefits of being regulated investment companies, and this may create tax problems. The IRS fully details the requirements, but for the basic ETF investor, there are few key points to ascertain.

A fund must pass these key tests in order to qualify as a regulated investment company:

- Of its annual gross income, 90 percent must come from dividends, interest, gains from sale or other disposition of stock, securities, foreign currencies, or other specific income sources.

- A fund must meet key diversification tests that are the same as those for a diversified fund, as specified in Chapters 2 and 5 in the discussion of fund-friendly indexes. These diversification requirements mean that the fund must have a minimum number of securities in order to be considered diversified. Based on these rules, the minimum number of securities required is 13. Of course, given the precise weights required with a fund of 13 securities, more securities are better for ensuring diversification when weights may change, possibly resulting from changing market capitalization.

- The fund must distribute, annually, at least 90 percent of its investment company taxable income.

Foreign Tax Credit

When investing in ETFs that own foreign securities, investors may have to pay foreign taxes on their income or other earnings abroad. U.S. taxpayers not only have to pay the foreign taxes, but they also must pay U.S. taxes on their income, meaning that U.S. taxpayers could face the possibility of double taxation on the same stream of income unless the ETF complies with tax regulations that allow U.S. investors to take a tax credit equivalent to the foreign taxes they paid. If this is the case, then U.S. investors can take a dollar-for-dollar credit off their actual taxes, thereby avoiding double taxation.

Consider two investors who have $10,000 in total income and owe $2,000 in foreign taxes on their overseas income. (See Figure 4-1.) Investor A invests in a fund that qualifies for the foreign tax credit. At the end, after the credit, she has $8,000 in after-tax net income. Investor B invests in a fund ineligible for the foreign tax credit, and he suffers from double taxation and winds up with $6,400 in after-tax net income, 20 percent less than Investor A.

Line	Item	Investor A	Investor B
1	Gross Income	$10,000	$10,000
2	Foreign Tax	$2,000	$2,000
3	Net Income (1) − (2)	$8,000	$8,000
4	U.S. Tax Rate	20.00%	20.00%
5	Deduction	$0	$2,000
6	Taxable Income (1) − (5)	$10,000	$8,000
7	U.S. Tax (4) × (6)	$2,000	$1,600
8	Foreign Tax Credit	$2,000	$0
9	Net Income after Foreign and U.S. Taxes (3) − (7) + (8)	$8,000	$6,400

Figure 4-1 Foreign Tax Credit versus Foreign Tax Deduction

How can an investor know he can obtain the foreign tax credit? The prospectus should disclose this material. For a registered investment company (this includes real ETFs, not look-alikes) that invests outside the United States, to qualify for the foreign tax credit, more than 50 percent of the value of the ETF, at year-end, must be foreign stocks or securities.[11] This has implications for so-called global funds that may invest in many countries, including the United States. If, at year-end, this fund has less than half of its assets as foreign stocks or securities, than the fund's investors are not eligible to take the foreign tax credit, with considerable tax consequences.

Regulations outside the United States

While the majority of the world's share of ETF (and ETF look-alike) assets are traded on U.S. exchanges, significant opportunities to invest in ETFs and related products exist outside the United States.

Figure 4-2 shows the ETF trading universe and associated regulators. ETFs do not trade in many countries, and the majority of the assets under management are in only a few countries. U.S. investors are advised to check with the regulators and their U.S. brokers on (1) whether they can legally access those markets, (2) ease of access to those markets, (3) the tax implications of investing in those overseas ETFs, notably whether any taxes can be taken as a credit dollar for dollar against the investor's U.S. taxes (creating a tax-neutral situation) or whether the taxes can be deducted only from the U.S. taxpayer's taxes, which is a less favorable outcome than a dollar-for-dollar credit.

Country	ETFs	ETF Assets	Global Share (%)	Regulator	Regulator Web Site
Australia	4	$794,620,270	0.13%	Australian Securities and Investments Commission	www.asic.gov.au
Austria	1	$88,076,499	0.01%	Financial Market Authority	www.fma.gv.at
Canada	24	$25,883,296,539	4.27%	Ontario Securities Commission	www.osc.gov.on.ca
China	2	$752,090,866	0.12%	China Securities Regulatory Commission	www.csrc.gov.cn
Finland	1	$211,843,388	0.03%	Financial Supervision Authority	www.rahoitustarkastus.fi
France	76	$29,725,620,664	4.91%	Autorité des Marchés Financiers	www.amf-france.org
Germany	99	$31,981,012,223	5.28%	Bundesanstalt für Finanzdienstleistungsaufsicht (BaFin)	www.bafin.de
Hong Kong	8	$9,407,002,845	1.55%	Securities and Futures Commission	www.sfc.hk
India	6	$290,852,300	0.05%	Securities and Exchange Board of India (SEBI)	www.sebi.gov.in
Ireland	6	$219,251,778	0.04%	Central Bank and Financial Services Authority	www.financialregulator.ie
Israel	14	$6,515,194,034	1.08%	Israel Securities Authority	www.isa.gov.il
Italy	2	$180,565,146	0.03%	Commissione Nazionale per le Società e la Borsa	www.consob.it
Japan	13	$32,793,557,121	5.42%	Financial Services Agency	www.fsa.go.jp
Korea	12	$1,651,759,349	0.27%	Financial Supervisory Commission/ Financial Supervisory Service	www.fss.or.kr

Note: Data as of February 28, 2007.

Figure 4-2 Countries Where ETFs Trade and Their Regulators

Sources: State Street Global Advisors (www.etfconnect.com/documents/ssga.xls) and International Organization of Securities Commissions.

(Continues)

Country	ETFs	ETF Assets	Global Share (%)	Regulator	Regulator Web Site
Netherlands	13	$2,641,729,656	0.44%	The Netherlands Authority for the Financial Markets	www.afm.nl
New Zealand	2	$73,125,197	0.01%	Securities Commission	www.sec-com.govt.nz
Norway	3	$114,912,631	0.02%	Kredittilsynet	www.kredittilsynet.no
Singapore	7	$909,584,157	0.15%	Monetary Authority of Singapore	www.mas.gov.sg
South Africa	7	$1,912,018,053	0.32%	Financial Services Board	www.fsb.co.za
Spain	2	$240,164,753	0.04%	Comisión Nacional del Mercado de Valores	www.cnmv.es
Sweden	5	$2,390,469,825	0.39%	Finansinspektionen	www.fi.se
Switzerland	18	$7,425,997,643	1.23%	Commission Fédérale des Banques	www.sfbc.admin.ch
Taiwan	2	$1,111,795,460	0.18%	Financial Supervisory Commission	www.fscey.gov.tw
Turkey	3	$43,666,431	0.01%	Capital Markets Board	www.cmb.gov.tr
United Kingdom	59	$17,563,275,658	2.90%	Financial Services Authority	www.fsa.gov.uk
USA	432	$430,663,629,692	71.12%	Securities and Exchange Commission	www.sec.gov
Total	821	$605,585,112,178	100%		

Figure 4-2 Countries Where ETFs Trade and Their Regulators (*Continued*)

For investors outside the United States who choose to invest in U.S. ETFs, they too will need to check whether they can legally buy U.S. ETFs and need to understand the tax implications of their purchases. Investors who do not have a U.S. tax ID (such as a social security number) may be subject to backup withholding, which means that the U.S. government withholds their taxes before they receive any dividends.

ETF Strategy

ETF regulations are there to protect the investor, so take advantage of what those regulations provide to better guide your investments. Investors need to understand the differences between ETFs, which are regulated under the Investment Company Act, and ETF look-alikes, which are not. The Investment Company Act serves to help investors, and you ignore it at your own risk. Regulations matter.

5

ETF INDEXES

"What did the market do today?" "The Dow went up 100 points." Why should it matter? People own individual stocks, not the Dow. For ETF investors, however, the question matters because the performance of their investment depends on an index that measures the prices of a basket of stocks, or other securities, and the nature of index construction can affect the probability of investors meeting their investment goals.

What Are Indexes?

Stock indexes provide a way of comparing prices over time, just as the consumer price index (CPI) measures changes in price levels, determining inflation rates relative to a fixed benchmark. Although it measures price changes, an index number does not have an actual value, as in dollars. It is simply a ratio of prices.

Consider a simple price index:

$$I = \frac{P_1}{P_0} \times 100$$

The index (I) measures the price (P) at time 1 relative to the price at (P) time 0. The value at time 0 is assumed to be 100. This ratio of prices, known as the *price relative*, is multiplied by 100 to create the new index level. For instance, $100 pays for a typical basket of goods in year 0. The same basket of goods costs $105 in year 1. The calculation is as follows:
Let

$$P_0 = \$100$$
$$P_1 = \$105$$

$$I = \frac{\$105}{\$100} \times 100$$
$$= 1.05 \times 100$$
$$= 105$$

Note that the index number does not depend on the currency because it has no unit associated with it. It is simply a measure of relative prices.

Consider one stock market with one company that only has one share trading. At time 0, the company has a price of $100. At time 1, the company has a price of $150. The new level of the market is 150/100 × 100, which is 150. The value of the market at time 1—relative to time 0—is 50 percent higher. This principle of measuring the value of basket at time 1 relative to time 0 forms the basis for indexing.

Here is the example worked out:

Let

$$P_0 = \$100$$
$$P_1 = \$150$$

$$I = \frac{\$150}{\$100} \times 100$$
$$= 1.50 \times 100$$
$$= 150$$

Indexes can be used to measure all types of relative changes—from consumer prices, to rainfall, to stock prices. The principle remains the same; only the data change.

Development of an Index

The development of an index is not complicated. The actual construction of the index involves three basic steps: selection, weighting, and calculation. In many ways, developing an index is similar to developing a survey to measure characteristics within a population.

Selection of Components

The first step is to choose a representative sample of the population. This consists of selecting the stocks from the universe of stocks that are considered representative of a particular investment strategy (e.g., large-cap stocks, the broad U.S. market, or the Spanish market) and assembling a suitable number of securities to create a representative sample. Some indexes select their components based on market capitalization or some other criterion, such as industry or value or any of the various criteria used to classify funds. Still, any decision couched in various airs of a scientific nature ultimately produces a product that probably has some bias. For example the Russell 2000 may be dominated with companies that are volatile because of their size. Investing in an index involves making a choice to invest in an instrument that will have some bias simply because of its components.

Weighting

Weighting is a method of assigning a value to each company in the index calculation. The Dow Jones Index is price-weighted, which means that it is a simple average — essentially the total share prices are summed and then divided by 30 to create an average number.[1] (Actually the divisor is less than 30 to account for various stock splits and stock dividends.) Those companies with higher prices have a greater weight on the index. (See Figure 5-1.)

The Dow method is not used today, except to calculate the Dow Jones Industrial Average, because it is a poor measure of an overall market — why should a stock with a high price simply move a market? But it persists simply because of the venerability and familiarity of the Dow Jones name.

The most common form of weighting is *market capitalization*, where the weighting factor *W* is based on the market capitalization, which is determined by multiplying the share price by the number

Price Weighted

Stock	Original Price	A Doubles in Price	B Doubles in Price	C Doubles in Price	A Halves in Price	B Halves in Price	C Halves in Price
A	$10.00	$20.00	$10.00	$10.00	$5.00	$10.00	$10.00
B	$20.00	$20.00	$40.00	$20.00	$20.00	$10.00	$20.00
C	$50.00	$50.00	$50.00	$100.00	$50.00	$50.00	$25.00
Average Price	$26.67	$30.00	$33.33	$43.33	$25.00	$23.33	$18.33
Index Number	100	112.5	125	162.5	93.75	87.5	68.75
% Change		12.50%	25.00%	62.50%	-6.25%	-12.50%	-31.25%

Capitalization Weighted

Stock	Original Price	Shares Outstanding	Market Cap	A Doubles in Price	New Capitalization	B Doubles in Price	New Capitalization	C Doubles in Price	New Capitalization	A Halves in Price	New Capitalization	B Halves in Price	New Capitalization	C Halves in Price	New Capitalization
A	$10.00	4000	$40,000	$20.00	$80,000	$10.00	$40,000	$10.00	$40,000	$5.00	$20,000	$10.00	$40,000	$10.00	$40,000
B	$20.00	3000	$60,000	$20.00	$60,000	$40.00	$120,000	$20.00	$60,000	$20.00	$60,000	$10.00	$30,000	$20.00	$60,000
C	$50.00	2000	$100,000	$50.00	$100,000	$50.00	$100,000	$100.00	$200,000	$50.00	$100,000	$50.00	$100,000	$25.00	$50,000
Weighted Average	$22.22				$26.67		$28.89		$33.33		$20.00		$18.89		$16.67
Index Number	100				120		130		150		90		85		75
% Change					20.00%		30.00%		50.00%		-10.00%		-15.00%		-25.00%

Figure 5-1 Effects of Different Forms of Weighting on an Index

of shares available to investors (as opposed to all of a company's outstanding shares).[2]

Calculation

Calculation is fairly straightforward. It consists of calculating the relative prices and producing the index number.

Trader's Notebook

Some new ETFs are based not on market capitalization but on fundamental factors, such as a firm's assets or revenues. Many of these new funds have been developed by Robert Arnott, a well-known financial expert. He has performed research that shows that indexes based on these fundamental weights, and rebalanced to stay in line with those weightings, may outperform market capitalization weighted indexes.

Index Diversity

Many indexes are not what they seem—especially in terms of diversification. Peter Bernstein, the well-known financial expert, has written that the S&P 500 cannot be considered diversified, because the 10 largest companies in the index account for 25 percent of the index's market capitalization, and the largest 25 companies make up 40 percent of the index's market capitalization. Other studies have shown, because of heavy weighting of large capitalization stocks, that the S&P 500 consists of 86 stocks; the Russell 1000 has 118. The performance of these indexes may be influenced significantly by a few of the biggest companies in the index, with the result being that investors are not getting the risk reduction, through diversification, that they think they are getting by investing in an index.

Major Indexes Measured by ETFs

There are many indexes out there—too many to cover in this chapter. Here, however, are some of the major indexes and their characteristics.

U.S. Indexes

The major U.S. indexes that have money attached to them are the S&P 500, the Nasdaq-100, Russell 2000, Russell 1000, the S&P 400, and the Wilshire 5000. The Russell 2000 is a small-cap index made up of all listed U.S. companies whose market capitalizations, based on size, range from the 70th to 97th percentile of market capitalization. Russell reconstitutes it annually, where it loses shares that fall into the Russell Microcap and Russell 1000 and gains from those that graduate from the Russell microcap and fall out of the Russell 1000. This high level of turnover with the opportunistic trading around the time of the reconstitution makes the Russell a somewhat problematic index in terms of costs and taxes for fund holders when capital gains are taken at the time stocks that drop out of the index are sold by a fund.

The Nasdaq-100 tracking stock tracks the 100 largest companies on the Nasdaq Index. This index is not highly diversified because many of the companies in the index are in the technology sector.

The Russell 1000 consists of the large-cap element of the Russell 3000, which is based on the 3,000 largest traded companies in the United States based on market capitalization.

The Wilshire 5000 Index is a total market index. It is important because it is the underlying index for Vanguard's Total Stock Market ETF (VTI) which is the largest of U.S. total market ETFs at the time of this writing.

ETF investors are not restricted to U.S. markets, however. It is often easier to buy ETFs based on foreign indexes than foreign securities.

International Indexes

There is a large universe of international and global indexes with ETFs associated with them. However, because of a combination of tax and regulatory restrictions, many of them are off limits to U.S. investors. To invest in overseas markets, most U.S. investors will be restricted to the Barclays Global Investor's iShares product lines, which are based on the MSCI indexes.

Figure 5-2 offers a sampling of major international and global indexes that are used to index significant amounts of money.

Region	Index
Canada	S&P/TSX 60
Europe	DJ Euro Stoxx 50
France	CAC 40
Germany	DAX
Hong Kong	Hang Seng
Japan	Nikkei 225
Japan	Topix
Sweden	OMX 30
Switzerland	SMI Index
United Kingdom	FTSE 100

Figure 5-2   Major International Indexes for ETF Investors

Tax Issues

When you're thinking about which indexes to use in investment strategies, it is important to keep in mind the costs of using different indexes. The major issue for investors is in the possible tax consequences of selecting an index. Although it may not be clear at first how a selection of an index can cost an investor money, consider our discussion of regulation in Chapter 4 and the various types of taxes that mutual funds pay that are mentioned in Chapter 3. Notably, if an index is assembled so that it does not comply with registered investment company (RIC) rules or properly structured if it is not an RIC, the fund will have to pay income taxes before any funds flow through to investors. This reduces the investor's return. A fund company that is in compliance with RIC rules will not pay taxes at the corporate level—all income will flow through to investors, who in turn will be responsible for their own taxes. In the case of ETFs held in a retirement plan, no taxes are paid until the money is withdrawn.

RIC Compliance

To create an RIC-compliant fund, the index the fund uses must meet certain requirements:

- At the end of each quarter of the RIC's tax year, no more than 25 percent of an index can be in the shares of a single issuer.
- At the end of each quarter of the RIC's tax year, at least 50 percent of the value of a fund's assets must be invested

in the shares of other issuers, but no single investment can exceed 5 percent of the value of the RIC's assets or 10 percent of the outstanding voting securities of the issuer.

These rules create certain minimum conditions for a diversified index. The first rule means that no company can account for more than 25 percent of the index. Of the remaining, smaller companies, the next 50 percent of the index needs a *minimum* of 10 constituents. This is to ensure that no company makes up more than 5 percent of this next 50 percent of the index. The final 25 percent of the index needs to have a minimum of two constituents to avoid violating the first principle. This means that the minimum size of the index is 13 securities. Of course, given how market valuations can change when a stock price moves, an index developer will add more shares to allow for movement in share prices to avoid violating these criteria.

Rebalancing and Taxes

One area where indexes require scrutiny, in a taxable account, is in the matter of rebalancing indexes, given the growth in equal and fundamentally weighted indexes. Consider a two-company index, with companies A and B each with a 50 percent share of the index, based on market capitalization at the index's inception. Over six months, Company A's value increases by 20 percent, so its market's share grows to 60 percent, and Company B's shares decrease by 20 percent, so it is now 40 percent of the market. To keep the weightings equal, some of A's shares need to be sold (at a gain), and some of B's shares need to be bought.

This rebalancing, usually done quarterly, ensures equal weighting, but it could also result in short-term capital gains taxes, which really hurt. However, this process of selling and buying to keep equal weights has two consequences—one is a higher cost because there are more transaction costs involved: (1) the commissions for buying and (2) taxes. To rebalance the fund, the shares that have increased in value will need to be sold, which most likely will result in capital gains taxes, thereby reducing the returns from the fund.

> **Trader's Notebook**
>
> Ultimately, when considering an index to use as a benchmark, it helps to look at the turnover of the index, because that could be an indication of the tax efficiency of the fund.

This also applies to the new fundamentally weighted RAFI (Research Affiliates Fundamentals Index) indexes, which weight by fundamental value factors as opposed to market capitalization. Taking gains creates costs and taxes. Rebalancing is not necessarily a costless activity when viewed in terms of taxes.

Foreign Tax Credit

The structure of ETFs with foreign components could determine their tax burden. This concerns global funds, which may have assets both inside and outside the United States. For global funds with assets in the United States, more than half of their assets must be outside the United States. Otherwise the fund cannot apply the foreign tax credit. This means that the shareholders of the ETF are not eligible to place a dollar-for-dollar tax credit on their U.S. taxes for any foreign taxes paid. While they can deduct taxes, the deduction is not as valuable as the tax credit that creates a tax-neutral situation for investors with money in a fund in a taxable account. Of course, this has less relevance for those with money in nontaxable accounts. However, it could be useful when choosing international indexes. Investors should consider indexes based in countries that do not tax foreign shareholders at all. The United Kingdom, for example, does not tax dividends of U.S. shareholders. This information should be discussed in the prospectus of the fund.

ETF Strategy

Understanding indexes helps investors choose ETFs. Although knowledge about indexes may not always help the investor to select winners, it can help investors avoid costs and reduce taxes. With ETFs, the question, "What did the market do today?" really matters.

6

THE ETF UNIVERSE

The ETF market has exploded, from one ETF in 1993 to over 600 in 2007, in the United States alone. Indexing once seemed simple, but just about everything is indexed, from dermatology and skin care products to barrels of oil. Are all those funds good investments? Probably not, according to John Bogle, the legendary founder of the Vanguard Group, who sees the multiplication of funds as being a long way from classic indexing. The wide range of choices, some that perfectly match what the investor needs and some that will not perform in line with expectations, creates confusion, as well as opportunity. With this plethora of ETFs in mind, intelligent selection begins with investigating the possible investments and then determining how to choose from among them.

ETF Investment Options

Investors face a confusing array of ETFs. How do the funds differ? Which ones should the investor buy? The simplest way to tackle the problem is to break the funds down into different categories and then examine their characteristics. (See Figures 6-1 and 6-2.)

Fund Type	Number of ETFs	Assets under Management as of April 30, 2007 (Millions)	Percent of Assets under Management	Representative Fund and Ticker Symbol
Broad	10	$14,049	3.05%	iShares Russell 3000 Index Fund (IWV)
Size	30	$151,326	32.83%	SPDR (SPY)
Style	46	$60,581	13.14%	iShares S&P 500/Citigroup Growth (IVW)
International	68	$120,003	26.04%	iShares MSCI Spain Fund (EWP)
Global	12	$3,564	0.77%	iShares S&P Global Telecommunications Index Fund (IXP)
Sector	123	$48,037	10.42%	Technology Select Sector SPDR (XLK)
Specialty	138	$22,088	4.79%	Claymore/Ocean Tomo Patent (OTP)
Commodity	17	$16,034	3.48%	United States Oil Fund (USO)
Currency	11	$2,128	0.46%	Rydex Euro Currency (FXE)
Fixed Income	20	$23,086	5.01%	iShares Lehman TIPS Bond Fund (TIP)
TOTAL	475	$460,896	100.00%	
Subcategory				
Broad	10	$14,049	3.05%	iShares Russell 3000 Index Fund (IWV)
Size—Large Cap	14	$113,314	24.59%	SPDR (SPY)
Size—Mid Cap	7	$19,507	4.23%	iShares S&P 400 ETF (IJH)
Size—Small Cap	6	$18,009	3.91%	iShares Russell 2000 Index fund (IWM)
Size—Microcap	3	$496	0.11%	iShares Russell Microcap Index Fund (IWC)
Style—Large Growth	7	$16,749	3.63%	iShares S&P 500/Citigroup Growth (IVW)
Style—Large Value	7	$17,744	3.85%	iShares S&P 500/Citigroup Value (IVE)
Style—Mid Growth	8	$4,626	1.00%	iShares S&P 400 MidCap Growth Index Fund (IJK)
Style—Mid Value	7	$7,107	1.54%	iShares S&P 400 MidCap Value Index Fund (IVE)
Style—Small Growth	7	$5,555	1.21%	iShares Russell 2000 Growth Index Fund (IWO)
Style—Small Value	8	$7,788	1.69%	iShares Russell 2000 Value Index Fund (IWN)
Style—All-Cap Growth	1	$287	0.06%	iShares Russell 3000 Growth Index Fund (IWZ)
Style—All-Cap Value	1	$725	0.16%	iShares Russell 3000 Value Index Fund (IWW)

Category	Number	Assets	%	Example Fund
International—Developed	49	$83,856	18.19%	iShares MSCI Spain Fund (EWP)
International—Emerging	19	$36,147	7.84%	iShares MSCI-Brazil Index Fund (EWZ)
Global	12	$3,564	0.77%	iShares S&P Global Telecommunications Index Fund (IXP)
Sector—Consumer Discretionary	7	$1,746	0.38%	Consumer Discretionary Select Sector SPDR (XLY)
Sector—Consumer Staples	10	$2,627	0.57%	Consumer Staples Select Sector SPDR Fund (XLP)
Sector—Energy	11	$8,015	1.74%	Energy Select Sector SPDR Fund (XLE)
Sector—Financials	14	$4,817	1.05%	Financial Select Sector SPDR Fund (XLF)
Sector—Health Care	33	$5,063	1.10%	Health Care Select Sector SPDR Fund (XLV)
Sector—Industrials	9	$2,650	0.57%	Industrial Select Sector SPDR Fund (XLI)
Sector—Material	6	$2,532	0.55%	Materials Select Sector SPDR Fund (XLB)
Sector—Technology	22	$7,857	1.70%	Technology Select Sector SPDR (XLK)
Sector—Utilities	6	$4,762	1.03%	Utilities Select Sector SPDR (XLU)
Sector—REIT	5	$7,968	1.73%	iShares Cohen & Steers Realty Index of Major REITs (ICF)
Specialty—Domestic, Dividend	15	$10,123	2.20%	First Trust Advisors Morningstar Dividend Leaders (FDL)
Specialty—Domestic, Other	105	$7,540	1.64%	Claymore/Ocean Tomo Patent (OTP)
Specialty—International, Dividend	15	$2,779	0.60%	iShares FTSE UK Dividend Plus ETF (IUKD.L)
Specialty—International, Other	3	$1,646	0.36%	Horizons Beta Pro S&P TSX 60 Bear Plus (HXD.TO)
Commodity	17	$16,034	3.48%	United States Oil Fund (USO)
Currency	11	$2,128	0.46%	Rydex Euro Currency (FXE)
Fixed Income	20	$23,086	5.01%	iShares Lehman TIPS Bond Fund (TIP)
TOTAL	475	$460,896	100.00%	

Figure 6-1 U.S. ETF and ETF Look-Alike Population as of April 30, 2007

Source: State Street Global Advisors (www.etfconnect.com/documents/ssga.xls and finance.yahoo.com).

Fund Type	Investment Rationale	Risk Factors
Broad	Chance to buy broad U.S. market with one investment. High level of diversification. Low, if any, turnover, which results in low taxes.	May underperform fixed-income investments. May underperform stock market strategies based on picking individual stocks. May underperform other markets. May underperform other market segments. May underperform other market sectors. Styles and weights may change over time.
Size—Large Cap	Blue chip companies that are leaders in their fields. Usually many of the most seasoned companies in the U.S. market.	Same as broad markets.
Size—Mid Cap	May outperform broad market and large-capitalization stocks in a given time period.	Mid-capitalization companies tend to have less diverse product lines than larger companies and thus could be more affected by problems that affect their product lines. The stocks of mid-cap companies may be illiquid and hard for an ETF to buy or sell, which could affect the ability of an ETF to match its index. Mid-cap stocks are more sensitive than large-cap stocks to negative economic and business factors.
Size—Small Cap	May outperform broad market and large-capitalization stocks in a given time period.	Small companies may be less secure financially than larger, better established companies. Small-cap companies may depend on a few key personnel and be more subject to personnel risk—the risk of key personnel departing the firm. Small-capitalization companies tend to have less diverse product lines than larger companies and thus could be more affected by problems that affect their product lines. The stocks of small-cap companies may be illiquid and hard for an ETF to buy or sell, which could affect the ability of an ETF to match its index.

Type		Risks
Size—Micro cap	May outperform broad market and large-capitalization stocks in a given time period.	Same risks as small-cap funds.
Style—Large Growth	Opportunity to seek out growth stocks, but with relatively solid companies.	Growth stocks lack dividend yield to cushion stock prices when market turns downward.
		May lack diversification resulting from concentration in a relatively small number of securities.
Style—Large Value	Allows the value-oriented investor to access a large selection of blue chips.	Value stocks may stay undervalued for long periods and may never reach their full potential value.
Style—Mid Growth	Access growth stocks in the mid-cap sector.	Growth stocks lack dividend yield to cushion stock prices when market turns downward.
Style—Mid Value	Access value stocks in the mid-cap sector.	Risks of mid-cap and value funds.
Style—Small Growth	Access growth stocks in the small-cap sector.	Risk of small-cap and growth funds.
Style—Small Value	Access value stocks in the small-cap sector.	Risk of small-cap and value funds.
Style—All-Cap Growth	Permits growth investing across the broad market.	Risks of broad market and growth funds.
Style—All-Cap Value	Permits value investing across the broad market.	Risks of broad market and value funds.
International—Developed	New economic opportunities	Illiquid inefficient securities markets.
	Economic diversification.	High price volatility.
	Currency diversification.	Exchange rate volatility and exchange controls. Withholding and other foreign taxes.
		Restrictions on repatriation of funds or other assets of the ETF.
		Higher transaction costs relative to the United States.
		Difficulties in enforcing contracts.
		Lower levels of securities regulation compared to the United States.
		Different accounting, disclosure, and reporting compared to the United States.

Figure 6-2 Summary of ETF and ETF Look-Alike Types and Risks

(Continues)

Fund Type	Investment Rationale	Risk Factors
International—Emerging	Opportunities to invest in rapidly growing economies. Because of regulations in many countries that restrict foreign ownership of individual equities, funds are the only way to invest in them.	More substantial government involvement in economic matters. Higher inflation rates than in the United States. Social, economic, and political uncertainty and risks of nationalization or expropriation of assets, and risk of war. High concentration in one sector for certain ETFs. Risks for international-developed funds with particular risks of unstable governments and risks for nationalization or expropriation of assets or war. Emerging market economies are dependent on exports, usually commodities and subject to effects of commodity price fluctuations. Emerging market economies often have high levels of debt and inflation. Emerging market countries are in parts of the world highly subject to natural disasters and effects of global warming.
Global	Invest in an industry across borders.	Risks of international funds. Eligibility for foreign tax credit.
Sector—Consumer Discretionary	Use as part of sector rotation strategy. Capture growth as economy grows and consumers spend more money on luxury and big-ticket goods.	Overall economic performance. Interest rates. Costs of necessities that may limit discretionary spending. Highly competitive markets. Subject to changes in tastes, fads, and demographics.
Sector—Consumer Staples	Use as part of sector rotation strategy. Use as stabilizer in portfolio, because many of these goods are necessities.	Government regulation of many companies. Subject to changes in tastes and habits.

Sector—Energy	Opportunity to benefit from rising energy prices.	Energy prices. Spending on exploration and production. Political instability in energy-producing regions of the world. Securities prices react rapidly to changes in supply and demand. Environmental regulations.
Sector—Financials	Play on interest rates, economic expansion, and consumption trends. Pay above-average dividends. Usually the most liquid stocks in international markets.	Governmental regulation. Subject to economic cycles, especially real estate. Insurance is highly competitive. Rising interest rates hurt business. Credit issues with borrowers.
Sector—Health Care	Benefit from changing demographics. Profit from medical advances and the biotechnology revolution.	Profitability related to patent protection—risk from patent expiration. Product obsolescence. Product liability issues. Products require FDA approval, which may take time. High level of competition, which makes it hard to raise prices and may lead to price discounting.
Sector—Industrials	Benefit from economic expansion. Profit from improved sales for particular products.	Obsolescence of products or manufacturing processes. Transportation stocks can be highly cyclical because of fuel prices, labor, and insurance costs. Environmental damage and product liability claims. Same risks as material sector.
Sector—Material	As economy starts to grow, the material sector expands. Take advantage of shortages of basic supplies, which cause price increases that benefit the materials sector.	Commodity prices. Factors affecting international trade, including value of the dollar. Economic cycles and overcapacity. Environmental regulations and liabilities.

Figure 6-2 Summary of ETF and ETF Look-Alike Types and Risks (*Continued*)

(Continues)

Fund Type	Investment Rationale	Risk Factors
Sector—Technology	Invest in a fast-growing, and often volatile, sector of the economy.	Highly competitive environments. Products subject to rapid obsolescence. Telecommunications companies are subject to governmental price regulation.
Sector—Utilities	Usually decent dividend yield. Above-average dividend yield and steady growth.	Subject to governmental regulation of rates. Inverse relationship of value to interest rates. Competitive pressures in deregulated markets. Compliance with environmental and nuclear safety regulations. Fuel price and weather risks.
Sector—REIT	Invest in real estate without the difficulties of actual ownership. More liquid than investing in real estate by buying property outright. Take advantage of real estate cycles—up or down. Good income stream.	Highly cyclical markets Adverse movements in national, statewide, and local real estate markets (such as oversupply of properties or too little demand). Obsolescent properties. Changes in availability, terms, and costs of mortgage funding. Impacts of environmental laws. Failure to comply with federal tax laws for REITs may mean taxation at the corporate level, which could reduce payments to shareholders.
Specialty—Domestic, Dividend	Income and stability from dividends. May outperform their comparable markets.	Weighted toward particular sectors.
Specialty—Domestic, Other	Access to new investment strategies. May allow access to hedge fund-style strategies.	May be gimmicky. New, less-tested investment strategies.

Type		Risks
Specialty—International, Dividend	Income and stability from dividends. May outperform their comparable markets. Diversification of economic risks.	Risks of international funds.
Specialty—International, Other	Access to new investment strategies and use hedge fund–style strategies in other currencies.	Risks of international funds and specialty funds.
Commodity	Hedge commodity prices, such as energy. Profit from demand for commodities. Access alternate investment markets.	Speculative. Fewer investment protections than for ETFs. Funds may have significant tracking error compared to commodity prices.
Currency	Use to hedge other investments from adverse currency moves. Speculate on currency fluctuations. Make long-term bets on currencies.	Speculative. Fewer investment protections than for ETFs.
Fixed Income	Obtain income. Diversify portfolio. Hedge against inflation with inflation-protected bonds. Profit from interest rate moves.	Bond prices move inversely with respect to interest rates. Long-term bonds have greater sensitivity to interest rate moves, economic events, and trends.

Figure 6.2 Summary of ETF and ETF Look-Alike Types and Risks (*Continued*)

The funds seek to obtain results that correspond to the price and yield performance, before fees and expenses, of the respective indexes that they track. The funds promise simple, low-cost investment. Yet that investment comes with risks.

The choice of an index implicitly selects styles and sectors. If that index drifts in its makeup, then its selection of styles and sectors will change, and investors may not end up with the portfolio they wanted at the time of their initial investment decision. According to a recent report titled *Assessing the Quality of Stock Market Indices: Requirements for Asset Allocation and Performance Measurement*, from the EDHEC Risk and Asset Management Research Centre:

> The style drifts of the indices are of concern to investors since we can conclude that broad market indices constitute specific choices of risk factors rather than a "neutral" risk exposure. This means that investors who passively hold an index or managers who select a market index as a benchmark can see their risk exposure being modified through time. As a result, it may happen that their risk exposure no longer corresponds to the initial asset allocation and thus no longer corresponds to their initial choice of risks.

Trader's Notebook

Investors have to keep in mind the generic risks affecting all types of fund investments. The market for the fund may be inactive, or illiquid, at times, thus making purchase, or sale, difficult. The shares could trade at a premium, or discount, to their net asset value, resulting in the investor possibly collecting less, or more, than the underlying value of the share. You need to remember that you are investing in a risky market— one not insured or guaranteed by any government agency. ETF promoters do not provide guarantees.

In addition to the problem of drift, funds using derivatives as part of a representative sampling strategy could incur risks of rapid, adverse moves in derivatives markets leading to greater losses than when a fund invests only in conventional securities. Investors have to watch, as well, for tracking error risk—the performance of a fund may not match that of the underlying index. Tracking error could arise from the rounding of prices, failure of a sample to match the target index, or fees and expenses that an index, being costless, does not incur.

Classification by Capitalization

Some funds invest in stocks based on their market capitalization. Large-capitalization (large-cap) funds typically invest in the largest companies in the U.S. market, generally the companies whose stocks make up 70 percent of the market value of all traded stocks. Mid-cap funds invest in a group of smaller companies whose total market value accounts for the next 20 percent of U.S. market value. Small-cap funds invest in even smaller companies whose value equals 7 percent of total market value. Micro-capitalization (micro-cap) funds put their money into much smaller firms, basically those in the Russell Micro-cap Index, which account for the remaining 3 percent of market capitalization. The various categories combine to make up the broad market, which includes large-capitalization, mid-capitalization, and small-capitalization stocks, but *not* micro-capitalization stocks.

Investors in capitalization-based funds must understand that a significant change in the market value of a component stock could move that stock from one fund to another. For example, if a company decreases in market capitalization, it may drop from the large-capitalization category to the mid- or small-capitalization category. This means that the stock can no longer remain part of a large-capitalization index. In turn, a fund based on that large-capitalization index may have to sell that security and replace it with another. Either way, the change in portfolio forces investors to pay taxes and expenses related to the sale of the security.

Broad Market Index

A typical broad market index covers 97 percent of the market capitalization of all publicly traded companies in the United States and its territories. The Russell 3000 Index fits into this category. It is a capitalization-weighted index of the 3000 largest publicly traded companies that are located in the United States and its territories.

When choosing to invest in a broad-based index, such as the Russell 3000, the main risk an investor faces is that the overall market may not perform as well as fixed-income investments or stock market strategies that select individual stocks or particular sectors. On the other hand, buying into a broad index frees the investor from making a lot of decisions about market sectors and might be the best bet for the amateur investor who wants to be in the market.

In reality, it is not easy to define the "market." An investor buying a broad market index purchases a portfolio whose weightings (in terms of market capitalization) reflect the market's opinion of the securities at that time. The weights of various stocks, or industries, in the index may change over time. For example, Microsoft was not part of the Dow Jones Industrial Average for many years, despite the firm's size and economic importance. Adding Microsoft to the Dow changed the weights of stocks in the Dow.

Even a fund based on a broad index could force its owners to pay taxes if stocks leave the broad capitalization index by going out of business, being bought out, or falling in market capitalization to the micro-cap category. These changes could present investors with capital gains taxes and transaction costs as funds trade stocks to match the index.

Funds Classified by Market Capitalization of Investments

Classification by market capitalization is one of the most basic ways to separate and classify stocks, because the criteria are straightforward—market capitalization is calculated by multiplying the number of shares available to investors by the most recent market price.

Size—Large Cap

Large-capitalization stocks make up 70 percent of the U.S. investment market, at least by definition. The S&P 500, the most important large-cap index, serves as the basis for the first and largest ETF, the SPDR (Standard & Poor's depository receipt). Although the index contains 500 stocks, in reality only a small number of the stocks influence its value because the index is weighted by market capitalization.

Although an index may be large capitalization, that does not make it neutral in terms of style or sector. The investor who chooses a particular index, which appears broad, really purchases the style and sector weightings inherent in that index or fund. These change as companies are added to or subtracted from the fund.

The Standard & Poor's 500 Index is a market capitalization-weighted index of 500 companies selected by Standard & Poor's for inclusion based on criteria known to its index committee. More money tracks the S&P 500 and its various components than any other index. Many funds are based on this index, or on other large-cap indexes such as the Dow Jones Industrial Average and the Russell 1000 Index of the 1,000 largest U.S. publicly traded companies measured by market capitalization.

Size—Mid Cap

Next in size come the mid-cap companies, which account for 20 percent of market capitalization. Mid-cap stocks have risks that distinguish them from large-cap stocks:

- Less diverse product lines than larger companies, which makes them vulnerable to problems in a particular product line

- Illiquid trading conditions for stock, making shares hard to buy or sell, which affects the ability of an ETF to match its index

- More sensitive than large-cap stocks to negative economic and business factors

The S&P 400, with its portfolio of 400 stocks, is one of the best-known mid-cap indexes.

Size—Small Cap

Further down in size are small-capitalization stocks, which make up 7 percent of U.S. market capitalization. Small-cap stocks have particular risks associated with them, some of which are similar to the risks of mid-cap stocks:

- Less secure, financially, than larger, better-established companies
- Dependent on a few key personnel and more subject to the risk of key personnel departing the firm
- Less diverse product lines than larger companies and thus could be more sensitive to problems affecting a particular product line
- Illiquidity of trading in their stocks makes it hard for an ETF to buy or sell, which could affect the ability of an ETF to match its index

The Russell 2000 Index, probably the best-known small-capitalization index, is a subset of the Russell 3000, which covers 97 percent of U.S. market capitalization. The Russell 1000 encompasses the largest 1,000 companies in terms of market capitalization. The Russell 2000 includes the next 2,000 companies in terms of market capitalization. The Russell 2000 is reconstituted every year in June, when companies that drop out of the Russell 1000 are added as well as those that graduate upward from the Russell micro-cap index. The nature of this index, with change at the top and bottom of the list, makes the Russell 2000 subject to a high level of annual turnover, which can make it a less tax-friendly fund. It is capitalization weighted.

Size — Micro Cap

Last, but not least, comes the Russell Microcap Index, comprising the remaining 3 percent of U.S. market capitalization. Micro-cap funds share the risks of small-cap funds. In addition, micro-cap stocks tend to be more volatile than those with larger capitalization.

Style

While capitalization is relatively straightforward, style investing is a more nebulous category due to some of the seemingly arbitrary classification criteria. *Style* describes a method of investing that looks at fundamental characteristics of securities and then classifies the securities according to criteria that enable the investor to make decisions and allocations based on those criteria. *Growth* and *value* are the two most common styles. Growth funds invest "primarily in stocks that are expected to increase in capital value rather than yield high income."[1] Barclays Global Investors, in its prospectus for the iShares Morningstar Large Growth Index Fund, designates the stocks in that fund as growth "because they are issued by companies that typically have higher than average historical and forecasted earnings, sales, equity and cash flow growth." However, growth stocks generally lack the dividend yields that can help cushion stock prices when markets slump.

Value funds invest in "shares of a company with solid fundamentals that are priced below those of its peers, based on analysis of price/earnings ratio, yield, and other factors."[2] Sometimes, though, as the impatient find out, the stocks may remain undervalued for long periods or, even worse, may never reach a normal valuation. Barclays Global Investors, in its prospectus for the iShares Morningstar Large Value Index Fund, declares that the stocks in the fund are designated as value "because they are issued by companies that typically have relatively low valuations based on price-to-earnings, price-to-book value, price-to-sales, price-to-cash flow and dividend yields." Funds classified neither as growth nor as value are considered *core*. However, there are too few core ETFs to warrant discussion.[3]

Figure 6-3 shows the formulas Morningstar uses to define the various styles. Other indexes may use different formulas. Investors need to understand that temporary changes in market perception (as evidenced by earnings projections or swings in the price/earnings ratio) could lead to ejection of securities from the fund, thereby leading to unnecessary tax consequences and expenses. These processes, although appearing very systematic, could easily

Value Score		
Time Period	Factor	Weight (%)
Forward Looking	Price-to-projected earnings	50.0
Historical	Price-to-book	12.5
	Price-to-sales	12.5
	Price-to-cash flow	12.5
	Dividend yield	12.5

Growth Score		
Time Period	Factor	Weight (%)
Forward Looking	Long-term projected earnings growth	50.0
Historical	Earnings growth	12.5
	Sales growth	12.5
	Cash flow growth	12.5
	Book value growth	12.5

Style Score	
Style Score =	Growth Score – Value Score
Growth Score	0 to 100
Value Score	0 to 100
Style Score range:	−100 to 100
	100 = Growth
	−100 = Value
Neither category:	Core

Figure 6-3 Morningstar's Style Breakdown Criteria for Determining a Stock's Style

Source: Morningstar Methodology Overview.

vary from one index developer to another. Morningstar designs its categories so that one-third of securities is designated as growth, one-third as value, and one-third as core. The style and market capitalization formulas are used to further classify ETFs, with the size (large, mid cap, small cap) used as an adjective and the style as a noun, creating for example, a large-cap growth fund or a small-cap value fund.

It is distinctly possible that if ETFs are constructed around these highly arbitrary definitions, they would exclude stocks that experienced investors would believe belong in the category. Definitions might snare growth stocks that do not grow and value stocks that don't have value. For example, in Figure 6-3, consider Morningstar's 50 percent weighting for earnings. Many value stocks do not

> **Trader's Notebook**
>
> It is possible that some style funds may not be very diversified because some assets are concentrated in a relatively small number of securities. This may make the fund more susceptible to risks associated with those companies or economic, political, or regulatory factors that might affect those companies.

have earnings; they have assets. Investors may not get what they want.

The capitalization and style categories can be combined to further break down the types of funds. Here are the characteristics of the major categories.

Large Growth

The large growth category consists of large-capitalization stocks with a growth bent, which is determined by the index provider.

Large Value

The large value category is made up of large-capitalization stocks with a value bent, which is determined by the index provider. According to the S&P 500/Citigroup Value Index, which contains the value-oriented members of the S&P 500, these companies constitute about 51 percent of the S&P 500.

Mid Growth

The S&P 400 Index is a prominent mid-cap index. Approximately 47 percent of the stocks in the S&P 400 fall into the growth category, according to the Standard & Poor's MidCap 400/Citigroup Growth Index.

Mid Value

The S&P 400 Index mentioned above also has been broken down into a value index. Approximately 53 percent of the stocks in the S&P 400 fall into the value category according to the Standard & Poor's MidCap 400/Citigroup Value Index.

Small Growth

The Russell 2000 Index is the best-known small-capitalization index. It, too, has a growth component. The iShares Russell 2000 Growth Index Fund (IWO) comprises about half the capitalization of the Russell 2000 Index.

Small Value

The Russell 2000 Index has a value component. The iShares Russell 2000 Value Index Fund (IWN) comprises about half the capitalization of the Russell 2000 Index.

All-Cap Growth

The all-cap growth category is composed of growth stocks within the all-capitalization, or total market, universe. One fund that seeks to capture the movement off all-cap growth stocks is the iShares Russell 3000 Growth Index Fund (IWZ) which tracks, appropriately, the Russell 3000 Growth Index.

All-Cap Value

The all-cap value category is composed of value stocks within the all-capitalization, or total market, universe. One fund that seeks to capture the movement of all-cap value stocks is the iShares Russell 3000 Value Index Fund (IWW) which tracks, appropriately, the Russell 3000 Value Index.

International Funds

The funds discussed above all focus on the United States. However, ETFs cover the world. An international fund invests outside the United States. Global funds, often headquartered outside the United States, invest in markets around the world, and this may include the United States. This distinction is important, because a global fund that has holdings both inside and outside the United States may create potential tax problems for investors, if the fund is not a regulated investment company. As mentioned in Chapter 4, if a fund investing outside the United States does not have more than 50 percent of its assets classified as foreign, its investors cannot apply the foreign tax credit to the overseas taxes they pay.

International funds may be subject to a number of risks, including economic and political events affecting securities markets as well as changing interest rates. There are some risks peculiar to investing in international funds, the principal one being currency risk. Since securities are priced in a different currency from that of the investor's home country, it is possible that exchange-rate fluctuations could impair the return to the investor. On the other hand, an investor living in a country with a weak currency could benefit from the change in currency values and might even buy into a fund for that reason.

Other risks that may characterize international investments include:

- Illiquid, inefficient securities markets

- High price volatility

- Exchange-rate volatility and exchange controls; withholding and other foreign taxes

- Restrictions on repatriation of funds or other assets of the ETF

- Higher transaction costs relative to the United States

- Difficulties in enforcing contracts

- Lower levels of securities regulation compared to the United States

- Different accounting, disclosure, and reporting compared to the United States

- More substantial government involvement in economic matters

- Higher inflation rates than those in the United States

- Social, economic, and political uncertainty and risks of nationalization or expropriation of assets; risk of war— these issues are a particular concern for emerging markets funds

International—Developed

One type of international fund tracks an index based on companies in developed countries, although there may not be a formal definition of developed countries in comparison to emerging markets.

Figure 6-4 shows the breakdown of the world according to ETF providers. Countries that are not included on the developed list probably fall into the emerging category, with the possible exception of European countries such as Denmark or Iceland.

Among the risks of investing in international funds is the possibility that an international fund may be dominated by companies in one sector, which means that the investment takes on the risks of one sector. For example, two of the three largest companies in the MSCI Spain Index are banks, which could subject the investor to a high degree of concentration in the banking sector as opposed to the whole economy.

Developed Markets	Emerging Markets
Australia	Argentina
Austria	Brazil
Belgium	Chile
Canada	China
Finland	Colombia
France	Czech Republic
Germany	Egypt
Greece	Hungary
Hong Kong	India
Ireland	Indonesia
Israel	Jordan
Italy	Malaysia
Japan	Mexico
Luxembourg	Morocco
Netherlands	Pakistan
New Zealand	Peru
Norway	Philippines
Portugal	Poland
Singapore	Russia
Spain	South Africa
Sweden	South Korea
Switzerland	Taiwan
United Kingdom	Thailand
United States	Turkey

Figure 6-4 The World According to ETF Providers

International — Emerging

Emerging markets refer to economies that are expanding and moving toward developed status. Brazil, Russia, India, and China, the BRIC countries, are well-known examples of emerging markets. In addition to the general risks facing investors in international funds, emerging markets have their own particular risks, most notably that they are often highly dependent on exports, especially of commodities, and are economically susceptible to fluctuation in commodity prices and the vagaries of international trade. In addition, these countries may have high levels of debt and inflation.

Many emerging markets exist in regions that are subject to natural disasters such as earthquakes, volcanic eruptions, and tsunamis that can adversely affect their economies. In addition, many developing countries are more at risk from the effects of global warming than are other countries. Think of flooding in Bangladesh or China running out of water.

International—Global

One important case to note for U.S. taxpayers is global funds, which invest abroad and may also have investments in the United States. Often these funds concentrate on one industry, which means that they are nondiversified. This increases the risk of the securities moving together in the event of an adverse shock to the industry and the risk of great price volatility.

> **Trader's Notebook**
>
> Funds can be classified as nondiversified because of the high correlation among the various securities. Nondiversified funds may have larger percentages of their assets in securities of smaller numbers of issuers, which makes them susceptible to the risks associated with these particular industries. Investors need to find out whether these funds qualify for regulated investment company tax treatment.

Holders of global funds that do not have more than half of their assets outside the United States are not eligible for the foreign tax credit (discussed in Chapter 4), which could reduce the returns to investors. Another risk factor can arise from the fact that foreign exchanges and foreign exchange markets may be open on days when a U.S. ETF does not trade, which means that the shares could change in value, even though a fund's investors cannot buy or sell the fund's shares.

Sector

Many ETFs select their investments from a particular industrial sector. State Street Global Advisors, one of the largest issuers of ETFs, divides the investment universe into 10 industrial sectors. The sectors, as classified by State Street, are:

1. Consumer discretionary
2. Consumer staples
3. Energy
4. Financials
5. Health care
6. Industrials
7. Materials
8. Technology
9. Utilities
10. REIT

Concentration in a particular sector makes a fund susceptible to any single occurrence, such as a political, economic, regulatory, or market event. Many sector funds are considered nondiversified, which means that they may be exposed to more volatility than more diversified funds. Being nondiversified, however, does not mean that a fund cannot also qualify as a regulated investment company, which is a means of avoiding double taxation for shareholders. The following overview of the sectors will help investors have a better idea of the holdings of the respective sector funds.

Consumer Discretionary

The consumer discretionary sector is composed of companies catering to consumer discretionary spending such as leisure, for example, as opposed to necessities, such as food, which is usually considered a consumer staple. The consumer discretionary category typically includes companies from these industries: retail, media, hotels and lodging, restaurants and leisure, household durables, textiles, apparel and luxury goods, automobiles and their components, leisure equipment and goods, and consumer services. These kinds of companies benefit from rising consumer income.

The investor in a consumer discretionary fund ties the success of the investment to factors related to consumer spending on items that are not considered necessities. Obviously, a key factor in that success is the performance of the economy where the companies operate, with a stronger economy tending to be better for these companies. Interest rates can affect the prospects of funds in this sector, too, because higher interest rates may negatively affect discretionary spending; for example, higher interest rates could result in fewer car loans and fewer car sales, while falling interest rates may result in more consumer purchasing or purchases on installment plans. Higher gasoline prices could reduce spending in restaurants, because more income is used to pay for basic transportation. These markets are also highly competitive. Just look at the amount spent on TV advertising to promote consumer discretionary products—companies aren't spending millions of dollars on Super Bowl commercials to sell stone and gravel. Demographic changes, such as an aging population or changing consumer tastes such as preferences for organic products, can dramatically and quickly affect the profitability of consumer products companies.

Consumer Staples

While some consumer discretionary items may be luxuries, consumer staples refer to necessities such as putting food on the table. Typically, the consumer staples sector includes food products, beverages, retailing of food and staples, household products, and personal products. Consumer staples companies generally provide the portfolio with steady growth and income, which are especially desirable traits when investors fear an economic downturn in other sectors.

Even consumer staples face risks, such as government regulation of the use of food additives and methods of food production that could affect the profitability of companies in the sector. Laws, regulations, and litigation can affect tobacco companies. Consumer trends, fads, and advertising influence food and beverage sales.

Energy

Energy is another of life's little necessities. With all the talk of high energy prices, shortages, and volatility in oil prices, energy funds may interest people who wish to invest in those markets in a diversified manner. Companies in this sector are engaged in oil and gas exploration and production and oil equipment, services, and distribution.

Because of concerns about global warming, energy companies are subject to government regulation and claims for environmental damages. Also, because oil is produced in some of the less politically stable parts of the world, geopolitical and political events can cause oil prices to jump dramatically thus affecting energy companies. Energy securities will react to changes in supply and demand, political events, the success or failure of exploration projects, tax, and government policies.

Financials

Providing the monetary energy that facilitates all parts of the economy, the financial sector consists of commercial banks, insurance companies, diversified financial services companies, securities brokers, thrifts, mortgage companies, real estate, and consumer finance companies.

These companies are subject to considerable governmental regulation, which can limit the size and types of loans they can make and the interest rates they can charge. Investment in this sector offers a way to play interest rates, economic expansion, and consumption trends. Financial companies normally pay above-average dividends. In some countries, financial firms are among the few actively traded securities, so investors who want to put money in these markets must invest in the financial sector.

Economic downturns, or business and economic developments, could depress the value of real estate, which adversely affects real estate lenders. Insurance company profitability moves in cycles. The profitability of financial services companies depends on the availability and cost of capital, and companies tend to do worse when interest rates rise. In addition, credit-related issues with borrowers can hurt lenders when borrowers fail to repay loans.

Health Care

Experiencing a tremendous influx of capital in recent years, the health-care sector is made up of pharmaceuticals, biotechnology, health-care equipment, health-care services, health-care providers, health-care technology, and life sciences tools and services firms. The sector has grown as a result of medical advances, thereby expanding personal income and changing demographics.

Companies in the health-care field are highly dependent on patent protection for their products. The expiration of those patents can affect company profits, as does product obsolescence. In addition, given the litigious atmosphere surrounding medical issues, companies in this sector often face litigation based on product liability issues and related claims. Many health-care products and pharmaceuticals require the approval of the Food and Drug Administration before they are permitted to come on the market. The approval process may take years. Denial of approval damages companies trying to bring products to market. In addition, health-care companies are often subject to high levels of competition that may make it hard for them to raise prices and may even result in price discounting.

Industrials

Sharing many of the product obsolescence risks of the health-care sector, the industrial sector usually includes transportation companies, aerospace and defense manufacturers, construction and engineering companies, manufacturers of capital goods (used to produce other goods rather than being bought by consumers), and various types of industrial and trading companies and distributors. Investors expecting economic expansion or improved sales for particular products will want to focus on this sector.

Obsolescence of products, or manufacturing processes, could adversely affect company profits in this sector. In addition, the stocks of transportation companies can be highly cyclical, with periodic sharp increases in costs resulting from factors such as changes in fuel prices, labor agreements, and insurance costs. Industrial companies are also at risk for environmental damage and product liability claims. In addition, industrial sector firms face many of the same risks as companies in the materials sector (discussed below).

Materials

Sharing many risks with industrial companies, the materials sector includes companies in chemicals, metals and mining, forest and paper products, containers and packaging, and construction materials. Companies in this sector benefit from economic upturns and shortages of supply of the particular material relative to demand, which will raise the price of the product. Many of these companies trade in commodities from around the world. Commodity price movements, a change in the value of the dollar relative to other currencies, import controls, and global competition (after all, a pound of copper is a pound of copper regardless of whether it comes from Arizona or Chile) can dramatically change the prospects for these industries. These industries are prone to overbuilding, and to economic downturns when the worldwide supply of many of these materials exceeds demand, and companies report large losses from operations.

Also, given the often dangerous and environmentally sensitive nature of materials extraction and refining, companies in these funds may face liability for damaging the environment and depleting resources. And they have to make large expenditures on safety and pollution controls.

Technology

The technology sector includes companies from the computer hardware and software, computer components, telecommunications equipment, telecommunications services, Internet service and software, IT services, and office electronics industries. Technology investors look for profitable innovations, benefit from an expanding economy, and expect high growth rates. Technology companies operate in a highly competitive environment. Many of their products are subject to rapid obsolescence. In addition, telecommunications companies are subject to federal and state regulation, and the telecommunications market has undergone considerable restructuring in the past few years.

Utilities

In contrast to the highly competitive technology sector, the utilities sector consists of regulated power, gas, and water companies, independent producers and/or distributors of power, and interstate pipelines. Utilities, in general, offer above-average dividends and steady growth. A key risk for regulated utilities is that regulators may delay or refuse to grant needed price increases, which leaves the utility collecting inadequate revenues while costs keep rising. Utilities operating in jurisdictions that have restructured their regulatory frameworks may face competition in some activities and regulation in others. The need to comply with environmental and nuclear rules adds another level to regulation. Investors in utility ETFs also confront commodity risks because the price of fuel can affect profits. In addition to operating and regulatory risks, investors should note that the value of utility stocks tends to move inversely in relation to interest rates.

REIT

REITs (real estate investment trusts) are companies that invest in real estate and pay their earnings as dividends to investors. REITs are vehicles for investors who want above-average dividends as well as growth from appreciation of real estate values. Although

investing in a REIT ETF allows investors to diversify their investments across different REITs, the investments are still concentrated
in a cyclical business where the companies' profits may be highly
correlated with these risks. This area has a number of particular
risks, in addition to those of industry concentration:

- Adverse movements in national, statewide, and local real
  estate markets (such as oversupply of properties or too little
  demand)
- Obsolete properties
- Changes in availability, terms, and costs of mortgage
  funding
- Impacts of environmental laws
- Failure to comply with federal tax laws for REITs may result
  in taxation at the corporate level, which could reduce
  payments to shareholders

Specialty Funds

The specialty category comprises fund categories that don't fit into
the other categories. As of April 2007, the specialty category
accounted for 29 percent of U.S. funds, but barely 5 percent of
assets under management. The category consists largely of funds
meeting certain dividend criteria (dividend funds) and the
"specialty—other" area. This "other" category is where many of the
gimmicky funds can be found. These include funds that select
companies based on various rules that may have worked well in the

past, but can fall apart when a fund actually trades based on them. These "other" funds may not have a clear investment rationale and may be expensive relative to other ETFs.

Domestic—Dividend

The dividend fund category accounts for more than half of specialty fund investment. These funds are usually selected based on criteria related to the payment of dividends such as dividend growth rate and dividend payout ratio as well as trading volume. This is to ensure that the ETF does not get stuck with illiquid investments. These funds tend to be weighted toward utilities, financial services companies, and consumer goods companies, which tend to pay decent dividends consistently.

Domestic—Other

This category comprises ETFs and ETF look-alikes that do not fit neatly into other fund categories. As of April 2007, these operations made up more than 20 percent of U.S. ETFs and ETF look-alikes, by number, but accounted for less than 2 percent of U.S. ETF assets under management. The low uptake may be related to the relative newness of the funds or, perhaps, a dim opinion of their investment value. Many specialty funds may be based on relatively untested investment concepts or theories. However, one group of specialty funds may be worth investigating—funds that use weightings that differ from the standard market capitalization weighted funds. These funds may use equally weighted indexes or weightings determined by fundamental factors, such as company assets. These funds are rebalanced periodically either to keep equal weightings of stocks or to keep capitalizations in line with some predetermined weight. This constant rebalancing may create superior investment returns—a fact known for nearly 40 years, but only recently put to use. However, it is less clear how the tax consequences of this rebalancing—the capital gains taxes incurred—could eat away at the superior returns.

The Claymore/Ocean Tomo 300 Patent Fund (OTP) typifies one of the more "out there" specialty funds. It is based on a sample of companies that have significant intellectual property in terms of patent holdings. Time will tell whether these specialty indexes offer diversification, low-cost investments, and returns that justify the risks and often higher costs compared to the more basic ETFs.

International—Dividend

The specialty international dividend category follows the same classification as the domestic dividend fund with companies chosen based on their dividend payouts, dividend increases, and other characteristics, but these companies are outside the United States.

International—Other

This specialty fund category also works outside the United States. Regulatory authorities have approved specialty funds outside the United States.

Commodity

The commodity-based funds have become very popular recently as an alternative investment. However, these commodity funds are usually not exchange-traded funds; they are grantor trusts that do not trade with the protections of the Investment Company Act. One of the best known of these commodity-based funds is the United States Oil Fund (USO), a grantor trust with tremendous tracking error, administered by Victory Bay Asset Management.

Currency

The currency trusts represent a way for investors to invest or, better still, speculate in currencies without trading an over-the-counter market or dealing with the futures markets. Again, these trusts are not ETFs in the sense that they are not covered under the Investment Company Act. Currency markets can be extremely volatile with rapid changes that may take investors by surprise.

> **Trader's Notebook**
>
> It may be best for novice investors to avoid currency instruments, unless they have a clear rationale and plan for trading them. If an investor desires currency diversification, it may be safer to obtain foreign currency exposure by investing in an ETF denominated by a different currency than one's home country.

When buying or selling a currency trust, investors make an explicit bet that a particular currency, or currency basket, will rise or fall relative to another one. Some investors may attempt to use these trusts to hedge a foreign currency investment without using futures or options contracts, but it is not clear whether these trusts are an optimal way to hedge, given the potential tracking error between the fund and actual exchange rates.

Actually currency trusts may be inferior to trading a futures, or options, contract, given that many of these currency trusts may have issues with tracking errors or construction that do not exist with a futures contract.

Fixed Income

ETFs can provide a way for investors to access the fixed-income market in a cost-efficient manner and to diversify their investments. Individual investors, for instance, may encounter difficulties in buying individual bonds.

On the other hand, some observers believe that because of inefficiencies in the bond markets, bond portfolio managers may ferret out and use knowledge of those inefficiencies to increase profits. Still, cost needs to be factored in, and bond ETFs are probably significantly cheaper than typical bond mutual funds. As for risks, a rise in interest rates can cause bond values to fall. Debtors could default on bond payments, thereby depressing the value of the bonds they issued. Bonds with longer terms to maturity have a greater sensitivity to changes in interest rates and economic events and trends.[4]

ETF Strategy

Investors need to understand the basics underlying the ETF or the ETF look-alike—the advantages and disadvantages, risks and potential rewards of each product—before choosing the fund. Just because a product category has been growing rapidly, it does not mean that an investor needs to jump in. Some of the fastest-growing products have also been some of the most problematic in terms of tracking their benchmarks. That, in fact, is one of the key points to remember. Although ETFs may have proliferated, the principles that relate to them remain the same—tracking an index. Many of today's products are not diversified and may not be well constructed in terms of how they track an index or limit costs and taxes. More is not always better.

7

SUPPORT AND RESISTANCE WITH PIVOTS

ETFs are growing. There are a number of new instruments filling financial pages. And as they do with stocks, commentators are telling the public where the buyers and sellers are. In fact, there are services that people can purchase, or they can use simple formulas and make their own determination.

With ETFs, knowing where there is support is key, especially if you are a short-term trader. The authors have seen short term being as short as three seconds or as long as three months.

The following explanation of pivot points is derived from a service known as the Pattern Trapper (patterntrapper.com), which is a trading-related educational Web site run by Bob Hunt. As traders, we can state that having some sort of support and resistance concept in mind is key to trading ETFs. Understandably, the public would rather listen to pundits and gurus for this information. However, we want you to stop trading as if you were the public.

Pivot Points and ETFs

There are many technical indicators. We believe that *pivot points* are the best way to look at the vast universe of ETFs.

The pivot point formula looks like this:

$$P = \frac{L + H + C}{3}$$

P, or the pivot point, is the average of yesterday's high (H), low (L), and close (C).

Example 1

Imagine a hypothetical ETF in which yesterday's trade ranged from a low of zero to a high of 10, with a closing price of 5. According to the formula above,

$$P = \frac{0 + 10 + 5}{3}$$

$$P = 5$$

The pivot point for today will be 5. That is the midpoint for this ETF.

The expected high (resistance) and low (support) for today are derived from equally simple mathematical formulas:

$$R = (P \times 2) - L$$
$$S = (P \times 2) - H$$

Therefore, using the data from our hypothetical market, the expected high (resistance) for today will be, $R = (5 \times 2) - 0$ (which equals 10).

Today's expected low (support) will be $S = (5 \times 2) - 10$ (which equals 0).

Putting it all together, if yesterday had a range of 0 to 10 and closed in the middle at 5, then we expect today to do exactly the same thing, namely, a high of 10, a low of 0, and a close of 5.

The bottom line for traders willing to take the opposite of your trade is that while generally they are looking only to buy the bid and sell the offer, at the support and resistance points they will get long or short. You as an ETF trader must always think, "Who would want to take the other side of my trade?"

Example 2

Let's say that yesterday's low and high are the same as in our previous example (0 and 10), but rather than a close of 5, let's say the market closed on its high: 10. Our equation will be as follows:

$$P = \frac{0 + 10 + 10}{3}$$

This will yield a pivot point of 6.67.

Calculate the new support and resistance numbers.

$$R = (6.67 \times 2) - 0$$
$$S = (6.67 \times 2) - 10$$

Today's high (resistance) is expected to be 13.33. Today's low (support) is expected to be 3.33. What has occurred is that the higher close has caused all the pivot points to slide a little bit upward. It's easy to see what would have happened if yesterday had closed on the low: all of today's support and resistance expectations would have slid down just a bit.

The pivot points have survived the electronic revolution intact. In fact, they have thrived. Modern technical theorists have taken the old support and resistance levels and created tiers of support and resistance (S1, S2, and S3 . . . R1, R2, and R3), all based on the same simple ideas and straightforward math as the originals. (See Figure 7-1.)

Figure 7-2 is a shortened version of the pivot formula if you decide to use an Excel spreadsheet. However, you will notice that we've added S3 and R3. No, these are not characters from *Star Wars*. They represent final support and last resistance. If these numbers are taken out and you are on the wrong side of the market, it will be time to cash in your chips.

Name	Formula	Comment
Pivot (Average)	a. (High + low + close)/3 b. (High + low + close + opening)/4	You may include opening as in *b*.
First Resistance	(2 × average) − low	Usually does not hold in volatile markets
First Support	(2 × average) − high	Public buys here
Second Resistance	Average − next low + next high	Breakout possible (Do not sell into this rally)
Second Support	Average − next high − next low	Watch for break (Do not buy into this break)

Figure 7-1 Formula Review

```
DP* (daily pivot)  = (H + L + C)/3
R1 (resistance 1) = 2 × DP − L
S1 (support 1)    = 2 × DP − H
R2 (resistance 2) = DP + (R1 − S1)
S2 (support 2)    = DP − (R1 − S1)
R3 (resistance 3) = (DP − S1) + R2
S3 (support 3)    = DP − (R2 − S1)
```

*DP = daily pivot point (average).

Figure 7-2   Expanded Version of Pivot Formula

Moving Averages and ETFs

Note that while the pivot point is useful in identifying daily buying or selling strength, it is subject to wide fluctuations in highly volatile markets. Because it is derived from prices for one day only, there is no direct correlation between it and situations in longer time frames.

The moving averages serve to smooth the daily fluctuations in the pivot points and provide an indication of market trend. When the pivot points are above the moving averages, a rising market is indicated (uptrend); conversely, pivot points below the moving averages indicate a falling market (downtrend). The premise behind the use of moving averages is that a trend once established is more likely to continue than to reverse. As a result, trades taken in the direction of the moving average result in buying strength and selling weakness.

Advantages of Moving Averages in Trend Trading

Use of moving averages in trend trading provides three key advantages for traders:

1. A trend-following technique is, by definition, objective.
   Variations can be back-tested to verify or optimize results.

2. Because action points are well defined, uncertainty is minimized.

3. By employing a trend-following method, it is impossible for a move to occur without increasing the general market participation. In short, as prices rise, volume increases.

Disadvantages of Moving Averages in Trend Trading

There are two major disadvantages in using moving averages in trend trading:

1. Whipsaws are frequent and inevitable, and all signals acted upon are late by definition. That's why you must anticipate 20-minute averages. (Whipsaws are a situation when a security's price first heads in one direction, then quickly moves in the opposite direction. The term comes from the push and pull actions that lumberjacks used to cut wood with a saw known as a whipsaw.[1])

2. Large numbers of long positions will be taken near the top of the range and short positions on weakness near the bottom. Since markets fluctuate in trading ranges most of the time, it seems clear that fewer than half of the trades will be successful. "Rules" developed in some markets will not work in others or even in the same markets during different periods. Attempts may be made to adapt the rules to volatility, but predicting volatility is no easier than any other kind of market prediction.

What about Swing Trading?

Using pivots for day trading ETFs is fine, but we have a little secret for you. Sometimes the pivots can be extended. How?

We merely take a three-day moving average of the pivot and then look at the average price of the ETF for the week. The Pattern Trapper (patterntrapper.com) shown in Figure 7-3 is free.[2] If you are a pivot trader, you want to be sure you are trading with the trend. In the fall of 2007 you would have to be long or be a buyer of the stock market. We are above the yearly pivot, and we have received no signal to be short. However, there are opportunities on the short side. And that is the beauty of ETFs.

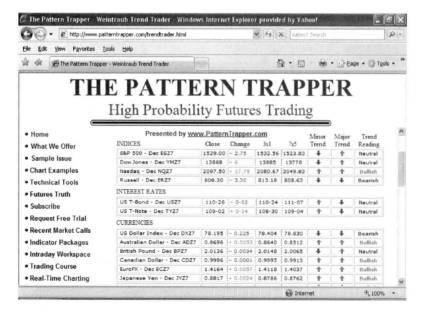

Figure 7-3 Free Trend Trader Originating from patterntrapper.com

Following are illustrations of several new sector ETFs, annotated with modern pivot point analysis.

Figure 7-4 shows the opening below the daily pivot and continuing below the pivot maintaining a negative initial 20-minute balance indicates likely weakness in the day time frame. The trader should look for an opportunity to go short at the pivot. There are several opportunities to do so. After establishing a short position, the trader should look to exit the trade at the S1, the first level of pivot support.

Figure 7-4   XLY; Pivot Point Example of Bear Move

The flag pattern (no real direction) that forms around S1 suggests that the market will likely see continuation on the downside into the close. On the break below the 1 p.m. (13:00 on figure) low, traders can easily establish another short position. They should then place a contingent stop close against the S2 support. In this case, they would have been able to buy back their short and get flat before the close.

Figure 7-5 shows a sharply lower opening. Even though traders will be sorely tempted to buy this S2 opening, they should refrain,

Figure 7-5 XLE

bearing in mind that the move below the daily pivot indicates a bearish tone in the day time frame.

However, in the late morning, as the market dipped all the way down to S3, traders might take a limited risk stab at establishing a short-term long position. If they do get long at S3, their profit target should be S2. This penetration deep into support is not a place to get greedy on the long side.

The best trade of this day will be the short at S1 at around 1 p.m. (13:00 on the figure). Traders have logical places to take partial profits. Their first profit stop should be at S2. After that they could leave half their position on for a possible run back down to S3 with a contingent stop close order to make sure they're out at the end of the day.

Figure 7-6 shows a good example of combining an idea of trend with support and resistance trading methodology. The open and initial balance of trade indicates a market that wants to go higher. The problem for traders is that they have only a very brief window (the third bar) to get long, the time before 10:00. If they're able to get in, then all is well and good—they can put in their profit stop at R1, the first resistance level.

Once the market gets past R1, it never really shows much initiative to go higher. The best the traders could do with a day like this is to accept that the direction is up. They could get long at R1. It would be an agonizing day. The market never really gives them satisfaction, nor does it prove them wrong. Traders should exit with a stop close.

Usually, a day like this will bring in the sellers. And as the market moves toward the close without ever even once letting the

Figure 7-6 XLU

shorts out, the likely outcome is a quick pop up on the close as the shorts run for the exits. This gives a small opportunity for the trend-aware trader to get long somewhere toward the late afternoon.

Figure 7-7 represents another instance in which traders would be well served to go with the direction the market shows early. The open is below the daily pivot. The telltale flag pattern shows up in the first 30 minutes, alerting traders to be ready for continuation to the downside.

The traders' best price to get short will be the break of S1 just after 10:00. They should exit at S2 and take their quick 20-cent

Figure 7-7 XLP

profit. They could then look to reenter on the short side just after noon on the retest of S1. They may or may not get executed, because the market never penetrates their price level.

The spike down to S3 at 2:00 (14:00) is a reasonable place for traders who are willing to go against the trend to take a shot at getting long. Again, since the market doesn't penetrate their price, they may not get their order filled. Traders with a slightly longer time horizon might be able to get short at around the 10:00 break to the downside (out of the flag pattern) and stay short all the way into the close.

This is likely to be one of those days in which traders look back at the chart after the close and think they should have made more than they did. But the reality is that this is a day full of "just misses," with only one or, at best, two quick trades.

Figure 7-8 is a classic trend day. This chart represents most sell-oriented traders' worst nightmare because the market did not "back and fill." If you are on the sell side, it is a loser from the get go. The psychology of most traders is that as soon as they realize that they missed their buying opportunity, they start looking for

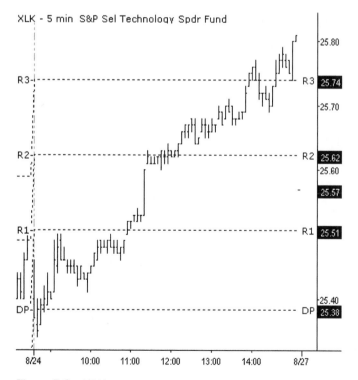

Figure 7-8 XLK

places to get short. Getting short on a day like this will be very bad business, which only points out the importance of including some sort of trend component in your trading strategy.

Traders probably won't be able to get long at the daily pivot, but they can surely get long at around 11:00 at the break above R1. They should peel off part of their position at R2.

The balance of their position should be exited using a contingent sell or at R3 OCO (one cancels other) stop close.

Traders should be particularly wary of the kind of trade that falls late in the day represented in Figure 7-9. A lot of traders will make

Figure 7-9 XLB

good money on a day like this. However, it's the type of day that will reinforce all your bad habits. Why? The only way to make money here is to go against the trend, and buy on the close that is dangerously close to the pivot.

It could possibly be argued that the first quick pop above R2 is a fairly reasonable place to put on a small test short. If you do, you should definitely exit at R1. Don't press your luck and look for the big continuation to the downside; more often than not, you won't get it.

A good idea would be to get long at around 10:00. You'd end up sitting on this trade for the next four hours. When should you give it up and get out? Look for the first full bar to form below R1. This comes at around 1:30.

If you are feeling aggressive, you could risk your profits from your 9:00 short and go short again here. Use a narrow stop (R1 is a good stop level), and OCO it with a buy stop on the close. Again, you should remember that if you do well on a day like this, it will make you feel smarter than you really are. The truth is that you hit on one of those one-in-ten trades in which you get paid to trade against the trend.

ETF Strategy

Above the daily pivot, you are bullish; below the daily pivot, you are bearish.

8

ETF MONEY MANAGEMENT

Successful traders will tell you that proper money management can contribute as much as 60 to 80 percent toward the success of a trade. In fact, assuming that you are trading in a liquid market, the entry is the least important component. The exit should be determined by profit objective, risk parameter, or the market not performing in a manner that is in sync with your style of trading. The last point means that if you establish a position in a market and it goes flat, starts trading erratically, or just starts trading in a manner that makes you uncomfortable, it is usually a good decision to exit the market regardless of the current disposition of your position.

Margin-to-Equity Parameter

One of the most important money management techniques, which practically every successful trader knows and practically every unsuccessful trader does not apply, is to establish a *margin-to-equity parameter.* What this means is that you never use more than a predetermined percent of your trading funds for any one position. For example, if you are using 10 percent margin to equity and the margin for the market you are trading is $1,000 per contract and you had $10,000 on deposit, then you should only be trading one contract. If your parameter is 20 percent margin to equity, you could trade two contracts with your $10,000 account. Depending on your tolerance for risk, bank account, market volatility, and so on, the parameters can vary; however, at no time should you exceed a 25 percent margin-to-equity ratio.

You must observe whatever margin-to-equity parameter you establish for yourself. Otherwise it is a wasted exercise. It does no good to establish sound trading rules and then not follow them. Mediocre trading rules, observed, are better than no trading rules at all. There are many reasons why new and poor traders lose money, but right at the top of the list is using most or all of the money in the trading account for margin. Even a 50 percent ratio, not to mention 80 to 100 percent, leaves no margin for error. Using too large a percentage of capital creates a situation in which you must be right on the first trade. Not only must you be right, but in order to not create a debit situation, the stop loss orders will probably be placed too close to the entry price, thereby not allowing the position to "breathe."

A stop order placed too close to the entry (because the trader is over-trading) creates a situation in which you can be stopped out of the market, at a loss, and then have the painful experience of watching the market turn around and move in the direction you had anticipated. Had you used a 10 percent margin to equity, you would have been in a comfort zone and been able to place the stops properly and, best of all, participated in the market move to the benefit of your account and mental health. As the account grows, the 10 percent, obviously, represents more dollars, and that translates into being able to comfortably trade larger positions.

Use Discipline

There is something very important to keep in mind, regarding margin to equity, using the above example of the $10,000 account and employing a 10 percent margin-to-equity rule. Let's say that you hold a position requiring $1,000 margin and the market goes against you; you are stopped out with a $200 loss. Assuming a $20 commission, your account would now be worth $9,780. Certainly not a disaster, but if you are going to be disciplined (and all successful traders are disciplined), your next trade must be in a market whose margin requirement is no more than 10 percent of $9,780, or $978. It is easy to convince yourself that it is only $220 and "for sure" the next trade will be profitable, and your account will be back to $10,000 or more.

This way of thinking, which unfortunately is the rule rather than the exception with most mature traders, is a major reason why most people lose money trading.

In 1998, one of the largest and best-known hedge funds was Long-Term Capital Management (LTCM). The principals of the fund were trading stars from major investment banks, plus two Nobel laureates. How could such an auspicious group ever be wrong? Unfortunately, that is what the members of the group thought. After an extraordinary early success, producing huge returns for themselves and their investors, they abandoned all discipline and leveraged the assets of the fund way beyond reason.

> **Trader's Notebook**
> Discipline is the key ingredient to successful trading. If you keep strict self-discipline regarding basic trading rules, such as those related to money management, you can make money trading without having any fundamental knowledge of the market. When your discipline goes, your money is sure to follow.

When you are leveraged to the hilt, all it takes is a slight market reversal to start dissipation of assets. And, in this case, when the positions are huge, the problem is exacerbated as you liquidate. In the end the losses were over $4 billion and LTCM was out of business.

Another example of discipline breakdown occurred mid-2006. Amaranth, at the time, was a $9 billion hedge fund that lost $6 billion in one week—yes, one week—and collapsed! How could this happen? Greed took over, and the discipline that was used to create a $9 billion hedge fund went out the window, and the money followed. One trader was allowed to amass a huge position in natural gas, a very volatile market, and when events didn't turn out the way he anticipated, the bottom fell out.

These two examples demonstrate that whether you are trading $10,000 or $10 billion, the same rules apply. And when smart people do dumb things, bad things happen.

Evaluate Others' Opinions

There are several aspects to money management besides margin to equity. One of the most common faults that some traders have is that they listen to opinions. Listening to opinions is not a bad thing to do if you are evaluating those opinions and not just looking for someone who agrees with you. Remember, your idea is as good as anyone else's. Too often you are unsure and end up in a position only because someone, who you think knows more than you do, recommends the strategy. As illustrated previously, smart people can be wrong. Also, your objectives and those of the opinion giver can be very different. You might be interested in a short-term trade of a few days or even a few hours—intraday. The person whose opinion you are adopting might be looking at a long-term position of months or years. Given that disparity, you could have exactly opposite views and both be right or both be wrong.

Avoid Overconfidence

Over-trading is a weakness of many traders. This type of trading comes from greed and hubris which, in many instances, follow a run of successful trading. Long-Term Capital Management and Amaranth are classic examples. Both amassed excessive positions after several years of extraordinary success, and they believed they could do no wrong. The market has a way of humbling you, and the key is to not to let it destroy you.

Overconfidence is a trap that can be fatal. You should have objectives for every trade and achieve these objectives before adding other positions. Also, be sure that you have an exit strategy if the market does not move your way; this will keep the loss manageable. Good traders need a humble attitude relative to the markets. You can never afford to be overconfident. Overconfidence allows you to let your guard down, which translates into lack of discipline.

Analyze Each Trade Separately

Every trade should be looked at objectively. Do not become a true believer. Circumstances and conditions change. In order to be a successful trader, you have to be agile. The good idea of yesterday might not be so good today. A trader should hate to lose but not have a fear of losing.

It is good to remember that you can have more losses than profits and, if you are following good trading rules, be successful. It is a common tendency for traders to lack discipline with money made in the market compared with money they have invested in the market. Once a trade is closed and the profit is in your account, that is your money. Money is money, and if you are reckless with the profits, that recklessness will run over into the invested money.

> **Trader's Notebook**
>
> A fear of losing is an emotion that will keep traders in a position too long, thinking that they can't take the loss and that the market will come back. When you give a trade more room, you are throwing good money after bad.

> **Trader's Notebook**
>
> One way to prevent falling into a reckless trap is to keep your account at a constant level. Draw down excess, and deposit it in a conservative place. The longer you hold onto money, the more likely you will consider it your own.

Staying on the Sidelines Is Also a Management Technique

Sometimes it is good business not to do business. Many times traders feel that they have to keep their money working and don't want to miss anything. This attitude usually produces over-trading, and we have seen what that can do to an account. There is always another bus. This means that just because the market is making a big move, doesn't mean that you have to respond to it. Sometimes the intelligent choice is to do nothing. There will always be other trading opportunities.

ETF Strategy

In speculation (trading) you do not have to be fully invested to realize great returns. High leverage (LTCM/Amaranth) is a destroyer of portfolios. Successful speculation involves vigilance and discipline.

9

SHORT SELLING: SECURITIES AND ETFs

M arkets react in one of three ways: they move up, move down, or move sideways. Trading opportunities exist in all three phases; however, the opportunities in a sideways market really occur only with certain option strategies. It is not the purpose of this chapter to discuss option strategies because the majority of non-professional traders rarely, if ever, trade options.

We are left, then, with two choices: buy or sell. The potential for gain, in trading, is as great in a down market as it is in an up market. In fact, generally, profits can come faster in a down market. Traders can take advantage of the opportunities presented in a down market by selling short. Although short selling is not very complex, it is not entirely simple either. Short selling involves certain risks and procedures that are unique and not inherent in buying long.

Short Selling Securities

Selling short is selling something you do not own. You are hoping to buy it back later at a lower price. Conceptually this is the same for stocks, futures, or ETFs. However, there is a major difference in the mechanics for short selling within these markets. In order to sell a futures contract short, it takes no more energy than buying long. However, selling securities and ETFs short is more involved.

You must borrow the number of shares of the stock or ETF that you wish to sell (this can usually be accomplished through your broker) in order to have securities to deliver to the buyer. Until this past year, you also would have had to wait for an uptick (that is, a price higher than the previous price) before you could sell. As of July 6, 2007, the SEC has removed the uptick rule for short selling securities, so now stocks as well as futures and ETFs can be sold short on a downtick, uptick, or zero tick.

When you buy a security, you are taking ownership of an asset. You are not agreeing to make or take delivery at a later date. Therefore, before you sell a security, you must either own it or, in the case of a short sale, borrow the appropriate number of shares from someone who owns the stock, or ETF, in order to make delivery to the buyer. The short seller now has the obligation to buy back the security, hopefully at a lower price, in order to return it to the entity from whom it was borrowed.

Short Selling ETFs

Futures are contracts to make or receive a specific asset at a future time. This means that there is no exchange of physical property until the specified delivery date. And in most contracts, with the exception of agricultural futures, delivery is satisfied in cash.

Not only do ETFs present an opportunity to trade sectors, but you can buy, sell, hedge, or arbitrage with equal facility. For example, if you want to trade the energy sector against the auto or airline sectors, all you do is buy one and sell the other. There exists a tremendous number of trading opportunities today, with the large and ever-expanding number of ETFs available.

There are now inverse ETFs. These are designed to go up when a particular sector or index goes down. Inverse ETFs can be bought the same as any other ETF. What this means is that if you are bearish about a sector, or just want to protect part of your portfolio, you buy the appropriate inverse ETF, which will appreciate in price if the selected market goes down. Some of the inverse ETFs available are real estate, consumer goods, technology, emerging markets, and China. You can also buy double-leverage ETFs that go up 20 percent for every 10 percent decline. You can hedge your portfolio by putting up only 50 cents for every $1 invested.

In short selling, you sell first hoping to buy back later at a lower price. An everyday example might be buying something on sale. You see a sweater in a store for $50. The sweater is something that you would really like to have but you feel that the price is too high and you know that the store is going to have its annual sale in a few weeks. The sale comes, and you are able to buy the sweater for $40, $10 less than the original price. In essence, you have just saved (made) $10. Of course, the risk, in this example, is that when the sale comes, the coveted sweater might be sold out or your size is not available. Even though you did not sell first, as in a true short sale, the practical effect is the same. You "made" $10 by avoiding buying at the higher price and, instead, purchased the sweater at the lower price. As in short selling, you incurred a risk—the chance that the item would not be available.

Hedging Your Portfolio

You might be thinking, "I'm not a speculator, I'm an investor. Why would I want to sell short?" The answer is to reduce long market exposure. By adding some short market exposure to their long equities holdings, investors can create a hedged or even a market-neutral portfolio. (Adopting this approach certainly would have been a great benefit during the 2000–2003 market downturn.)

To be sure, if your portfolio is hedged, you will not receive full benefit from market rallies. Therefore, a hedged portfolio requires some maintenance; that is, you should actively manage any short strategy. Even during a strong bull market, some short exposure can be appropriate for some investors. An investor whose portfolio has generated substantial gains might want to establish a partial hedge to protect the profits in the event of a market downturn. If the market continues moving up, this investor will not benefit fully; however, the protection and peace of mind would be worth the cost. Historically, bull markets are followed by bear markets, so if investors believe that the bull market has run its course or is close to running its course, they might want to initiate a short position.

There is a story, supposedly true, about Jesse Livermore, one of the most famous stock speculators of the 1920s. In October 1929

> ### Trader's Notebook
>
> Hedging is like buying life insurance. We pay the premiums, hoping that no one will ever collect—but someone always does. Bull markets always correct themselves at some point, and when that happens, investors can collect on the "premiums" they have paid.

the stock market crashed, and many rich people became poor in one day. Mr. Livermore's wife heard the news of the crash and panicked. She promptly sold all the furnishings and artwork from their house thinking that they, like most people, were broke. When Mr. Livermore returned home, he naturally asked his wife what had happened. After she explained, he told her that he had just had the most profitable day of his career. He had been short. As discussed earlier, all bull markets come to an end and are followed by a bear market. Sometimes, near the top of a bull market, the stampeding bulls are kicking up so much dust that you cannot see the approaching cliff.

ETF Strategy

To the inexperienced, short selling can be a difficult concept to get comfortable with. But when you understand the fundamental differences between shorting stocks and shorting ETFs, it becomes apparent that selling short is as easy as buying. As stated at the beginning of this chapter, markets do only three things: they go up, down, or sideways. Assuming that traders are trading up or down markets, then if you do not avail yourself of the opportunities in a down market, you are greatly reducing your chances for success.

10

ETF ARBITRAGE AND SPREADING

T he *Merriam-Webster's Collegiate Dictionary* defines *arbitrage* as: "The nearly simultaneous purchase and sale of securities or foreign exchange in different markets in order to profit from price discrepancies." Distilled down: buying low and selling high.

In futures trading, the term *spreading* is generally used instead of the word *arbitrage*; however, as markets have become more global, arbitrage seems to be used as the descriptive word for this type of market activity. Arbitrage has been also known as a "riskless profit," originating from the security arbitrage opportunities when a trader would buy a particular security on one exchange and simultaneously sell the same security on another exchange at fractional differences, but enough of a difference to cover transaction costs and leave a profit. Opportunities like that were more prevalent in the days before advanced computer trading. Traders would communicate by phone, which was not as efficient as today's computer trading, and the lack of efficiency created many arbitrage opportunities for the alert and agile trader.

The term *riskless profit* is really a misnomer. Any competitive trade has risk, even the type described above. Often the first part of the trade was made (buy or sell), and the other side would not be available. For example, a trader buys 100 shares of General Motors (GM) on the New York Stock Exchange. When she made the buy, there was a good quote for 100 GM at a higher price on another exchange. However, markets change, and the apparent advantage would be lost.

Forms of Arbitrage

There are several forms of arbitrage transactions. In futures, the trader might buy the current contract month and sell the three-month-out contract, the strategy being that one believes that the nearby market will tighten (less supply, bad weather, big exports, etc.) in relation to the succeeding delivery months. This trade is directionless; that is, the trader does not care if the market goes up or down, the concern is solely the difference between the two trading contract months. There is a different dynamic from the one that exists in an outright long or short position.

> **Trader's Notebook**
>
> In the 1980s, risk arbitrage became the strategy du jour. This is a strategy in which you identify companies that are targets for takeover and buy the stock of the company. If your research proves to be correct, you are able to resell the stock at a profit when the takeover is announced and the stock appreciates. This also became a popular strategy for insider trading, an illegal activity that landed many of those who participated in it in jail.

In futures, if you buy one delivery month and sell another delivery month, in the same market, you would have an *intramarket calendar spread*. If, on the other hand, you bought futures in one market and sold futures in another market, you would have an *intermarket spread*. There are also *interexchange spreads*. *Hedging* is a type of arbitrage or spread. Being long a security and short a related ETF is a hedge, as is being long financial instruments and short financial futures.

Money markets present opportunities for arbitrage. These opportunities usually involve money market instruments in one market trading at a different yield from a similar instrument in another market. For example, a trader buys a Treasury note at 4.5 percent yield and in turn sells a Eurodollar note, having the same face value, at 4 percent.

ETF Arbitrage

ETFs trade in the open market with their prices set by market demand. Therefore, any ETF may trade at a premium or discount to the value of the underlying assets. For example, if the underlying ETF is trading at a significant premium to the underlying assets, the arbitrageur will buy the securities that comprise the ETF, convert them to shares in the ETF, and then sell them in the open market. The exact opposite action can be taken when the ETF trades at a significant discount to the underlying. The arbitrageur will buy the ETF shares, exchange them for the underlying securities, and sell the securities for a profit. This activity is not only profitable for the arbitrageur but also provides liquidity and keeps the ETF prices in line with the underlying assets. This type of arbitrage requires a larger capital base than the more traditional form of arbitrage.

A type of ETF arbitrage, which is popular and more available to the smaller independent trader, is like the aforementioned futures arbitrage or spread. For example, a trader is of the opinion that higher fuel prices will negatively affect prices for the airlines and auto companies. The trade then would be to buy energy-related ETFs and sell airline- and/or auto-related ETFs. Today there are ETFs in so many different markets that the arbitrage opportunities are limited only by the traders' imagination and abilities.

Advantages of Spreading

Why should a trader spread? Wouldn't it be easier to just concentrate on being long or short and not worry about a more complex position? One advantage of spreading is that spread positions tend to trend more reliably and more dynamically than outright positions. This is mainly because spreads trend without the noise caused by computerized trading. A lot of the intraday moves and head fakes are greatly diminished, if not removed, because both sides of the spread are generally affected by these interfering factors, but the spread price—the difference—remains. Since the only thing that concerns a trader with a spread position is the difference (remember this is a directionless trade), the intraday market gyrations are of no consequence.

Also, it generally is not necessary, or even advisable, to watch a spread position all day. In fact, you really do not need real-time quotes. (This obviously is a great advantage for the person who has a day job.)

Besides creating liquidity for markets, arbitrage also causes prices to converge. As a result of arbitrage activity, securities trading in different markets, commodities, and currency exchange rates tend to converge in all the markets in which they are traded. The more efficient the market, the faster the convergence. This convergence characteristic is the result of the very human trait of wanting to buy the less expensive and sell the more expensive. In addition, international arbitrage activity in commodities, securities, and currencies influence exchange rates thus creating parity in purchasing power.

Identifying Arbitrage Opportunities

Much of the information needed to have an informed opinion is readily available. Many brokers provide newswire service. There are paid subscription services that advise on arbitrage opportunities. There is also software available that helps people locate undervalued securities that could present an ETF arbitrage possibility.

It would seem that with the opportunities available in arbitrage, there should be a large number of diversified investors trading small positions—taking advantage of the anomalies presented in a dynamic market. In fact, however, ETF arbitrage is conducted by a relatively small number of large investors. The fact that these large and sophisticated investors are doing ETF arbitrage suggests that there are considerable profit possibilities.

ETF Strategy

Granted, many of the opportunities are not available to the smaller trader because of their lack of capital, expertise, information, and the like. However, many opportunities do occur on a regular basis, and the alert and diligent trader can take advantage of these situations. As previously stated, arbitrage/spread positions generally require less maintenance and stress than do other positions, so arbitrage trading is definitely a style of trading that is worth learning about.

11

OPTIONS FOR ETFs

Options are the right to buy (call) or to sell (put) a particular ETF at a particular price and on a particular date. This right has value and is bought and sold, much as the underlying ETF is traded. The value of the options is based not only on the price of the ETF but also on the time remaining until the option expires and on the volatility of the underlying market. That is, every option has three specifications: expiration, price, and, in this case, the underlying ETF. (Options are not unique to ETFs so, depending upon the market, the option's underlying instrument could be a security, futures contract, or anything with a fluctuating value.) All option contracts expire on a specified date. The contract will specify a strike or exercise price at which the purchase or sale of the underlying will occur. An option can be bought or sold at any time before expiration.

Four Basic Strategies

There are four basic strategies for option investors:

1. Buying calls

2. Writing calls

3. Buying puts

4. Writing puts

A call contract gives the right to buy, and the put contract is the right to sell. If you buy a call (go long), you have the right to buy a particular ETF at the strike price before expiration, assuming that you choose to exercise this right. If you write (sell) a call, you have the obligation to sell the underlying ETF at the strike price, if the buyer chooses. Buyers of a put own the right to sell the underlying instrument at the strike price before expiration, if they choose to exercise that right. And if you write a put, you have the obligation to buy the underlying at the strike price, if the buyer exercises the right. Buyers of an option are in control. It is their choice whether to exercise or not. This is why buyers pay a premium when buying an option. They want to exercise their right to buy or sell because this means that the underlying is trading at a price higher (for a call) or lower (for a put) than the strike price.

Sellers collect a premium when they sell the option and will keep it if

> **Trader's Notebook**
>
> Buyers have rights, and sellers have obligations. That is, the buyer has the right to exercise or not, and the seller has the obligation to buy or sell the underlying at the exercise price if the buyer so chooses.

the option expires. The maximum profit the writers of an option can make is the premium they receive when they write the option. It is important to know that even though the profit potential for writers of an option is limited, the risk potential is unlimited. That's right! If you sell an option, your risk is unlimited.

Option Terminology

People who deal with options use various terms that are unique to this market. Some of the basic terms are:

- In-the-money
- At-the-money
- Out-of-the-money
- Intrinsic value
- Breakeven
- Premium

A buyer wants the option to be *in-the-money* and the seller does not. A call is in-the-money when the market price exceeds the strike price. Or, in the case of a put, when the market price is below the strike price. An option buyer will exercise, at expiration, an option that is in-the-money.

At-the-money refers to a situation in which the market price, of either a call or put, is equal to the strike price. Buyers will not exercise at-the-money because, when you factor in the premium, they would be buying at a loss. Sellers get to keep the premium.

An option is *out-of-the-money* when the market price is below (for a call) the strike price or above (for a put) the strike price. At expiration, if an option is out-of-the-money, the sellers will keep the premium without obligation, which means that the buyer's right of an option to buy or sell, at the strike price, no longer exists.

Intrinsic value is the amount the option is in-the-money. A call has intrinsic value when the market price is above the strike price. A put has intrinsic value when its market price is below the strike price. The amount of intrinsic value for a call is determined by subtracting the strike price from the market price. Intrinsic value for a put is found by subtracting the market price from the strike price. Intrinsic value can never be a negative number.

The *breakeven* for a call is determined by adding the premium to the strike price. Any price above this point will be profitable for the call buyer. The breakeven for a put is the strike price minus the premium. The put buyer's position is profitable at any price below this point.

The price of an option is the *premium*. Option premiums are quoted on a per-share basis. Therefore, to determine the dollar amount of the premium, you multiply the quoted premium price by 100. For example: A particular ETF is trading at $84.25. The $85 December calls are trading at $6. If you buy the $85 December calls, you will pay a $600 premium ($6 × $100) and have the right to buy the ETF at $85 per share any time from the time of the trade until expiration. Remember, in doing this, you have added $600 to the price of the ETF, making your breakeven price $91. However, you have limited your risk to no more than $600.

The option premium is composed of two values: intrinsic value and time value. *Time value* is the market's perceived value of the time remaining to expiration. An option will have time value any time the option's premium exceeds the intrinsic value. The more time remaining, the greater the chance there is for a price change. The further the expiration, the greater the time value. At expiration there is no time value.

The factor with the greatest influence on premium is the volatility of the underlying ETF. The greater the volatility, the larger the premium. Premiums for options fluctuate much like the price of the ETFs. If the underlying price should rise, then the premium for the call premium would rise and the premium for the put would fall. You can see how traders can trade options in much the same way that they trade the underlying market.

Option Strategies

Although trading options can be a cheaper way to trade ETFs (you pay only the premium) and will provide the trader with a defined risk (the amount of the premium), using options to protect a position is, perhaps, the best reason for market participants to have an understanding of various option strategies. (There are many different option strategies, and it is not the purpose of this book to get into that, but it is worthwhile to mention a couple of the basic strategies that will serve the reader well.)

If you are long an ETF, using options can protect you against the market risk of the position. It is, in effect, buying insurance. You buy a put, pay the premium, and now know exactly what your risk is.

Another strategy to mitigate your risk is to sell a covered call. Assume you are long an ETF and you sell a call option at a higher strike price than the current market price. You will receive the premium which, in turn, reduces the cost of the ETF position. The downside to this strategy is if the market continues to rally, your short call position will be exercised, and you will lose your original position to the call buyer and will not participate in any further upside market move. However, your realized profit will have been enhanced by the premium you collected when you sold the call to cover the position.

There is also a way to hedge your downside risk on a long position without cost. This is called a *collar*. Assume you are long at 70 and buy a 65 put at 5 (costing $500) and sell an 80 call at 5 (collecting $500). The premium you have paid is offset by the premium you have collected. If the market goes down, you can "put" your position at 65. Therefore, your risk is limited to $500. As in the case of a covered call, the upside is limited (in this example) to 80, or a $1,000 profit.

> **Trader's Notebook**
> Check out CheattheStreet .com for some new and facile ways of trading ETF options.

ETF Strategy

Understanding options provides market participants with the means to garner more consistent profits and, at the same time, help to manage risk. Not all ETFs have options, so you must determine your strategy before you trade, not during the trading. Options are more of a hedging vehicle. If you have a definite opinion, skip options. If you are not sure, you can generate income by selling options.

12

EVALUATING ETFs

Whether you are a novice, an intermediate, or an experienced investor, you should understand stock valuation. Evaluating a particular ETF will take you only so far. By applying some very basic valuation methods, you can greatly improve your chances for becoming a successful investor.

Price/Earnings Ratio

One of the most popular valuation methods is the *price/earnings (P/E) ratio*. The P/E ratio is calculated by dividing a stock's price by its earnings per share. There are a couple of ways of looking at this ratio. One is that a company with a high P/E ratio reflects the market's expectation of future performance. Therefore, companies with high P/E ratios should show greater performance in the future than companies with low ratios. Other people feel that high P/E ratios can possibly be evidence of an overvalued company and that the lower ratio represents an undervalued situation and a possible buying opportunity.

There is truth in both positions, and this is one reason why you can have two divergent positions on the same security by two qualified analysts. A company might have a low P/E ratio because of no or minimal growth. Obviously, if this is the case, the low ratio would not represent a buying opportunity. The authors believe that the best application of the P/E ratio is for comparing similar companies within the same industry. Remember, it is only one of several tools you can use when evaluating securities.

Price/Sales Ratio

Another ratio is the *price/sales (P/S) ratio*. This one is calculated by dividing the stock's price by its sales (revenue) per share. When calculating this ratio, it is best to use the revenue from the latest four quarters; that is, on a trailing basis. Trailing basis means the revenue numbers are from past (realized) earnings, as opposed to projected (future) earnings. Since sales (revenue) are a more strictly defined number than earnings, the P/S ratio gives a more reliable number than the P/E ratio. As evidenced by the corporate scandals of the recent past, there are a number of ways that management can tamper with earnings. (It is definitely more difficult, and probably fraudulent, to tamper with revenue numbers.)

The P/S ratio will vary from industry to industry; however, the rule of thumb is that a stock with a ratio below 0.75 is undervalued. A ratio above 3.0 is evidence of overvaluation and, therefore, should be avoided. As is the case with most generalities, you should be cautious of certain situations. One situation is that a company on the verge of bankruptcy very often will have a low P/S ratio. This occurs when sales have only a slight drop, but the stock price drops precipitously.

Another situation could be if a company has a high debt load and, even though it is showing a low P/S ratio, the company is unprofitable because it cannot cover its interest obligations with operating income. Always bear in mind that P/S ratios will vary significantly from industry to industry.

Financial Ratios

Financial ratios are numbers from the balance sheet, or income statement, expressed as ratios. Financial ratios allow you to compare a company's financial strengths and weaknesses to those of other companies within the same industry and to its own past performance. Some of the financial ratios that are commonly used are debt-to-equity ratio, bond ratio, common stock ratio, and preferred stock ratio.

Debt-to-Equity Ratio

The *debt-to-equity ratio* is the total long-term debt divided by the total shareholders' equity. This ratio is the measure of leverage—the use of long-term financing—to increase earnings. Debt can enhance earnings, but it also may increase risk to the common-stock holder of this particular company. If a company has a large amount of debt, there could be the possibility that it will have difficulty in meeting its financial obligations in the event of an earnings downturn.

Long-Term Debt/Capitalization

Long-term debt/capitalization is similar to the debt-to-equity ratio. *Long-term debt/capitalization* compares total long-term debt to total capitalization rather than to shareholders' equity. Or, to state it another way: it measures the percentage of total capitalization provided by long-term debt financing.

Common Stock and Preferred Stock (Capitalization) Ratios

The common stock ratio and the preferred stock ratio are computed by taking the value of the respective class of stock and dividing it by the total capitalization of the company.

Analyze the Company's Profitability

> **Trader's Notebook**
>
> Consider an example of a company where common stockholders have invested $100 of equity and the company has borrowed $100. Its total capitalization is $200. The common stock ratio is $100/$200, or 50 percent. Avoid stocks with a ratio of 30 percent or less. Also note that the higher the ratio, the more secure the company is from a creditor's point of view.

Income statements are used by analysts to judge how efficiently and profitably a company is operating. The income statement summarizes a company's revenues and expenses for a fiscal period. It compares revenue with costs and expenses during a particular period. Some of the components of the income statement are: operating income, interest expense, net income after taxes, earnings per share, and retained earnings.

Determine Working Capital

One way to find out a company's ability to meet its current financial obligations is to determine its working capital. Working capital is found by simply subtracting current liabilities from current assets. Working capital will be a dollar figure and, by itself, does not allow analysts to compare companies. To compare companies, you must use the current ratio. This ratio is the current assets divided by the current liabilities. You are now comparing the current assets with a company's current financial obligations, regardless of the company's size or business.

> **Trader's Notebook**
>
> The most stringent ratio of a company's liquidity is the cash/assets ratio. Cash/assets ratio is determined by dividing cash and cash equivalents by current liabilities.

Identify Operating Income

Operating income is also referred to as operating profit, operating margin, or earnings before interest and taxes. This is simply a company's profits from its business operations. Interest expense on a company's debt is not an operating expense. Interest expense is deducted from taxable income, which leaves pretax income. If a company pays dividends, the dividends will be paid out of net income after taxes. Dividends on preferred stock are paid first, and the remaining income can be paid to the common-stock holders or reinvested in the business. Earnings per share are what remain after interest payments, taxes, and preferred-stock dividends are paid. Earnings per share are determined by dividing net income after taxes, interest, and preferred-stock dividends by the number of common shares outstanding. *Retained earnings* are earnings not paid out in dividends. This can also be called *earned surplus*.

Calculate Cash Flow

The cash flow calculation does not include cash obtained from financing. As a result, it is a good way to determine a company's ability to grow internally without it borrowing cash or issuing more shares (a dilutive measure) to raise funds for expansion, factory and equipment upgrade, or acquisitions. Companies that generate substantial cash flow from operations find themselves in a good position to create greater shareholder value.

> **Trader's Notebook**
> Companies with good cash flow are in a position where they might be able to acquire other businesses at an opportune time. Acquisitions are often an effective means through which corporations can expand, diversify, and sustain above-average levels of growth; all of which can result in higher returns, which is good news for the shareholders.

A company with good cash flow is in a position to pay dividends. Dividends, however, are not always the best use of funds. For example, in the case of a new and/or growing company, it is usually a better decision, for the long term, to invest excess cash back into the company.

There are a couple of other options available to companies with strong cash flow. One of these options is to pay down debt. Debt requires servicing (interest payments) and, therefore, it is often a good practice to eliminate, or at least reduce, debt obligations, which, ultimately, will work to the benefit of future cash flow.

At certain times a company may choose to buy back some of its outstanding common shares. The company will issue a notice stating the percentage of outstanding common stock it plans to buy back as well as the price and time period. Companies buy back shares when they feel their shares are undervalued. Because this reduces the amount of shares outstanding, the result is usually an increase in the value of the remaining outstanding shares. However, there are situations in which a company's stock is lagging for good reason, and the buy back will result in a temporary uptick in price.

Understand the Competitive Advantage

Research and development (R&D) is an excellent avenue for a company to spend excess cash, particularly with technology-based companies. In all businesses, but particularly in technology, the competitive advantage lies in staying one step ahead of the competition. And with abundant cash on hand, a company is in position to ensure that it stays ahead of its competition in equipment, research, and product development.

Research the Backgrounds of Management

There is always the human factor to take into consideration. In order to become and remain successful, a company must hire the best people. Therefore, it is important to research the background of the top managers of any company you are considering investing in. Also, you want to invest in the company that has the leading products in the sector in which it operates. Not surprisingly, this usually favorably correlates with the company with the best management. Look at the salary of the CEOs. Are they dining on caviar while the workers are being laid off? Is their salary off the charts? Maybe it is time to lighten up.

Getting the Research Done

The authors know that many people will read this and feel that there is just too much research to be done before they can make an informed investment decision, and they do not have the time, expertise, or, in most cases, either. Don't give up. There is a lot of help available. It is not the purpose of this book to promote one brokerage company or another, but most of the major companies, and many of the smaller boutique companies, provide a range of services to assist you in doing your own research or in making recommendations to the client that the companies' analysts have researched.

Many brokerage companies will provide a list of the most popular ETFs with investors or list ETFs by asset class, style, market cap, region, sector, or sponsor. There are some companies that will list ETFs based on the parameters that you, the potential investor, provide. This last service is particularly handy for people who enjoy doing much of their own homework but do not have the time or inclination to cull through several hundred ETFs to find a potential investment. Full-service brokers will provide these services, but with a little digging you can get most of this done on your own and save money by using a discount broker.

Trader's Notebook

There is no rule to success that works unless you do. To be a successful investor requires effort. And as with any skill, the more you work at it, the better you become. The great thing about developing a skill in investing/trading is that it can be fun, as well as financially rewarding.

Do not be intimidated into believing that the brokerage companies' recommendations are always right. Just remember Enron, WorldCom, and Global Crossing, to name a very few of the past companies that ended in disaster. Your opinion is as good as the next person's, and if you learn how to do research on your own, you will develop a skill that will serve you forever.

ETF Strategy

There are several essential tools for analyzing a security or ETF. As you become proficient in using these tools, you will find the ones that work the best for your objectives. Look at the leading stocks in an ETF and apply the analysis to the top stock in that ETF. Most ETFs "follow the leader," and a poor first place will drag down the entire complex. By applying this method, it will not be necessary to analyze *every* stock.

13

ETFs AND MARKET ACTIVITY

Whenever the decision is to be made whether to buy or not, where to buy, when to buy, and what to expect as a result of that decision, the best and most reliable information comes from the market itself. Markets, by themselves, are neutral. They produce a constant flow of information that provides the same opportunities for everyone. How to take advantage of those opportunities is what reading and understanding market-generated activity is all about. There is an expression: "If you want to make rabbit stew, first you have to catch the rabbit." The same is true in trading. In order to take advantage of an opportunity, first you have to recognize that one exists.

What is market activity? It is the distillation of all buy and sell decisions being made in the marketplace from all participants, from the most sophisticated and highly informed to the novice and least informed. Market activity finds expression in the form of the high, the low, and the close for any time period, be it yearly, monthly, weekly, daily, or intraday, in whatever time frame one chooses to view the market.

Yes, this is about bar charts, but not in the conventional sense of technical analysis. Most forms of technical analysis utilize past-tense price activity and impose current activity upon it in the hope or expectation of determining future market direction. Sometimes it works, and just as often, it does not.

Market activity does look at past behavior to determine where the market has indicated there are important support and resistance areas. However, to determine whether to buy or sell, and where and when, the best indicator is present-tense market activity. In other words, what is the market revealing about the current collective buy-sell decisions being made now, and can that information be used to define an opportunity? The answer to that question is: absolutely!

Read the Trends ... and That Includes ETFs

In all ETF markets there are three different phases: uptrends, downtrends, and trading ranges. There are transitions between each phase that occur to signify when a change may be getting underway. The classic signs of a trend change are the buying climax ending an uptrend and a selling climax ending a downtrend.

All markets are a function of supply and demand. Sometimes market phases will end as a result of a subtle change in supply or demand. In an uptrend, demand is in charge. This is apparent by daily bar ranges, the price fluctuations between high and low, that are wider as the market advances and volume activity is stronger. Declines within an uptrend tend to have narrower bars and less volume activity.

A lack of demand, evidenced by smaller ranges as price rallies and not strong volume, will eventually invite supply. Selling forces will recognize that the strength of buying has receded, and sellers will become emboldened and more active in their selling. Eventually, price will give way, or not hold, and start a new trend to the downside.

The same is true for market declines, only in reverse. Supply dominates as price declines. At some point, supply will abate, and buyers will take note and start to become more assertive in their activity thus causing prices to start to rise.

> **Trader's Notebook**
>
> Volume is another important piece of information as market activity develops. Volume is underutilized as a decision-making tool because it can be confusing and occasionally appear to be misleading. (For these reasons, volume is not a part of this discussion.) However, when properly integrated with market activity, it can be very revealing as confirmation of how the market is developing.

These are generalizations; there are myriad ways in which markets start, develop, and end, but as guides, these observations are accurate. With this information in mind, one can now take a look at what constitutes market activity, in a few examples, and how it can be used in the present tense to make informed buy and sell decisions.

Read Price Behavior Patterns

Markets being neutral, all any market can do is generate price information. That's all! How one chooses to interpret and deal with that information is a different story. It is important to realize that it is not about being right or wrong. Right or wrong does not exist in the market because the market is never wrong in what it does. It just is. If you have no idea of the trend, then don't trade.

The market does advertise itself through behavior patterns, and it does so in a way that reveals what you might anticipate as a result and in a way that enables one to make a relatively informed decision for a proper trade.

> **Trader's Notebook**
>
> In working, you have to do things right. In trading, you have to do the right things. Therein lies the rub.

A proper trade is one that has the likelihood of a favorable result. It does not ensure that a profitable result will follow, but it does mean that by making only proper trades, the likelihood of success is more probable than otherwise.

The results of an individual trade cannot be known in advance. However, by understanding the statistical nature of probabilities, the consistent application of making a series of proper trade decisions arising from reading market activity should result in an overall positive. This is your market edge—your advantage in successful trading.

Market activity is reading the price behavior that results from the collective buy and sell decisions from all participants. It is what determines how wide a price range will be for the time period. Where price closes at the end of the day determines who won the battle between buyers and sellers.

In an uptrend, the daily range tends to show wider ranges as the price advances. This is because demand is greater, and buyers are willing to participate as the price goes higher. Closes also tend to be in the upper end of the range, which is further evidence of demand being in control.

Declines in an uptrend tend to have smaller ranges because buyers are fewer in number, and it is more difficult for sellers (supply) to move the price lower, and the number of sellers is lower than the number of willing buyers.

This general description of market activity occurs in all time frames and conveys the same information. As stated previously, when you're looking at the various time frames, it becomes apparent that what appears as a weakened market in one time frame is just a slight reaction in a larger time frame. The overall direction remains intact. It pays to be aware of all time frames because it better identifies high probability opportunities.

For example, a market in decline for several days may seem discouraging for those who are long, maybe even to the extent that they exit the position. However, a monthly chart reveals that the daily price decline is coming into an area that has proved to be strong support in the past. It simply does not show up on a daily chart. Instead of worrying or selling out, it may be a great opportunity to enter more positions at a minimal risk with the probability of positive results.

Trade in Terms of Probability

There is no such thing as certainty in the markets, with one exception. The most reliable certainty is that anything can happen. With that in mind, one needs to develop an approach to investing in terms of probability. Such an approach allows for the possibility of being wrong.

While no one likes taking losses, it can get worse when one refuses to acknowledge when one is wrong by hanging onto a loss, hoping it gets better. It rarely does. Initially, being wrong is acceptable. Staying wrong is not. For the few occasions when overstaying a position does improve, it creates a bad precedent that will repeat itself with the inevitable negative results. Discipline cannot be overstressed if one wants to succeed.

> **Trader's Notebook**
>
> As common as the notion of preservation of capital is, it is, or should be, the cornerstone behind every decision-making process. Learning how not to lose is more important than learning how to win. Being wrong in the market usually entails losing capital. Knowing how not to lose capital gives one staying power and the continued opportunity for gain.

Each market is unique in how it unfolds, from a choppy, go-nowhere trading range to a steady, directional move, up or down. Thinking in terms of probabilities allows for more flexibility in expectations. That, in turn, leaves one more open and objective in reading a market as it develops.

Avoid Fixed Expectations

Having fixed expectations leaves one to focus on that market information which will reinforce those expectations at the expense of ignoring or not seeing other activity that could be detrimental to a fixed expectation and result in overstaying one's position.

What does this have to do with reading developing market activity, and why is it important? A closed mind will see only that portion of market activity viewed as favorable and not see the red flags as warning signs appear. Fixed thinking prejudges and prevents one from seeing all of a market. The last thing one needs is inadequate market information.

The markets offer unlimited opportunities that repeat themselves over and over, that offer unlimited amounts of money every day, week, or month. A well-defined market approach and the right mindset can put one in harmony with this unlimited flow of opportunity for success.

Take Responsibility for Your Trading Decisions

> **Trader's Notebook**
>
> Access to charts portraying an ETF is key for identifying trends. Before you trade any ETF, punch up a daily chart, then a weekly chart, and finally a monthly chart. The market loves to test old highs and lows. Don't place orders until you have analyzed your charts.

It is worth remembering that the markets cannot do anything to you. The markets are neutral and simply generate price information that is a mirror of the collective participants. That is all a market is as it facilitates trade between buyers and sellers. The market does not know if you have a position, long or short, at what price, and so on. That is a personal decision you make. The feelings in response to your decisions are yours and yours alone—not the market's.

Learn to accept responsibility and accountability for each decision you make. Let every decision be the result of diligent preparation that defines your entry and risk level at the same time. The market cannot do anything that you do not allow. It merely reflects your decision making and how well prepared you are.

ETF Strategy

If you're an investor, review your ETF portfolio once or twice a year. Does volatility make you nervous? Stay with bond ETFs. If you're a trader, are you beating the market, including commissions? If not, consider dollar cost averaging. Are you a speculator? Chances are you will not beat the market, unless you have a trading edge. Remember that your software, hardware, commissions, and time must make speculating in ETFs worth your while.

If you have a $100,000 account, spending 5 percent on advice from a guru results in a $5,000 drawdown in your account. There are many unscrupulous newsletter writers who charge between $3,000 and $5,000 a year for ETF advice. That means the advice must overcome the price of the so-called tips and make an additional 3 to 4 percent to beat the market. Use a search engine on the Internet. Most advice can be found for free.

14

DESIGN, MAINTAIN, AND MANIPULATE YOUR ETF PORTFOLIO

Let's begin this chapter by creating a portfolio of ETFs using Yahoo! Finance. To create a portfolio in Yahoo!, you must register; this registration will give you your very own Yahoo! e-mail address. If you don't want many of today's advertising materials filling up your inbox, make sure to decline any e-mail offers while signing up. Let's assume that you now have a unique Yahoo! user ID and are logged in.

Develop Your "Watch List" of ETFs

You can access the Yahoo! Finance page by either clicking on the Finance tab on the home page or you can go to

Figure 14-1   Yahoo! Finance Home Page

http://finance.yahoo.com. On this page you will see the following tabs: Home, Investing, News & Opinion, Personal Finance, and My Portfolios. (See Figure 14-1.)

Click on *My Portfolios*, and the pull-down menu will open. (See Figure 14-2.) Then click on *New Portfolio*, and a new page will open. (See Figure 14-3.)

Click on *Track a symbol watch list* to open another page. The page should appear as shown in Figure 14-4.

Create a name for your ETF portfolio inside the box next to "Portfolio Name." In the symbols box under step 2, enter the symbols representing various ETFs you are planning to track. You can

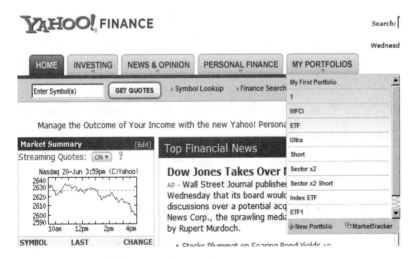

Figure 14-2   My Portfolio Pull-down Menu

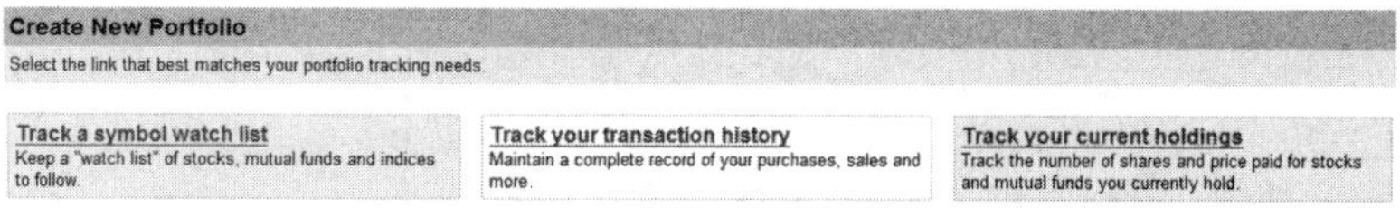

Figure 14-3   Create New Portfolio Page

select as many as you like and enter any new ones that may interest you. Yahoo! Finance allows for a maximum of 200 symbols in one portfolio. If you need or want more than 200, you can just create a new portfolio. (Refer to Appendix A; it provides you with the symbols for most of the ETFs traded on the major exchanges in the United States.)

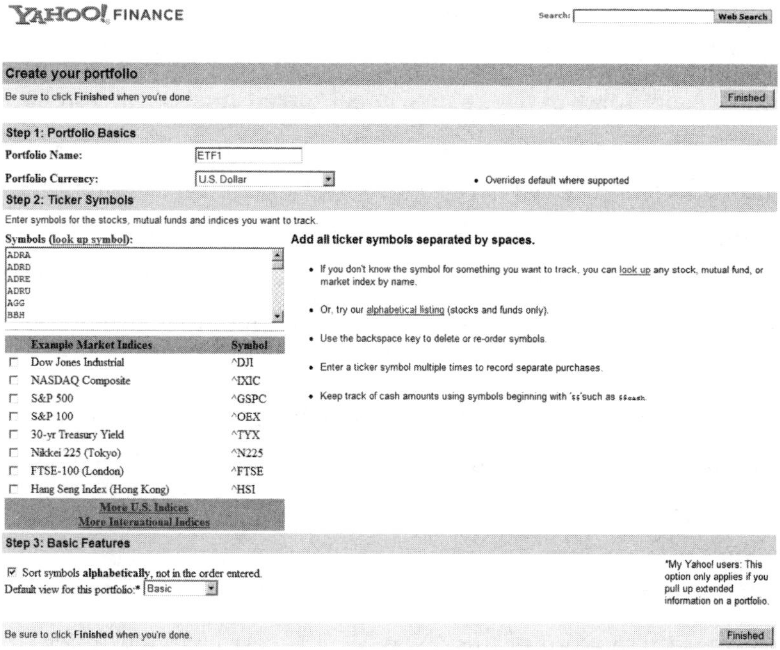

Figure 14-4   Create Your Portfolio Page

After you have entered all your symbols, click on the box *Sort symbols alphabetically* in step 3 if you want the symbols listed in alphabetic order. Finally, click on the *Finished* button in the bottom right corner of the screen.

Yahoo! Finance provides four built-in views for your portfolios. (You also have the option of creating your own.) You can choose to display up to 16 types of data out of the 65 available on Yahoo! Finance; i.e., Ask, Bid, P/E Ratio, etc.

Export Your Portfolio into Excel

Now that your portfolio on Yahoo! Finance is complete, let's export it to Microsoft Excel. Start by opening Microsoft Excel. Click on *File* → *New*. You will have a new Excel spreadsheet open. You now have a bold box in cell A1 (column A, row 1). Click on *Data* → *Import External Data* → *New Web Query*. (See Figure 14-5.)

You now have the "New Web Query" window open. On the top of this window, in the address box (like the one in your Web browser), key in http://finance.yahoo.com and click on *Go*. (See Figure 14-6.)

Pull up your portfolio just as you did before and choose the desired one you wish to export into MS Excel. Once your portfolio screen is up, you will see black sideways arrows within yellow boxes.

Click on the arrow next to the symbol column, and it will turn green. At the bottom of this "New Web Query" window, click on

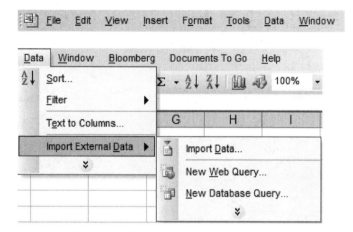

Figure 14-5 New Excel Spreadsheet

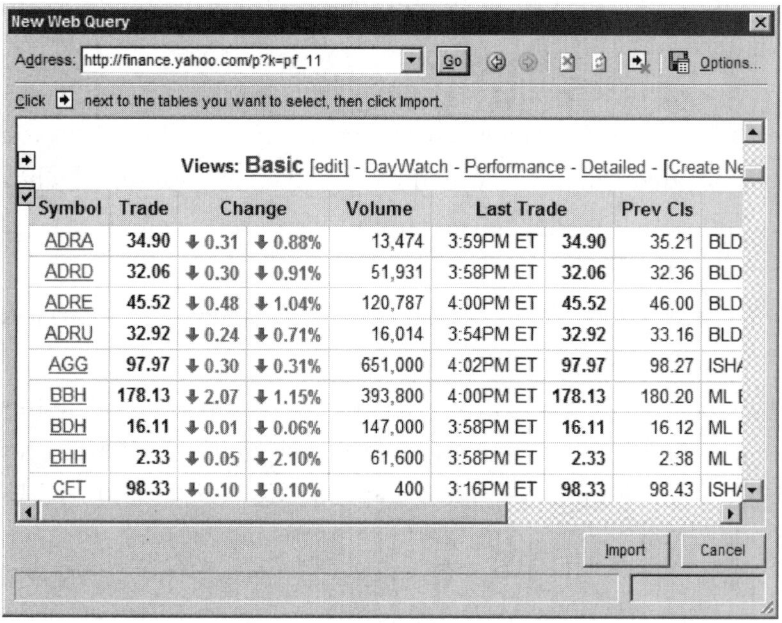

Figure 14-6 New Web Query Page

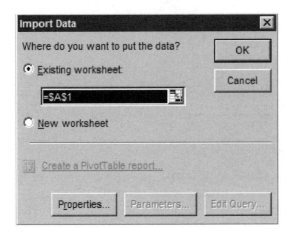

Figure 14-7 Import Data Window

Import. This will lead to the "Import Data" window shown in Figure 14-7.

Here you have the choice of importing data at the place you originally were (cell A1) or any other place on the worksheet. After you have decided where you would like the data to be inserted, click on OK. This will now give you a new external data toolbar, as shown in Figure 14-8.

To refresh these data, click on Refresh Data icon  . This will refresh all the data on the spreadsheet.

Yahoo! Finance gives you free quotes, so you can update this anytime and as many times as you wish during the day. Once your data are successfully imported, your spreadsheet should look like the one shown in Figure 14-9.

Figure 14-8 External Data Toolbar

	A	B	C	D	E	F	G	H	I	J	K	L	M	N
1	Commission	Trade Date	Price Paid	Shrs	Holdings Value	Symbol	Trade	Change		Volume	Last Trade		Prev Cls	Name
2		-	-	-	-	ADRA	34.9	0	0.00%	0	20-Jun	34.9	34.9	BLDRS ASIA 50 FD
3		-	-	-	-	ADRD	32.064	0	0.00%	0	20-Jun	32.064	32.064	BLDRS DEV MKTS 100
4		-	-	-	-	ADRE	45.52	0	0.00%	0	20-Jun	45.52	45.52	BLDRS EM MKTS 50
5		-	-	-	-	ADRU	32.924	0	0.00%	0	20-Jun	32.924	32.924	BLDRS EUR 100 FD
6		-	-	-	-	AGG	97.97	0	0.00%	0	20-Jun	97.97	97.97	ISHARES LEH AGG FD
7		-	-	-	-	BBH	178.13	0	0.00%	0	20-Jun	178.13	178.13	ML BIOTECH HLDR12/39
8		-	-	-	-	BOH	16.11	0	0.00%	0	20-Jun	16.11	16.11	ML BRDBND HLDR12/40
9		-	-	-	-	BHH	2.33	0	0.00%	0	20-Jun	2.33	2.33	ML B2B HOLDRS12/40
10		-	-	-	-	CFT	98.33	0	0.00%	0	20-Jun	98.33	98.33	ISHARES LEHMAN CREDI

Figure 14-9 Sample Spreadsheet

Maintain and Manipulate Your Portfolio

> **Trader's Notebook**
>
> You may also want to look for a low-cost broker, but remember to be careful as to how your broker executes your orders; some brokers charge extra money for orders other than market orders, such as stop and stop limit orders.

Now that you have your portfolio list for ETFs, let's talk about strategy. If you are a short-term trader and plan to hold for a few weeks or less, focus only on ETFs with a decent trading volume. The higher the volume, the higher the liquidity, and thus the smaller the price difference between the bid and ask. This price difference is a built-in trading cost as most of us buy at the ask price and sell at the bid price.

The biggest advantage of trading ETFs is that your risk is spread over all the underlying stocks comprising the ETF. For example, if you want to trade SPY, a basket of all 500 stocks of the S&P 500 Index, your risk is spread over the entire index. If you want to trade QQQQ, a basket of the 100 stocks of the Nasdaq-100 Index, your risk is spread over 100 stocks. If you buy individual stocks, your risk is solely based on a single company. Thus, if anything were to go wrong with this company, such as an analyst downgrade, accounting irregularities, or product delays, you will be put at considerable risk.

Many ETFs are based on industry sectors. Almost all industries have a historical pattern of outperforming the markets during a certain time within their economic cycles. You can buy

> **Trader's Notebook**
> Risks associated with individual stocks do not have the same impact on ETFs.

ETFs when they are at the bottom of their respective cycles and sell when they are near the top, or the end of the cycle.

There are also leveraged ETFs that work on both directions of the markets. This leverage can be multiplied up to two times. These types of ETFs are good for retirement accounts where leverage through margin and shorting are not allowed. Since self-directed retirement accounts do not allow margin trading, you cannot utilize classical leverage or shorting. In the case of addressing leverage, if your analysis is convincing you that the Nasdaq-100 is going up and you would like to utilize leverage but cannot through margin, you can buy QLD. QLD is an ETF that moves at twice the rate of the Nasdaq-100. However, due to the inability to short, in a falling market retirement accounts have two choices, either to ride out the storm or to cash out and enjoy the money market interest rate. The problem is that you cannot take advantage of the falling market by taking a short position. If your analysis is telling you that the Nasdaq-100 is heading south and you want to take advantage of a falling market while at the same time using leverage, you can buy QID. QID is an ETF that moves at twice the rate of the Nasdaq-100, but in the opposite direction. Thus, if the Nasdaq-100 falls 2 percent, the value of your long position of QID will gain 4 percent. If your analysis is wrong, you will lose twice as much money as anticipated. This allows you to capitalize on an expected correction (or reversal) of an expanding market. Thus, in a limited retirement account where shorting stock or leveraging through margin is not allowed, you can use ETFs. Most common index ETFs like the Dow Jones, Nasdaq-100, S&P 500, and Russell 2000 are available for trading.

Two Significant Trading Strategies

We now discuss two trading strategies: momentum and value.

Trading Based on Momentum

Momentum traders usually buy when prices are making new highs. This kind of trading is characterized by:

- Buying when the closing price of an ETF is at a 20-day high.
- Buying when the close is above the 50-day moving average.
- Buying when the close is above the 200-day moving average.
- Buying when the close is above the last few weeks' high.

You can also use moment retracement. For example, instead of buying after the stock makes a high, you can wait until the price backtracks (or retraces) about 38 or 50 percent, and then buy on reversal.

Trading Based on Value

Another strategy is to trade based on value. Here, look for an industry at the bottom of an economic cycle that is ready to rebound. At this point in the cycle, everybody is nervous and nobody can really tell what the future will hold for this industry. Historically, this is the time to buy. You are likely to see industry prices making multiyear lows—here will be a panic sell-off or two. If you recall when crude oil was selling around $10 a barrel in 1998, you know what happened after that.

Trader's Notebook

When using a value strategy, you should buy after everyone has sold or sell after everyone has finished buying. When using a growth strategy, you will be buying as earnings or stock price starts an upside momentum and you will ride as long as this momentum exists. For many industries, this is an industrial cycle within an economic cycle. If you are holding ETFs based on a particular industry, you will be holding them for a long period of time. Remember though, it will be very difficult to buy at the bottom of the cycle and sell at the top.

If you are a short-term trader, there are many ETFs that have good trading volume and liquidity. In this case, you can use technical analysis for your entry and exit. Always remember to enter your predetermined stop loss as soon as your position is confirmed. Once you determine your stop loss, DO NOT CHANGE.

You can also spread one ETF against another—buy the strong and sell the weak. For example, when risk premium is high in the market, buy the Dow Jones Index (low-risk index) and short the Russell 2000 Index (high-risk index); because when the market takes a turn, the Russell will be down more percentage points than the Dow.

These are the basic concepts. Remember, even though your risk is spread over many stocks when you are trading ETFs, it doesn't necessarily mean that you can't lose—big.

ETF Strategy

Finally, remember that the markets can be nonrational longer than you have the money to sit through them. Never, ever risk more than a certain percentage of your account on any one trade.

15

EUROPEAN ETFs

The United States is the largest ETF market in the world, based on both the number of ETFs traded and assets under management. Over 70 percent of the world's ETF assets trade on U.S. markets. Japan is in the number two spot, followed by Germany and France. Europe as a whole, however, nails the second spot, with 285 funds that had $93 billion in assets under management, as of February 28, 2007. Americans seeking to diversify outside the U.S. market should consider Europe in making investment decisions.

The size of the average ETF in Europe tends to be smaller than Asian and U.S. ETFs. The major markets are in Germany, France, the Netherlands, and Switzerland. The other European markets are relatively small. Only four European markets have more than 1 percent of global ETF assets. Still, the market is growing, with new ETFs being added to the list on a regular basis.

Invest in European ETFs

When it comes to investing in Europe, Americans have two basic choices. They can invest in ETFs on U.S. exchanges that track European markets (such as those that follow the MSCI (Morgan Stanley Capital International) indexes), or they can invest directly in European ETFs that trade on European markets.

In deciding, which course to take, investors need to consider the following factors:

- **Can investors buy the funds?** There may be legal restrictions on U.S. citizens investing in European ETFs, or it may be difficult for U.S. brokers to buy and sell on European markets.

- **Tax aspects:** How will the funds be taxed, and how will that taxation affect the investment? Are there tax treaties that can ease the tax burden?

- **Costs:** Which is cheaper? The MSCI indexes tend to be more expensive to trade than many European ETF indexes.

- **Diversification:** Some European ETFs may be highly concentrated, which is characteristic of many MSCI indexes. In addition, some European ETFs do not have many components. The main Belgian and Portuguese stock indexes have 20 components, which limits their value as diversified investments.

ETF Choices

The ETF choices can be broken down into four areas:

1. **Investing in pan-European ETFs:** Covering many countries.

2. **Country ETFs:** Indexes based on one country.

3. **European sector ETFs:** Sectors across different countries.

4. **Currency baskets:** Track the euro or other European currencies.

One risk that international investors face is that they are buying investments in foreign currencies—using dollars. At some time, while holding the investment, that foreign currency may depreciate relative to the dollar, which would reduce the value of the investment in U.S. dollars. On the other hand, the currency may appreciate while the investor holds the investment, which would increase the value of the investment when translated into U.S. dollars. Investors must be aware of these risks when making their investments and understand the potential impact of exchange-rate fluctuations on the value of their investments.

ETF Managers—Europe and the United States

The U.S. ETF market is dominated by four managers: State Street Global Advisors (SSgA), Barclays Global Investors (BGI), Vanguard, and the Bank of New York. Together, these four managers control nearly 93 percent of U.S. ETF assets, as of October 1, 2007. The top 10 advisors manage over 99 percent of U.S. ETF assets, as of October 1, 2007.

In Europe, the market is also highly concentrated with four top companies: BGI, Lyxor, Axa Gestion, and Credit Agricole. These companies manage over 80 percent of European ETF assets with the top 10 managers controlling over 95 percent of European ETF assets, as of February 28, 2007.

In both markets, BGI is the leading, if not dominant, player with roughly 60 percent of U.S. ETF assets and about 50 percent of European ETF assets under management. BGI's presence in Europe *doubled* when, in 2006, it purchased INDEXCHANGE from HVB (a large German bank). INDEXCHANGE, a pioneer in European ETFs under the leadership of Andreas Fehrenbach, its managing director, is now iShares Germany. (See Figure 15-1.)

In addition to US ETFs, as mentioned above, another 285 ETFs traded in Europe (as of February 28, 2007). U.S. investors might want to trade in the European markets directly, although as we will see, this approach may lead to significant complications.

Before trading directly in European markets, consider the fact that the ETFs traded in European markets may not differ much from the choices in U.S. markets. First, many European ETFs are not based on European markets, but on U.S. and other markets, so U.S. investors can access those markets through U.S. ETFs. Second, a significant number of the European ETFs, mostly in the United Kingdom, are commodity funds. U.S. investors can buy

ETF Manager	Fund	Ticker
Bank of New York	BLDRS Europe 100 ADR Fund	ADRU
BGI	iShares MSCI-EMU	EZU
BGI	IShares S&P Europe 350	IEV
BGI	iShares MSCI Austria	EWO
BGI	iShares MSCI Belgium	EWK
BGI	iShares MSCI France	EWQ
BGI	IShares MSCI Germany	EWG
BGI	iShares MSCI Italy	EWI
BGI	iShares MSCI Spain	EWP
BGI	iShares MSCI Sweden	EWD
BGI	iShares MSCI Switzerland	EWL
BGI	iShares MSCI Netherlands	EWN
BGI	iShares MSCI United Kingdom	EWU
Rydex	Currency Shares Euro Currency	FXE
Rydex	Currency Shares Swiss Franc	FXF
Rydex	Currency Shares British Pound	FXB
Rydex	Currency Shares Swedish Krona	FXS
State Street	DJ STOXX 50	FEU
State Street	DJ Euro STOXX 50	FEZ
State Street	SPDR S&P Emerging Europe	GUR
Van Eck	Market Vectors Russia ETF	RSX
Vanguard	European	VGK
WisdomTree	Europe Dividend	DEB
WisdomTree	European SmallCap Dividend	DFE
WisdomTree	Europe High-Yielding Equity	DEW
XShares	HealthShares European Drugs ETF	HRJ

Figure 15-1 Major European ETFs for U.S. Investors

commodities through the U.S. futures markets. Third, many of the European ETFs track broad market indexes. The MSCI indexes that form the basis of many of the iShares products also track a broad market in those European countries. The European ETFs that track broad market indexes, however, tend to have lower expense ratios. For example, iShares MSCI Germany has an expense ratio of 0.54 percent, while iShares Germany's DAX Ex ETF has an expense ratio of 0.15 percent.

The main differences between the European options open to U.S. investors and those open to European investors are that European investors have more access to:

1. European sector funds

2. A greater variety of indexes based on capitalization

3. European debt product ETFs

4. Growth and value ETFs

5. Leveraged funds

U.S. investors have the opportunity to invest through U.S.-based ETFs in a broad range of European countries, in pan-European indexes, and in some specialty funds, such as dividend funds based on European equities. In many ways, offerings for U.S. investors are similar to the options for European investors. For instance, many European funds actually track U.S. indexes and other non-European markets, and U.S. investors have the same if not more tools to track these same markets, at lower cost, and with lower taxes and lower transaction costs. Many European ETFs simply track broad European indexes, and in many cases, there may be considerable overlap with the MSCI indexes that U.S. investors can buy, so the difference in performance may not differ significantly.

In addition, WisdomTree has a range of dividend funds that tracks European stocks using fundamentally weighted strategies. The main gap between what an American or European ETF investor can get may lie in the ability to purchase certain specialty funds, because each country has different regulations regarding what kind of ETFs may trade on its respective market. The U.K.

market features a number of commodity funds, and the French markets feature leveraged ETFs.

Taxes

The tax angle can be very important for U.S. investors. If U.S. investors put their money in a U.S. fund, they can at least get an idea of their tax situation by reading the prospectus and related information from the fund. If they invest in a fund based outside the United States, they may face foreign tax liability and U.S. tax liability on income from dividends or capital gains. Tax treaties may apply in certain cases which permit U.S. investors to apply tax credits that neutralize the effects of foreign tax payments.

> **Trader's Notebook**
>
> Taxation varies by country. Investors should determine the potential tax liabilities that result from investing in particular countries. Capital gains taxes tend to be a U.S. phenomenon, but other countries may tax dividend income. Consultation with knowledgeable broker or tax advisor will provide insight before investing.

In the event that investors buy a fund that includes both European and U.S. companies, they will want to make sure that the fund has more than 50 percent of its assets in securities that are domiciled outside the United States in order to qualify for the foreign tax credit. If a fund does not qualify for the foreign tax credit, then investors can use their foreign tax payments as a tax deduction. However this is a less satisfactory alternative because investors are doubly taxed on their foreign earnings, whereas the foreign tax credit means that earnings are taxed only once, by the foreign country.

Regulation

U.S. investors need to be aware of regulatory issues related to investing in European markets. When investing in a U.S.-domiciled regulated investment company (RIC), investors have the protection they are entitled to under the 40 Act. Investing outside the United States usually means that the funds are subject to the regulations of the country where the fund is managed, or perhaps to the exchange where it trades. Protections for investors may be stronger or weaker than regulations in the United States.

It is important to remember, regarding securities regulation, the words of Andreas Fehrenbach, the head of iShares Germany, "Europe is not one country." Each country in Europe has its own securities regulators with their own rules. ETFs may not be permitted in some countries. Other countries may have regulations that favor domestic fund managers. Germany, for example, has much stricter regulations on the governance of investment funds than the United States. In Germany, the owners of fund managers may not have representation on the fund's board—all the directors must be independent of the fund. In the United States, funds usually have representatives of the fund's owner on the board.

For some U.S. investors, the discussion of regulation may be moot because it may be difficult or impossible for them to buy a non-U.S. ETF. Some countries may restrict foreigners from investing in their markets, U.S. brokers may not have access to those markets, or rules may prevent certain customers from buying the securities.

Strategies

Strategies discussed in Chapters 7 through 14 can be applied to European as well as U.S. ETFs. Going long or short are basic strategies. (Some investors may be interested in spread trades which are discussed in Chapter 10.) For example, a trader, based on analysis of economic or market issues, feels that the Swedish market is undervalued relative to the Spanish market. The investor expects the Swedish market to converge with the Spanish market. In this case, the investor could go long a Swedish ETF and short a Spanish ETF in the hope that the markets will move closer, in which case the investor will sell the Swedish ETF and buy back the Spanish ETF, hopefully at a profit. The investor will profit from a narrowing of the spread. In the event that the spread widens, the investor will incur a loss. If the investor, on the other hand, expects the spread to widen, the investor would go short Sweden and long Spain in the hope of profiting from the widening spread. This is a type of market-neutral strategy, because it does not depend on the performance of *any one* market but the relationship *between* the two markets.

European Currency ETFs

Other investors may wish to spread various European currencies against one another, to profit from changes in demand for different currencies. Still, the currency markets are highly volatile and not suitable for a buy and hold investor. A trader who desires to speculate in currency ETFs should carefully study the Forex markets and how they operate. In addition, currency ETFs may not be the best way to trade currencies. Traders who wish to speculate in these markets may be better served by trading in the futures or options markets, which may have greater liquidity.

Europe Is *Not* One Country

Countries have different characteristics and markets. Europe is not one country. The European Union plays an important role in European economies, but each country has its own securities regulator. There is no EU-wide securities regulation, although there have been efforts to harmonize financial reporting standards and other issues related to securities markets, such as what investments are suitable for different types of investors. The matter of EU securities regulation is discussed in the One-on-One Interviews section, following Chapter 16, in the interviews with Andreas Fehrenbach of INDEXCHANGE and Dimitris Melas of MSCI BARRA.

Eurozone Issues

In Europe, many countries have entered the eurozone, meaning that they have a common currency—the euro—and that their central banks have surrendered control over many elements of economic policy, such as setting interest rates. Interest rates and economic policy set at a European level may be less than ideal for individual economies.

The countries within the Economic and Monetary Union (EMU) of the European Union are economically interdependent. The member countries of the European Union, including the eurozone countries, may have heavy investments in Eastern Europe and may face risks—and can also reap rewards—from those investments. The eurozone consists of Austria, Belgium, Finland, France, Germany, Greece, Ireland, Italy, Luxembourg, the Netherlands, Portugal, Slovenia, and Spain.[1]

Eurozone countries have replaced their former national currencies with a single currency—the euro. Countries that have adopted the euro are parts of the EMU. Membership in the EMU requires these countries to comply with restrictions on inflation rates, government deficits, debt levels, and tight monetary and fiscal controls. (The country-specific information that follows can be found in its original form in iShares MSCI Series: Prospectus, January 1, 2007.)

U.S. investors can invest in 11 eurozone countries through the iShares MSCI EMU Index Fund (EZU). Other major country investments are described here, to be read in conjunction with Figure 15-1.

Austria

The Austrian economy is tightly interwoven into the economies of Europe, especially Eastern Europe, where it has many key trading partners. Austrian companies have economic holdings in Eastern Europe that allow investors to access those markets, indirectly, while still investing in a developed market economy, the Austrian economy. So one doesn't have to directly put money into Eastern European markets that may have governance or regulation issues and less stable currencies than the euro.

Belgium

The Belgian economy, given its relatively small size, is dependent on the health of the overall European economy. It trades heavily with its European Union partners. The Belgian economy is highly dependent on exports. Belgium lacks natural resources and depends on imports to meet its commodity needs. Commodity price fluctuations, or shortages of commodities, could have a significant effect on the Belgian economy.

France

France's economy is highly intertwined with that of Western Europe: 70 percent of its exports go to other EU member states. France is one of the world's largest agricultural producers, with one-third of the EU's agricultural land, and is highly susceptible to forces affecting agricultural markets, such as droughts, labor issues, and crop failures.

France faces a number of structural risks to its economy that could affect the performance of its markets, including social unrest and high levels of unemployment. Labor unrest often comes in the form of nationwide strikes that affect critical infrastructure, such as railroads. These labor actions can have deleterious effects on the French economy.

In addition to labor unrest, the French government plays an extensive, often interventionist, role in the economy and controls a large share of economic activity through ownership of shares in corporations in the banking, energy, automobile, and transportation sectors. Government spending can account for over half of GDP, one of the highest ratios in the industrialized world. The government heavily regulates labor and other markets, which may at times hamper French economic growth.

Germany

Germany is the largest trading nation in Western Europe and one of the world's largest exporters. Exports account for more than one-third of economic output and are a major factor in Germany's economic growth. Germany is heavily intertwined with the European economies, given that it is a key trading partner with many European economies.

The German economy faces certain structural risks that could affect its markets. Certain areas of Germany, primarily the former German Democratic Republic, have experienced significant unemployment levels and social unrest, resulting from the slow pace of integration of the former East Germany with West Germany. These problems may affect the German stock markets. In addition, the German economy is subject to high levels of regulations of labor and other markets. At times, these regulations may hamper economic growth.

Italy

The Italian economy depends on the performance of other European economies because these are its key trading partners.

The Italian economy faces a number of difficulties, including poor infrastructure, corruption, high government spending, and frequent changes in governments, which can affect Italian investments.

Italy suffers from high levels of unemployment, accompanied by labor and social unrest. This labor unrest can manifest itself in nationwide strikes. With increased globalization, Italy has seen some of its markets, in lower-end industrial products, hurt by competition with lower-cost economies, such as China.

As part of the EMU, Italy is subject to governmental budget restrictions. Recently it has had large budget deficits and a high level of public debt that has caused Italy's sovereign credit rating to be cut by credit-rating agencies. The EMU has warned Italy to reduce public spending and debt. This high level of debt and government spending may slow down the Italian economy.

Netherlands

The Dutch economy is dependent on other economies within Europe, where it has many key trading partners. The Dutch economy, because of the Netherlands' geography, being partly below sea level, is subject to risks from environmental events, notably flooding and storms. In addition, being near the center of Europe's transportation system makes it vulnerable to environmental events such as pollution and oil spills that can adversely affect the Dutch economy and trade.

In addition to having geographic risk factors, the Dutch economy has sustained high levels of unemployment and is heavily reliant on trade in its gross domestic product. In recent years, the Netherlands has been less competitive because of increased labor costs and competition within the European Union.

Spain

The Spanish economy and stock market have been, in recent years, among the best performers in Western Europe. However, the market is quite volatile and highly exposed to the Spanish real estate sector, which has cooled off recently. There are a number of risk factors related to investing in the Spanish economy and stock market. Spain has had trouble with domestic terrorism, including a large bombing by Islamic terrorists on March 11, 2004, and Spain harbors a terrorist group known as ETA, which seeks independence for Spain's Basque region. ETA and other Islamist terrorist groups may adversely affect the Spanish economy.

Spain faces a number of challenges from globalization. Its export capabilities have declined because of its higher labor costs relative to its competitors. In addition, Spain has a high unemployment level, although it has been declining. However, the labor market lacks flexibility, and the country has not solved the problem of low productivity growth.

The economy is not highly diversified and is heavily dependent on the real estate market to support its construction industries. Decreasing levels of real estate development could hurt the construction sector and may affect the banking sector. In addition, Spain's adoption of the euro, which has been a strong currency, has raised concern that Spanish exports are priced out of the range of foreign buyers. In addition, Spain's R&D levels fall short of many of its EU counterparts.

Sweden

The Swedish economy, like that of most other countries in Europe, is highly dependent on inter-European trade. The Swedish workforce is over 80 percent unionized, and the government funds an extensive social welfare system. It is possible that these factors may, at times, reduce economic growth. In addition, Sweden's economy depends on the export of natural resources and derived products. Changes in these sectors, notably the prices for products or the overall demand, could adversely affect the Swedish economy.

Sweden, although a member of the European Union, is not a member of the eurozone. Sweden's currency is the Swedish krona.

Switzerland

Switzerland has a considerable ETF market, despite its small size. Again, as in other European countries, the economy is intertwined with other European nations. In addition, the United States is a large trading and investment partner with Switzerland, so the Swiss economy is also subject to the ups and downs of the U.S. economy. This aspect may make investing in a Swiss ETF less diversifying compared to other European ETFs for U.S. investors. On the other hand, this may make the Swiss economy less dependent on the overall European economy compared to other countries in Western Europe.

The Swiss economy faces considerable commodities risk because it lacks natural resources. It relies on imports for its commodities needs. Price fluctuations or shortages could have a major impact on the Swiss economy.

Another risk, which may surprise investors who think of Switzerland as a haven of economic tranquility, is the fact that the Swiss economy has recently been experiencing a near-record-number of bankruptcies. The bankruptcies are the result of restructuring in the Swiss economy and may increase further. These bankruptcies could adversely affect investment in the Swiss economy and the rights of investors to reclaim assets of bankrupt corporations.

Switzerland is neither a member of the European Union nor the eurozone. Its currency is the Swiss franc.

United Kingdom

The United Kingdom is one of the most important economic entities in Europe, with London, its capital, a major center of world finance. The United Kingdom may hold particular appeal for U.S. investors because it does not tax dividends for foreign investors, meaning that investors get to keep more of their earnings. The United Kingdom, like Switzerland, has more diversified trade patterns than many other European nations because of a high level of trade and investment between the United Kingdom and the United States. This relationship can be a source of diversification of the economy, but it also exposes the U.K. markets to economic movements in the United States.

The United Kingdom, similar to Spain, faces terrorist threats that may affect the British economy. In recent years, the United Kingdom has suffered attacks from Islamic terrorists that have targeted transport facilities. The British government has tended to intervene less in the economy and in corporate ownership and governance than the governments of other European countries.

The United Kingdom, although a member of the European Union, is not a member of the eurozone. Its currency is the pound sterling.

Russia

Until recently, the Russian market had not had a U.S.-based ETF. In 2007 that changed with the launch of Van Eck's Market Vectors Russia fund (RSX). It needs to be made clear to investors that this is a highly speculative market. Investors face risks unlike those in the United States or Western Europe. Russia is an emerging market, which means that it is subject to rapid changes. In addition, in times of market unrest, emerging market companies may have difficulty tapping foreign capital and credit markets.

Russia may experience less economic, political, and social stability than the United States or Western Europe. The Russian government has not hesitated to take action against corporations that the government does not like or regards as threatening to its control. Russia's currency, the ruble, could undergo significant fluctuations resulting from interest-rate changes, monetary policies of various governments or international agencies, imposition of currency controls, or other political or economic developments.

Russia is a major exporter of oil and gas, which makes its economy highly dependent on the price of oil and gas. Falling oil and gas prices could have a major negative impact on the Russian economy and the Russian markets. Terrorist actions against Russian oil and gas infrastructure could affect Russia's ability to keep supplying those products, which could hurt the country's economy. Russia has experienced many acts of terrorism in recent years.

Problems in other emerging markets may cause investors to decide to dump Russian stocks, as well. Russia is not a member of the European Union.

ETF Strategy

Investing outside the United States allows investors to diversify their portfolios and seek new investment opportunities that may not be available in the United States. Europe provides a number of markets for U.S. investors to explore and different investment themes to exploit. European ETF markets are growing rapidly. Investors need to understand the risks and potentials of these investments, including changing exchange rates. Europe is not just for tourism; it's also for investing.

16

ETF PRACTICAL APPLICATIONS

When putting together an ETF portfolio, the more research you can do on your own, the more money you will certainly save. Even though there are many newsletters available, you have to do your own research.

Also, there is a little known strategy that we like to use with ETFs. For every dollar you make trading, take 20 cents of it and invest it in the most safe, secure investment you can locate. If it's another ETF, be sure it is an investment insured by the U.S. government. If it isn't, some sort of fixed income will do. Now here's the good news. It's that 20 percent over a 10-year period that will determine your eventual financial success.

Navigating Web Pages

There are seven steps you should address *before* you start trading ETFs:

1. **Set a goal:** What do you hope to accomplish, and in what time frame?

2. **Allocate resources:** Make sure you have a mixture of ETFs that will make it possible for you to reach your goal.

3. **Write it down!** The authors are amazed by the number of traders and investors who do not have a written plan. If you can't write it down, then at least dictate it to somebody. If you plan to retire at 40, show me your written plan.

4. **Select a good broker:** You may want to take half of your investments and give them to a full-service broker. At the end of the year you can determine who was the better trader—you or the broker.

5. **Have a rebalancing strategy:** The markets change. There are hundreds of ETFs. You have to know when to change your investment philosophy. If the Federal Reserve raises interest rates, fixed-income securities are going to look very, very attractive. If inflation begins to rear its ugly head, those gold and silver ETFs are going to skyrocket.

6. **Put a monitor on your portfolio:** Every time your doctor takes your blood pressure, go home and monitor your portfolio's health. Are there signs of trouble? Are you going to let your portfolio explode because of a diet of day trading and penny stocks? Monitor your portfolio.

7. **Know what you don't know:** There are great brokers out there. Even if they're full service, they're worth their weight in gold. Many brokerage firms have full-time analysts whose only job is seeking out new, innovative, and profitable ETFs. You may never see them on CNBC, but the leading brokerage firms employ the best and the brightest. And there's no law that says you can't get on the phone and speak with them.

Examine Typical ETF Screens

There are many ways to break down ETF Web screens. The following are the most typical.

Most ETFs are broken down by style, sector, and region. However the really important aspects are value, blend, and growth. Once you know that, the concept of size becomes the focus.

In Figure 16-1, there are five ETFs that are large value funds. They are: First Trust Morningstar Div Leaders (FDL), iShares Morningstar Large Value index (JKF), PowerShares Dynamic Large Cap Value (PWV), iShares Dow Jones Select Dividend index (DVY), and Rydex S&P 500 Pure Value (RPV). The optionsXpress software lists the five top funds in the category. So if you want to start a portfolio that is "large value," the work has been done for you.

As we move horizontally along the Style Box, we highlight the Large Blend square. (See Figure 16-2.) This contains funds whose objectives are to invest in securities with large market cap and offer a combination of value and growth stocks. As you will note,

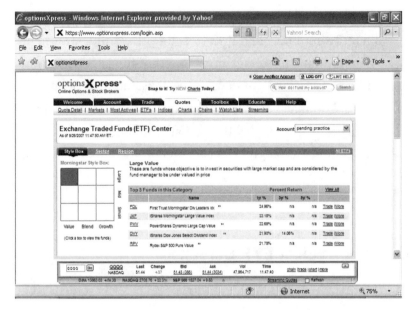

Figure 16-1 Large Value Funds

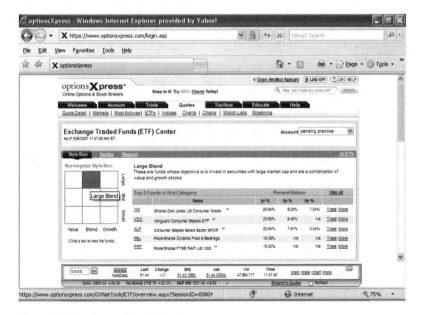

Figure 16-2 Large Blend Funds

the top five funds in this category include: iShares Dow Jones US Consumer Goods (IYK), Vanguard Consumer Staples ETF (VDC), Consumer Staples Select Sector SPDR (XLP), Power-Shares Dynamic Food & Beverage (PBJ), and PowerShares FTSE RAFI US 1000 (PRF).

The top row of the Style Box in Figure 16-3 highlights large growth. The ETFs represented here are focused on long-term growth. Look at the fourth ETF, PowerShares Aerospace & Defense. To the right of that listing you will note over a 10 percent return. Much of it was the result of military spending in the Middle East.

The middle row of the Style Box in Figure 16-4 shows mid-value or mid-cap investments. In this category you are seeking securities that are undervalued in price. Note that each of the funds listed contains the word *value* in its name.

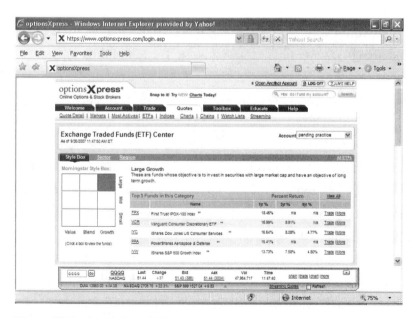

Figure 16-3 Large Growth Funds

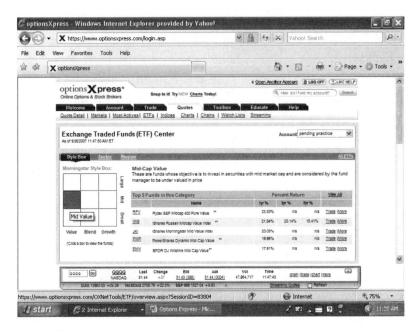

Figure 16-4   Mid-cap Value Funds

The mid-cap ETFs shown in Figure 16-5 are a blend of value and growth. Please note each symbol to the left of the funds. As in all screens, by clicking on these symbols, you can "drill down" for more information. However, for now, our strategies are based on value and growth.

In Figure 16-6 the top five funds are designed for long-term growth. Usually ETF investors look for a three-year growth factor. With these particular ETFs, there are only two with a three-year growth factor: iShares Russell Midcap Growth Index and iShares S&P MidCap 400 Growth Index.

When the foundation of your ETF is small value stocks, you are looking for more than average return. However, these ETFs are fairly new and reflect the bull market in 2006–2007 and should be used sparingly in 2008 and 2009. (See Figure 16-7.)

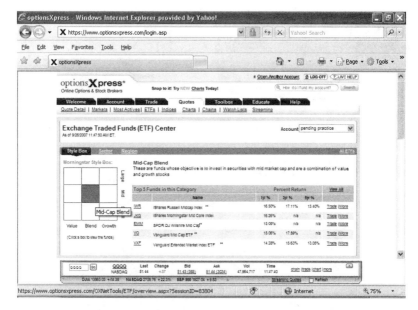

Figure 16-5   Mid-cap Blend Funds

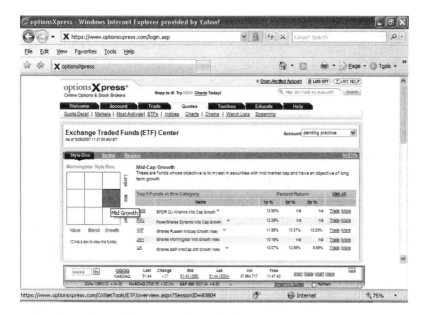

Figure 16-6   Mid-cap Growth Funds

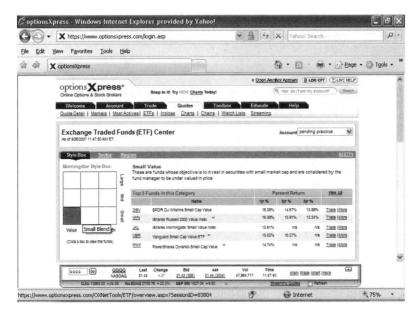

Figure 16-7   Small Value Funds

Small blends are new to the ETF game. (See Figure 16-8.) However, notice the name brand players behind them. They include Vanguard and SPDR. Now a word of caution. These merely represent the top five. You should explore a little deeper and speak to your brokerage firm. Fidelity, for example, has funds that are very similar. The difference is going to be execution and service.

Figure 16-9 shows the last category—small growth. This category represents small companies with big ideas. (Remember, Microsoft was once a small-growth company.)

These ETF screen shots are divided into style, sector, and region. Many traders follow one or two basic investment styles: value and/or growth. You have to decide for yourself what type of ETF trader you want to be. Value traders attempt to buy a buck's worth of assets for 50 cents. Price matters. They are very concerned with the price they

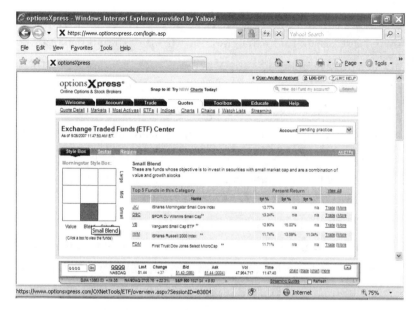

Figure 16-8   Small Blend Funds

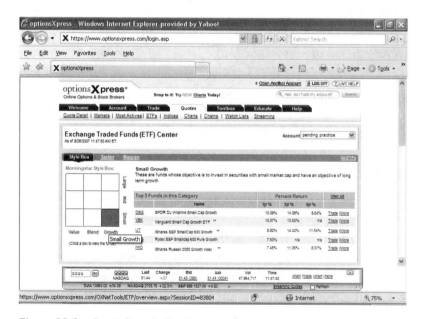

Figure 16-9   Small Growth Funds

paid for an ETF. As you probably can guess, growth managers and growth traders seek ETFs that are growing faster than the economy. They are not as concerned about price as they are about growth.

Today, traders may use a combination of both, and you can find ETFs that are based on market capitalization and investment style. Note that in the ETFs just presented, we were taking a long bias. Obviously, if we're looking to short an ETF, we're looking for companies that are poorly managed, poorly run, losing money, and may be going out of business.

Many ETF traders will look at the previous charts and merely pick the ETFs with the single largest return. They think that since they would like to gain 9 percent every year, all they need to do is simply eliminate asset classes that don't return at least 9 percent. Makes sense, right? Wrong! This is an example of naive mental accounting. What you lose is the power of diversification. For example, if you fixate on high-yield bond ETFs, you might ignore their diversification benefits for the portfolio as a whole. (No one can predict the future, and today's beauty contest winner can be tomorrow's wicked witch of the west.)

Herd Mentality

There's a tendency to pick ETFs with stocks that we have heard of. This is simply called "herd mentality," and when you open up and dissect an ETF, you may be amazed that its performance is based on stocks you've never heard of. Consider the Energy Select Sector SPDR (XLE). XLE is made up of major energy stocks, such as Exxon Mobil, Chevron, and ConocoPhillips. Another interesting aspect of trading XLE is related ETFs. The optionsXpress system has the capability for traders to view a screen to see what "people who traded XLE have also traded." The question on everyone's lips is, people who traded XLE tend to trade such stocks as Google, Apple, Goldman Sachs, and WXI Pharmatech, so where is the connection? There is a tendency for people to trade stocks that are leaders in their respective portfolios. It makes sense, doesn't it? People like to buy stocks that are leaders in their field. And here's the best part, the computer will automatically tell you what holdings people tend to be drawn to and cluster around, based on previous purchases. This is really common sense. Let's face it. People who tend to gamble in Las Vegas would certainly be open to solicitations from establishments in Reno and Nassau, right? Well, people who like big, fat energy stocks can't get enough of them. They are like layers of meat on a submarine sandwich.

ETF Spreads

Buying strength and selling weakness is as old as trading, and it's no different when it comes to ETFs. There are three great things about spread trading:

1. Increased flexibility

2. Allowing traders to take advantage of price disparity

3. Usually lower margin

Look at Figure 16-10. The top line in the graph is going to the right corner "top," and the bottom line is going to the right corner

Figure 16-10 Daily Snapshot Comparing the S&P Homebuilders to the Nasdaq Market QQQQ

"down." The top is the Nasdaq-100 Index Tracking Stock (QQQQ), and the bottom is the SPDR S&P Homebuilders ETF (XHB). Note, this screen shot was taken during the summer of 2007; even though the homebuilders looked weak, their performance continued to deteriorate into the new year. In essence, what we are doing is trading homebuilders against technology. So, why trade spreads? I may not know what's going up and what's going down, but I do know what are strong stocks and what are weak stocks, and I can profit by buying strength and selling weakness in any type of market environment.

Here is an example of stock indexes both moving in the same direction. As you can tell from Figure 16-11, both indexes were up, but one was up 20 percent, while the other was up 10 percent. Please note that the really important factor in trading spreads is

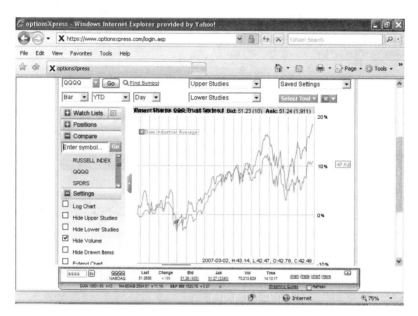

Figure 16-11 Comparing Stock Indexes

volatility. Many people have said trading spreads is like watching paint dry. That's because people are trading the wrong spreads. Put a little Tabasco sauce on your portfolio and they'll rocket.

Screens such as this are the most frequently used. Why? Because you know where the ETF is trading during the day in relation to the opening price. Before we leave these screen shots, you must know the components of an ETF. In short, how are they "sliced, diced, chopped, and mashed." Or as people say, "What are the ingredients?" To accomplish this, merely enter in the ETF symbol, as shown in Figure 16-12. You will see the price and volume for the symbol you entered.

As we examine the information on this particular ETF shown in Figure 16-13, we can see a 52-week range as well as the daily range, along with a simple chart. Note that there are over 600 ETFs.

Figure 16-12 XLE Price and Volume

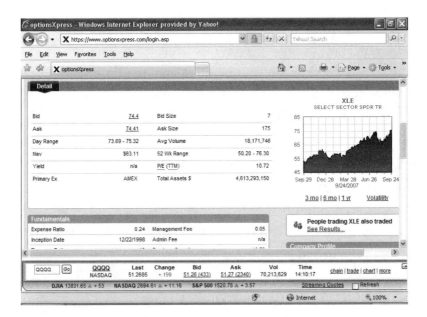

Figure 16-13 Detailed Price and Volume Statistics for the Energy Select Sector SPDR (XLE)

We are merely using XLE as an example and are not endorsing this particular fund. However, if there's no energy in your portfolio, what are you thinking?

Figure 16-14 provides important information about expenses, style, and returns of the Energy Select Sector SPDR (XLE). We can see 5-year, 3-year, and year-to-date returns, as well as the industry breakdown. (The industry breakdown pie chart is in the lower right-hand corner.)

The performance of an index is ultimately determined by the performance of its components. Figure 16-15 shows the top 10 components of the Energy Select Sector SPDR (XLE), which account for almost two-thirds of the weighting of the index. These companies have a major impact on the index's performance. Exxon Mobil alone accounts for over one-fifth of the performance of the

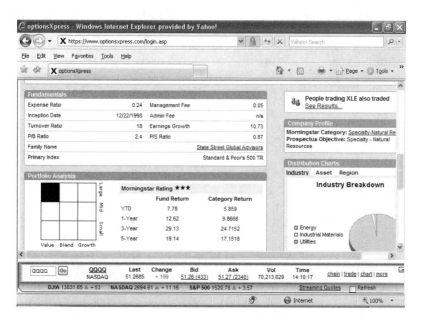

Figure 16-14 Look for the Rating

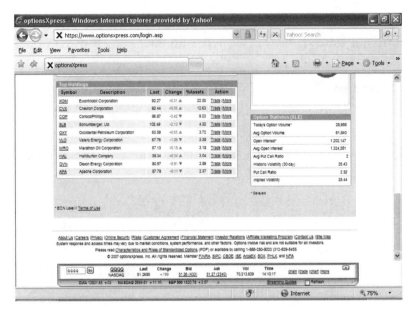

Figure 16-15 Major Components of XLE and Respective Weights

index. It is becoming increasingly apparent that I can buy 10 of the leading energy companies at one price, without risking massive amounts of capital. This particular page is updated in real time during the trading day.

ETF Strategy

Previously, we mentioned that with ETFs you could be your own hedge fund. ETFs provide you that role. You can now manage cash, fixed income, and equities, as well as hard assets. You can decide to enhance your portfolio or cut down your risk and have your ETFs take the opposite side of your portfolio. Good luck in your ETF trading.

Screen shots in this chapter, as well as Figure C-16 in Appendix C, are provided courtesy of optionsXpress, Inc., for educational and informational purposes only. optionsXpress, Inc., does not guarantee, approve, or endorse the content of this publication, nor does the display of optionsXpress screen shots indicate any association with or approval by optionsXpress. optionsXpress is not associated with, does not endorse, and does not sponsor the author or publication. optionsXpress, Inc., makes no investment recommendations and does not provide financial, tax, or legal advice. Any stock, options, index, or futures symbols displayed are for illustrative purposes only and are not intended to portray a recommendation to buy or sell a particular investment.

ONE-ON-ONE INTERVIEWS
Leading ETF Providers

This book discusses a number of concepts that may seem irrelevant to the ETF trader and investor. However, the following interviews with leading professionals in the ETF, index, and exchange worlds reveal how items such as regulation, tax laws, and principles of index construction are truly major issues. Many of the providers' concerns are not covered in their fund documentation or by the reporting of the financial media, but their words provide the "reality" of the ETF world.

AMERICAN STOCK EXCHANGE
The Birthplace of
Exchange-Traded Funds

The American Stock Exchange is responsible for launching the first exchange-traded fund—the Standard & Poor's depository receipts, the SPDR, in 1993. The ensuing years have brought forth a whole ETF industry.

Scott Ebner, senior vice president of the ETF marketplace at the American Stock Exchange (Amex), is responsible for both product development and the marketing of ETF products at the exchange. Mr. Ebner joined Amex in 1998, early in his career, and has been instrumental in expanding Amex's ETF business to the point where Amex has more ETF listings than any other exchange in the world. Mr. Ebner received a bachelor's degree from the College of William and Mary with a dual concentration in economics and international relations.

How do you feel capital markets have changed in recent years, especially with the ETF revolution?

ETFs have made things a lot easier for both the advisor community and the retail investor community. I think ETFs may have helped change the landscape, but they are also a good product for a changing landscape.

There has been a strong trend of firms increasingly offering fee-based financial advice, and ETF products are well suited for these fee-based platforms. ETFs are relatively low cost, extremely flexible, diversified, tax-efficient, and they don't have sales loads. More and more advisors, who are being paid for their advice, are looking for the best possible tools to use to implement strategies for their clients. Advisors realized that they don't have to be threatened by ETFs. They have found that clients were coming to them to seek advice on which ETF to buy, and how to meet their investment goals using ETFs, or combinations of ETFs, mutual funds, single stocks, and other financial products. This fit, with changes in the financial advisory community, is complemented by the continued growth in popularity of ETFs with self-directed individual investors and institutions.

Retail investors, institutional investors, and advisors have all found ETFs useful. At some point, for almost every investor, an ETF will be their best investment choice.

One issue that keeps cropping up is liquidity, especially on the short side. What does Amex do, through its oversight with its specialists, to ensure liquidity?

Liquidity in the ETF market is not defined entirely by trading volumes. Because institutions have the ability to create shares on an ongoing basis, specialists and other market participants have the ability to tap into the liquidity of the underlying securities and convert it into liquidity for an ETF. While higher trading volume can improve the liquidity in the ETF market, liquidity in the product is not bound simply by the trades. Liquidity can be transferred among the underlying markets, futures markets, and options markets. Investors concerned with liquidity should look at the size and depth of the quoted markets for an ETF in addition to trading volume.

Many market makers in ETFs maintain an inventory of ETF shares for lending at commercial margin rates. Short interest in many ETFs is quite large. The liquidity from market makers and specialists in both the quoted market for ETFs and the stock loan market can make a great deal of difference to the success of an ETF.

Do you have an opinion on the matter of weighting?

Many new indexes for ETFs have been created that use alternative weighting methods to construct index portfolios. Most are modifications of existing methods that have been around for years. Alternative weighting methods have been used by individual investors and professional asset managers alike and have frequently been used in other financial products such as index options, unit investment trusts, mutual funds, and structured products. It is good for the ETF market to have products based on indexes that offer an increased variety of construction and weighting methods.

What happens when an ETF shuts down?

There have only been a few ETFs that have been closed down. There are strict liquidating procedures. Announcements are made well in advance of closing the fund to notify investors that the ETF will be closing, and usually a liquidating distribution based on the NAV [net asset value] of the ETF is paid to shareholders. The liquidating distribution reduces the impact, but a fund closure has a tax consequence similar to a sale of the shares.

Who is your competition?

At one time we were the only game in town because we built this market, but the ETF market has matured and become very competitive. We now compete with all of the other exchanges. Nevertheless, Amex continues to be the largest ETF listing market, and we continue to attract the largest number of new ETFs.

It's better to be in a successful market, and competing well, than to be in an unsuccessful market.

When you look back on your career, are you surprised you are doing what you are doing?

When I first began working with ETFs in 1998, I thought ETFs were a great product that should be very successful, but I don't think anyone could have predicted this kind of success. It has been my good fortune to be involved in an exciting market for so long. It's very satisfying to see a product succeed, and it energizes you to work harder and help the products grow. Exchange-traded funds are great products with a lot of room for continued growth.

DOW JONES

Dow Jones develops, maintains, and licenses indexes for use as benchmarks and as the basis of investment products. It is best known for the Dow Jones Industrial Average that was started in 1896 with 12 stocks.

John Prestbo is manager of Dow Jones's index operations. He started working for the *Wall Street Journal* in 1964 and has spent his whole career with the Dow Jones organization. He has written a number of books on finance and investing. He is best known as one of two gatekeepers of the Dow Jones Industrial Average, which is the oldest and best known of stock market indexes.

Given your extensive experience in the capital markets, how do you think they have changed with the rise of ETFs?

It seems every day that people are paying more attention to indexes. The idea of index investing that John Bogle started was a major advance in investing. The development of ETFs is a continuation of those innovations. Indexes are far more in the spotlight than before. From a handful of indexes that few people/nobody paid attention to, now indexes make headlines. It seems that new indexes are created every week.

Dow Jones has a long history in the index business. It was the first to the market with a stock market average, with its Dow Jones Industrial Average over 100 years ago. Standard & Poor's came much later to the business.

What are the criteria that you use to set up an index? I noticed that Dow Jones recently set up a Grand Prix Index, based on companies that support or supply Formula One motor racing teams. It didn't seem diversified.

The Formula One Index was designed to bring attention to the index business.

I'll say. It was all over the news in Spain, even in news outlets that fail to cover the IBEX 35.

Apart from that, our indexes play an important role in financial markets. They are used for asset allocation purposes and benchmarking. The Dow Jones Wilshire 5000 index is the most accurate representation of the broad U.S. market. Other indexes, such as the Dow Jones Industrial Average, are made up of blue-chip stocks that are some of the largest companies in the USA. The Dow Jones Industrial Average is not a complete representation of the markets.

In determining how to set up an index, it's important to first determine its purpose. For example, are you interested in covering a complete market or a piece of a market? We try to provide as complete coverage as possible. Other indexes are specifically designed for the creation of financial products, such as structured products, notes, swaps, and ETFs.

What importance do you give the RIC/UCITS rules in putting together an index?

Compliance with RIC and UCITS rules is not important to index providers, but to funds that use those indexes. Some indexes may be representative of an industry but are not RIC-compliant due to the concentration within an industry; the telecom industry comes to mind.

An RIC-compliant telecom index would not be an accurate representation of the market. An index is about measuring a market. A fund can choose which indexes it chooses to license.

Another example of a problematic area related to RIC rules is the energy sector, where a few big companies dominate the market, although there are many small companies.

The RIC rules were set up in the 1930s as a way of providing protection for investors. They are not a guide on how to set up a benchmark. A benchmark needs to be about measuring a market, not complying with the RIC rules.

How does Dow Jones help investors understand the impact of taxes on their investments?

To help clients, and investors, understand the tax impact of certain indexes, we provide data showing gross returns and net returns after taxes. These data can be customized for clients depending on tax jurisdiction. In Europe, the default rate is usually Luxembourg. (Luxembourg's tax rates are commonly used because many European investment funds are located there.) Withholding taxes can be calculated by country, as needed.

In recent years, there have been a number of alternatively weighted indexes produced that underlie different investment schemes. How does Dow Jones approach weighting?

Market weighting is the accepted norm for almost all benchmark indexes. The Dow Jones Industrial Average will remain price-weighted, given its long history, to ensure the continuity of the index.

Dow Jones has also produced alternatively weighted indexes, such as the select dividend indexes. These indexes are becoming more accepted every day.

As you look back on your career, are you surprised you're doing what you are doing?

No. But as my career unfolded, I was fortunate having stayed with the same company for all of my career. I started out reporting and editing for the *Wall Street Journal* and developed an interest in these hidden areas of finance, such as indexes. The simple but successful practice of index investing has had tremendous repercussions for investors. Ultimately, the history of indexing has shown that good baskets of stock are better for almost all investors than are individual securities.

iSHARES GERMANY

iShares Germany, also known as INDEXCHANGE, was formed after Barclays Global Investors purchased INDEXCHANGE, Germany's leading provider of exchange-traded funds in 2006. iShares Germany was the first German company to offer exchange-traded funds. iShares Germany manages over 18.5 billion euros with some 80 exchange-traded index funds that track equity, real estate, and commodity indexes.

Andreas Fehrenbach holds a distinguished position in European ETFs. He saw an innovative trend happening in the United States—ETFs—and decided to bring them to Germany. It was not an easy matter because he had to overcome resistance from his employer, an active asset manager. However, he persisted, and INDEXCHANGE, the company he started as a subsidiary of HVB, a major German bank, quickly became one of the world's largest ETF providers. It is now part of the iShares group, as iShares Germany.

Given your extensive experience in the capital markets, how do you think they have changed with the rise of ETFs?

I think for Europe with ETFs a lot of things have happened. Before that, there were only a few investment products available, such as futures and options.

Before the arrival of ETFs, the only way to trade complete markets was to use derivatives. However, many institutional investors in Europe could not, and still can't, use derivatives. This is a major difference between Europe and the United States. ETFs have allowed many institutional investors to make short-term investment decisions, such as tactical over- or underweighting.

In America there is an issue of getting market makers for ETFs. Is this a problem in Germany?

Yes and no. At the beginning it was a big, big problem. At first when we started INDEXCHANGE, everyone said no. In Germany, market makers are known as designated sponsors. They are obligated to make a market in a particular stock. At first, the only designated sponsor we could get was HVB, which was the bank that owned INDEXCHANGE. But a few months later, it changed dramatically. Institutional demand took off quickly. More and more of the designated sponsors changed their minds due to the demand for the product. Within six months all the major market makers were on board—Goldman Sachs, Lehman, HVB, Arcalon Flow Trader, Deutsche Bank, and Commerzbank. Today, as we speak, many major firms are designated sponsors for our products.

Now, as we launch our fixed-income products, we are seeing the same difficulty of getting designated sponsors as we had with our equity products. Designated sponsors are now fine with equity products, but we only have a few for our fixed-income products. Still, the liquidity on these fixed-income products is higher than fixed-income products in the United States.

One problem with trading some ETFs in the USA is the lack of liquidity on the short side. Have these issues surfaced in Germany? How do you ensure liquidity?

Liquidity on the short side is a problem. In some cases there is no real lending market, or in other cases, the lending market for certain ETFs is developing in Germany. It is hard to get shares to go short. Part of it is that going short on an index requires new thinking about investments for many market participants who could not short an index before. Still, the options market is growing, which does create alternative ways of going short. Still, we have a long way to go to enable investors to go short on ETFs. At the moment, investors may be better off using futures to short an index.

On the long side, we have great liquidity, especially on the DAX index. The short side is still an issue.

Who is your competition?

In Germany, we have had a very big certificate market that has been our main competition. Certificates are a particular German investment product that are fixed income but have their performance correlated with the market. They are issued by banks. They really are like a fixed-income investment—a bond with equity performance. They have had tremendous tax advantages for investors. However, that advantage will go away soon.

These tax issues affect the growth of ETFs throughout Europe. In each country in Europe there are different issues. For example, in Spain, as far as I know, it's still not clear, from a tax point of view, whether an ETF is a share or a fund.

In addition, our competition consists of other investment funds located here in Germany and large savings banks.

Who are your customers? Retail? Institutional?

Up till now it has been nearly 100 percent an institutional market. About 95 percent of the market is institutional, and 5 percent is retail investors. The United States has more retail level usage.

Here in Germany, funds use ETFs for liquidity management, "equitizing" cash [putting cash to work in the marketplace], and hedging.

Expanding the retail market is difficult because that market is dominated by "push," where banks are pushing the product. To enter that market requires us to pay commissions, which ETFs are not equipped to pay, given their low cost structure. That's a big issue. Still, discount brokers, or online banks, may represent a new way to reach the retail market.

It will take time and education to sell these products more to retail customers. This contrasts with the United States, where a large part of the population has exposure to investment funds through their involvement in retirement plans.

Still, there is more and more demand for low-cost and efficient products, and ETFs are the most efficient product.

How do you see the market evolving? Do you see INDEX-CHANGE going outside Germany?

In thinking about cross-border operations, it is important to remember that Europe is not one country. While there are Europe-wide securities guidelines, they have to be implemented by each country, which has its own securities regulator, regulatory environment, and culture. That's the reason we have iShares dominating the UK, Lyxor dominating France, and INDEX-CHANGE dominating Germany, Switzerland, and Austria. If we try to sell a product in France, cultural and regulatory issues make it difficult for us to compete. There are differences in reporting and accounting regulations.

There are regulations unique to Germany. For example, German funds face very strict regulation—all board members need to be independent of the fund's owner. In fact, the BAFIN, the German regulator, prohibits the owner of a fund from having any representation on the fund's board. The reason for that rule is that every asset manager in Germany is owned by a bank. When HVB owned INDEXCHANGE, the bank had no representation on the board; it had no influence over any asset management decision or any management decision.

Since we are a German fund, our main market is German investors. Still, we do business in Austria and Switzerland.

What do you think of moves toward actively managed ETFs?

That's a good question—a really, really interesting question. At INDEX-CHANGE, if there is a rule on how to invest, a very clear rule, we might think about setting up a fund based on that rule. However, if there is any space for human decision, we won't do it. That's our golden rule. For example, we have a few funds which have dividend criteria, but they are clearly rule based.

I really don't think you can do actively managed ETFs, because the market makers will have a problem because they won't know what the members of the index are. I don't think you can do it.

Many of our readers are familiar with the RIC rules in the USA and how these companies can pass through their earnings to shareholders, without taxation at the corporate level, but they are not familiar with UCITS [Undertakings for Collective Investment in Transferable Securities] rules. What does UCITS compliance mean for investors?

UCITS is an effort to harmonize European securities regulations. Each country in Europe has its own securities regulators. UCITS tries to bring EU securities regulations together. UCITS funds have advantages such as being able to list across borders in the European Union. Some investors can't invest in funds that aren't UCITS compliant. One UCITS requirement is that a single security in the fund cannot have a weight of more than 10 percent.

When you look back at your career, are you surprised you are doing what you are doing?

I started out in retail banking and then moved into active asset management. I saw the need for passive investment products in Germany. At that time, there were a few passive mutual funds, but no one knew about them. After I learned about the success of ETFs in the United States,

I decided that they were right for us in Germany. I tried to get the products going in the asset manager where I was working. It wasn't easy. Fortunately, at HVB I was not only a product manager, but also a sales executive. It sounds really funny, but I think it is the perfect combination. I think that helped. I was in a position to see what customers demand or what they will demand. My position gave me a better view of the demand for our product.

KEEFE, BRUYETTE, AND WOODS (KBW)

K eefe, Bruyette, and Woods is an investment bank that specializes in the financial services sector (banking, insurance,
and capital markets). In fact, that's all it covers. This specialization
and its depth of coverage of the sector make its indexes very important for traders and other investors in this sector, especially for risk
management purposes. KBW's indexes underlie a number of ETFs
that State Street Global Advisors offers, as well as a series of stock
index options that help create liquidity in the marketplace for these
indexes. Note that this interview took place in July 2007, when the
U.S. subprime lending industry was undergoing a shakeout.

John Howard is the director of research at KBW, and **Siddharth
Jain** is the research department's index specialist.

What are your criteria that you use to set up an index?

Howard: In developing indexes, first and foremost there are very specific risks.
There are distinct risks within financial services. There are very distinct risks
in capital markets. We are trying to segregate the risks. Our competitors do
not qualify the risks. Our bank indexes do not look like our competitors. Our
competitors do not qualify the risks within the industries we cover.

Jain: People talk about correlation among subsectors of financials as one [a perfect correlation]. What we have brought to the table is the ability to explain
and show that there is a difference in correlation among subsectors of

financials. When you put together a basket of financials, banks do not trade the same way as insurance companies or mortgage companies or capital markets companies. Even within the banking sector, large and regional banks do not trade in the same way.

We use a number of quantitative and qualitative criteria to select the components of our indexes. These criteria include liquidity, volatility, and certain index-specific characteristics, such as regional diversification of a bank's deposits and earnings mix for our regional banking index.

KBW has the depth and breadth of coverage to look at the broad market.

Howard: We are very much bottom-up in our approach to selection of companies to include in our indexes.

Jain: We slice and segregate risk to present it to our customers in a carefully defined manner.

Howard: No one else does what we do. Our competition produces poorly structured products. It mystifies me that the marketplace has not demanded good indexes that properly capture subsectors.

Jain: We don't throw products at a wall to see if they stick. The products are tested before they are brought to market. We carefully select the components. A large-cap bank needs to behave like a large-cap bank for the index to perform as expected. Our products are tested for a long time and checked for internal tracking error before they are released.

Howard: We don't tolerate anything that doesn't capture a specific risk. We are constantly looking at the performance of each basket of stocks. Stocks are dropped if they will affect the basket. We do an annual review of each index, a quarterly rebalancing, and a monthly meeting on each index to review the behavior of the components. Mergers of companies within the index are a cause for change. Unlike other index providers, KBW removes companies when mergers are announced, not when they are completed. This is because the presence of merger arbitrage essentially takes a security out of the risk pool, which could make the basket less representative of the market.

Jain: For example, we recently removed Doral Financial Corporation from one of our indexes as it was not tradable, because it had failed to make SEC filings. If something is not tradable, it cannot be in our indexes because the specific risk of the market is now tied to that one stock. Readers can get a better idea about our index selection from criteria from our report, "Introduction of KBW Regional Banking Index and KBW Mortgage Finance Index" that can be found on our Web site: www.kbw.com. [A brief selection from that report, which outlines KBW's approach to component selection, follows.]

> For indices comprised of publicly traded companies, index constituents will be chosen on the basis of relevance to the market sector in question and, after due consideration, on certain trading criteria, including but not limited to stock price, stock price volatility, stock price correlation to index price, average daily trading volume, optionability of stock, market capitalization, country of origin, listed exchange, and perceived viability of listed company.
>
> Such metrics are necessary to ensure that the chosen constituents are not only reflective of the intended market segment, but are also tradable — i.e., they provide sufficient liquidity to enable market participants to effect basket trades for purposes of hedging, etc. Specific quantitative bounds will be followed for the above criteria (as guided by the relevant exchange rules). KBW product development and corporate research staff will consider these boundaries to ensure that the constituents are both representative and tradable.
>
> Specifically, the indices will be designed and maintained so that financial instruments based on them will be in compliance with necessary listing/maintenance criteria dictated by subsections (b) and (c) of Rule 1009A (Designation of the Index) on the Philadelphia Stock Exchange. Component securities that fail to meet these standards will be replaced within the index according to the above described policies and procedures.

What particular expertise does KBW bring to index development for ETFs?

Howard: KBW has more analysts covering the financial services sector than any other bank. This expertise is unique to KBW. For example, we have a panoply of components across all sectors that represent the risk of a particular market in our mortgage finance index. We have regional banks, mortgage lenders, and title insurance companies. This design creates a much better index that reflects mortgage risk. Sometimes we have to tell ourselves to stop from slicing even more finely than we do.

Jain: Our mortgage index has had loads of hits lately.

Howard: For us, developing these indexes is intuitive. We don't need clever tricks to determine constituents. The more we have gotten into index development, the more we see a crying need for someone like us to design index products, because there is a lot of junk out there.

MSCI BARRA

M SCI BARRA develops and maintains equity, hedge fund, and REIT (real estate investment trust) indexes that serve as benchmarks for managing over $3 trillion globally. It produces some of the most widely used indexes for markets outside the United States. Morgan Stanley, a global financial services firm, is the majority shareholder of MSCI BARRA; a minority share is held by Capital Group International, Inc.

Dimitris Melas is the executive director and head of research in Europe, the Middle East, and Africa for MSCI BARRA. He manages the firm's index operations in Europe and deals with matters related to index methodology, analytics, risk management, and portfolio construction. Prior to working at MSCI BARRA, Melas worked in fund management and quantitative research at HSBC. He has a master's degree in electrical engineering and is a chartered financial analyst (CFA).

What are the criteria you use to set up an index?

At MSCI BARRA, we construct indexes that reflect opportunities available in the investment markets based on securities available in the marketplace. There are four main reasons that we develop indexes:

1. **Research purposes.**

2. **To aid in asset allocation:** For example, by using indexes, it is possible to see how a domestic equity portfolio could be affected by adding international exposure to it.

3. **Performance analysis and attribution:** Using indexes makes it possible to compare a fund's performance with the market and to see if it justifies its costs.

4. **Investment product creation:** Indexes serve as the building blocks for mutual funds and ETFs.

Standard indexes are passive reflections of markets. MSCI BARRA seeks broad coverage of the investment opportunities that reside in a particular market. Each market has its own investment characteristics that guide the makeup of an index.

In the U.S. for example, there are many securities that create a diversified and complex market. In Finland, on the other hand, the situation is completely different. One company dominates the movement of the market, and that fact needs to be reflected in the index.

The index business is not static because our indexes both reflect and incorporate the changes in the market environment, such as trends in asset management. For example, MSCI BARRA creates customized indexes for clients or benchmarking needs. Indexes can be created around a certain type of company or other rules, such as socially responsible investing (SRI) indexes.

In recent years, there have been a number of alternatively weighted indexes produced that underlie different investment schemes. How does MSCI BARRA approach weighting?

We will create customized indexes based on client needs. As I just mentioned, for our public or standard indexes, we are trying to provide broad coverage of investment opportunities, and we tend to use market capitalization weighted by free float. This weighting has inherent advantages as it provides for automatic rebalancing and is a low-cost index to track.

A number of index providers have seemingly arbitrary classifications of growth and value stocks, wherein stocks fall into one or the other category. How does MSCI BARRA make the distinction?

Value and growth needed to be defined separately—a stock should not be classified as value simply because it is not a growth stock. For example, it is inappropriate to classify a stock as growth simply because it has a high price-to-book ratio. Growth should be based on an analysis of historic and forward earnings. Companies can have both value and growth characteristics. Some stocks are neither value nor growth.

In the European Union, UCITS is a series of EU rules that regulate funds sold across borders in the European Union. Many investors cannot invest in funds that are not UCITS-compliant. UCITS requires a level of diversification for indexes used to underlie ETFs. How does UCITS work? Does UCITS compliance affect your development of European indexes?

In regard to your first question, UCITS compliance confers considerable benefits on markets. UCITS directives are an effort by the EU to harmonize securities regulations. Investors need to understand that these directives need to be translated into state law by each of the member countries.

As to the second question, MSCI BARRA creates customized indexes that allow funds to meet various UCITS requirements, notably the 10/40 rule. The 10/40 rule states that no mutual fund can have more than one security making up more than 10 percent of a fund, and those securities that have more than 5 percent weighting in a fund cannot make up more than 40 percent of the total capitalization of the fund. Within these constraints, there is a lot of flexibility to develop various indexes. Customers can request custom indexes.

Does MSCI BARRA have or could MSCI BARRA develop any indexes friendly to short sellers?

At the moment, we don't have any indexes specifically targeted at short sellers. We could, however, make an index that replicates the payoff from the mechanics of short selling. It could be based on the whole shorting process with borrowing the stock and paying interest to lenders of shares. That could be a useful product. It could be useful to institutional investors, speculators, and those seeking to hedge a position. It could be used to create a short ETF portfolio.

Could you describe your methodology for producing indexes and the types of indexes you produce?

In developing an index, we consider market capitalization and available shares (free-float weighting)—which means that we subtract strategic stakes held by managers or governments, as these shares are not freely available to investors.

We take the perspective of institutional investors in considering weighting. For example, a stock with large capitalization but little float is not readily available to institutional investors.

We also create customized indexes for our clients. For example, in a defined benefit pension plan for Company X, we can create an index that does not include that company in the index.

That's good, because putting pensioners' money in their own company is not good risk management. Many Enron employees, who were already exposed to the risk of Enron investing by being employees doubled up on their risk by investing in Enron as part of their retirement planning, and when the company went bankrupt, they lost their jobs and their retirement savings.

Another example of a customized index that is a bit more complicated is creating an index for an investor or fund that wishes to stay out of a particular sector. For example, consider a state-sponsored pension fund from a country that has a lot of revenue from oil. It doesn't want increased exposure to that sector. MSCI can create an investable index that meets those needs.

ETF managers may choose to license our indexes. We are not linked to investment managers, which is a regulatory requirement in most jurisdictions. Investment managers can use our indexes to create an investable product. MSCI BARRA can handle the regular calculation and dissemination of indexes. [Regulators require that the calculation and dissemination of indexes be separate from the fund manager to avoid conflicts of interest or market manipulation.]

How does MSCI BARRA help investors understand the impact of taxes on their investments?

We calculate total return indexes with gross versus net return. We calculate tax rates on dividends by jurisdiction. In Europe we typically use Luxembourg's withholding tax rates on dividends because it is home to many offshore mutual funds. We will calculate liability by domicile or as needed by our clients.

When you look back on your career, are you surprised you are doing what you are doing?

This is a natural continuation of my work in investment research, where I engaged in risk modeling and portfolio development. The design and analysis that goes into creating an index is similar to managing funds. The research needs are similar when creating an index and managing funds.

VAN ECK GLOBAL

Founded in 1955, Van Eck Associates Corporation was among the first U.S. money managers to offer investment opportunities outside the United States. It offers global investment choices in hard assets, emerging markets, precious metals including gold, and other specialized asset classes.

Adam Phillips is the director of ETF sales at Van Eck Global, where he works with institutional sales desks, hedge funds, and pension funds. Prior to working at Van Eck, Phillips was an ETF trader on the floor of the American Stock Exchange. This background in trading makes his insights highly relevant to our readers.

Given your lengthy experience in financial markets, how do you think capital markets have changed in recent years with the advent of ETFs?

These days asset allocation is at the forefront for investment advisors. ETFs are great for asset allocation. They open up new asset classes to investors. Investors now have easy access to commodity-based investments.

ETFs enable investors to create mini-endowments of different asset classes. They can invest in various segments of the investment universe and obtain broader exposure to investment opportunities.

In many emerging markets, or rapidly changing and growing industries, it can be hard to pick stocks, as some may not be closely followed.

In these areas, ETFs allow investors to choose a basket of securities and obtain exposure to a sector with diversification.

In addition, ETFs can be used in all sorts of ways. They can be used for hedging and theme-based investing; and they can be subjected to technical analysis. These funds allow access to certain areas of the economy that may not have been accessible earlier.

How did you come up with the idea for these products?

Van Eck has had a 50-year presence in hard asset funds. Van Eck set up the first gold mutual fund, and it has created many innovative products in the hard asset area. It has now created ETFs in environmental services and the first Russian ETF in the United States. Van Eck has gone into areas that have not been well represented before. Van Eck has been the first in many of these areas in creating differentiated investment products. Van Eck does not do the supermarket approach to fund development where funds seek to have, and do, everything. Van Eck creates products with a unique compelling theme. These funds can be combined, often with other products, to create a broad, overall portfolio.

How does Van Eck approach weighting?

Van Eck funds use a modified market capitalization scheme. The weights of the components in the fund are set to ensure that the funds meet the RIC rules. Consequently, the funds comply with the RIC rules, which means that the earnings are passed through to investors and not taxed at the fund level. The modified weighting is based on equal dollar weighting. Weightings in some funds are capped at 10 percent for the four largest components. The smallest five companies are assigned another 10 percent of the capitalization. This allows the mid-cap companies, which have many innovative technologies especially in the alternative energy area, to make a significant contribution to the portfolio. For the Russia fund, this weighting scheme ensures that the index is a broad-based sampling of the economy and not just oil and gas companies.

One area where some ETFs have fallen short is in liquidity, especially on the short side. How is Van Eck doing here? Have you had difficulty getting market makers?

Our products have plenty of market makers and specialists to provide depth and liquidity. Volume is comforting. People look for it. Volume is important. Talk to any hedge funds, and they want to see trading volume. You don't want to have to rely on just the liquidity of the underlying securities. Our goal is to list options on these ETFs to drive order flow and create more liquidity. The short side is a different story. It is a function of security lending at brokerage firms.

Will expense ratios on Van Eck's funds go up after 2008, once their one-year cap expires?

The expense ratios are capped for one year, as stated in the prospectus. At this time, it is not our intention to raise them.

Who is your competition?

Our competition consists of other mutual funds, other ETFs, and single stocks in related areas. In addition, there are a number of index options such as ones on gold, silver, and steel that trade, for example, at the Philadelphia Stock Exchange.

How do you see change in the economic outlook influencing sales?

Van Eck's ETFs are part of a global growth story. Infrastructure and infrastructure investments are a major investment theme. Van Eck's products also allow investors to capture a large slice of emerging markets. Obviously, alternative energy funds could be hurt if oil falls to $10 per barrel.

When you look back on your career, are you surprised you are doing what you are doing?

As a former ETF trader, I am bullish on ETFs. They have tremendous positives. This market is just beginning.

WISDOMTREE

In recent years, there has been extensive interest in the theory of fundamentally weighted ETFs. These ETFs are based on indexes that are not capitalization-weighted, but weighted on other criteria, such as assets, dividends, and earnings, among other measures. One company that has based its whole investment philosophy on fundamental weighting is WisdomTree. WisdomTree has attracted a range of investment luminaries to work with it, including legendary hedge fund manager Michael Steinhardt, former chairman of the Securities and Exchange Commission Arthur Levitt, and the University of Pennsylvania's Professor Jeremy Siegel.

Luciano Siracusano, III, is WisdomTree's director of research.

Given your long experience in financial markets, how do you think capital markets have changed in recent years with the rise of ETFs?

One of the major trends of the last decade has been more disclosure to investors and more transparency in the financial markets. There has been another big trend, the move toward indexing of equity investments. The ETF structure capitalizes on all those trends. ETFs are transparent, with lower fees than actively managed mutual funds. They give investors a level of disclosure, in real time, that you don't necessarily get in a traditional mutual fund. It is possible to actually see the holdings in the portfolio.

One of the big events in our industry has been the whole reform that has come out of the mutual fund scandal in the past three to five years. Investors are becoming much more educated about the costs inherent in mutual funds and a lot of the hidden costs they were not aware of. I think cost, generally, is becoming more of a factor in how people evaluate financial products. When people shop for personal items, cost matters. But, for a long time, it hasn't really mattered for financial products. People are coming to understand the relationship between how much they pay for a financial product and how much that return is over time. No one has done more work than Jack Bogle in educating people about the relationship between high costs and high management fees and investor returns over time. It's one of the reasons why indexing has taken off the way it has and why exchange-traded funds are so popular, because they marry this movement toward indexing your assets with a structure that is, in our opinion, a better mousetrap than a traditional mutual fund.

Another thing I think people are becoming more aware of, after the stock market crash in 2000, is just how important it is to be diversified in their holdings and how important asset allocation is. I think that people may have learned a lesson about what happens when you become overweighted in any one sector, because a lot of people got stuck due to the technology bubble, and that had a real material impact on their returns. Now I think they are more conscious of being well diversified, and I think they are more sensitive to the kind of risks that are inherent in some of the different stock markets around the world.

How did you develop the idea for WisdomTree's methodology?

The WisdomTree index methodology was created by Jonathan Steinberg and me. The two of us are the inventors. Our names are on the patent. We created the proprietary index methodology. Michael Steinhardt, our lead investor, asked us to validate what we had done with an independent third party. We looked around to see if there was precedent that could back up what we had done, but there wasn't any at the time. There was very little we could find in the literature that explains what happens when you weight by the dividend stream. Our intellectual property was circulating in the venture capital community many months before Robert Arnott even published a paper on the subject. There wasn't even Research Affiliates data to point to. We went to Jeremy Siegel and asked if there was a way to confirm, or validate, what we had done. He said he was independently writing a book on dividend-paying stocks and did a lot of research on what happens when you tilt the portfolio toward higher dividend-paying stocks. All his independent research was consistent with what we had done, and he was so impressed that he decided to join the company and become formally involved with it. It was the incandescence of the WisdomTree intellectual property that attracted people like Jeremy Siegel to the company.

What are your opinions on weighting, especially the debate over equal weighting, cap weighting, and fundamental weighting?

With equal weighting, you give equal weight to all stocks in an index. These funds have a bias toward small- and mid-cap stocks. Equal-weighted indexes do not lend themselves to much investment capacity. A fund tracking an equal-weighted index will soon come up against capacity constraints—it can't be easily scaled up.

A fundamentally weighted index from WisdomTree gives you a lot of characteristics of a capitalization-weighted index in the sense that it scales—larger companies get larger weights—but once a year we adjust the portfolio for what we think is relative value. We're anchoring the initial weights once a year on a fundamental measure; by dividend for dividend funds and by earnings for earnings funds. There hasn't been a lot written about fundamental weighting, but a lot of people have practiced it, starting with Goldman Sachs in the early 1990s. The idea is not novel. What is novel is the debate that has been spawned by it, and WisdomTree's ability to commercialize it across the board in 38 ETFs is what has focused everyone's attention on us. Now people have a real alternative to cap-weighted index funds that they can use in broad asset allocation. Anywhere in the world they're using a cap-weighted index fund, WisdomTree is going to give them a fundamental weight alternative. That's where a lot of the excitement comes from.

The problem with modified equal weighting is that it creates a mid- and small-cap bias in a portfolio. It doesn't lend itself to broad asset allocation. People want a certain amount in large cap or large-cap value. With modified equal weighting, size drift creeps into the portfolio, meaning that the portfolio differs from the intended asset allocation of a financial advisor. Financial advisors dislike style drifts because they are paid to produce a particular asset allocation. If an index doesn't give them precise cuts, they don't want to use it. Unlike modified equal weighting, WisdomTree's fundamental weighting methodology gives precise cuts of the market. Our large cap is more large cap than is the Russell 1000 or S&P 500. Our small cap is more small cap than is the Russell 2000 or S&P 600. The reason for that is that we select stocks based on market capitalization and weight on a fundamental measure. WisdomTree gives investors broad market coverage, but we change the way the portfolio is weighted because we don't weight based on market capitalization. Fundamentally weighted funds are a real alternative to cap weighting.

One area where some ETFs have fallen short is in liquidity, especially on the short side. How is WisdomTree doing here? Have you had difficulty getting market makers?

Liquidity is not an issue we've come up against. People don't typically want to go short our ETFs because when you short one of our ETFs, you're responsible for paying the dividend yield to someone else. All of the research we've done shows over time that if you want to do a long/short strategy, our ETFs would make more sense on the long side. Investors could short a cap-weighted ETF and go long on one of ours.

Liquidity is fine. It is determined by liquidity in the underlying securities. We are dealing with index funds that cover trillions or hundreds of billions of dollars of capitalization. One person's purchase of $10 million or $100 million of our ETFs doesn't affect the prices of the underlying securities. That's why the bid-ask spreads on our funds can be so tight.

Our bid-ask spreads are around 3 to 5 cents on our domestic funds and 8 to 10 cents on our international funds.

One related issue to liquidity concerns specialists. Specialists provide the seed capital to launch ETFs through the creation process. With more and more ETFs, it may be hard to get a specialist to put money up front to seed the fund. If funds do not have specialists willing to put up capital, that will be a barrier to entry going forward. Not for WisdomTree, though.

Who is your competition?

On the one hand we compete against other index providers—Standard & Poor's, Dow Jones, MSCI, and FTSE on the index side.

On the ETF side we also compete against Barclays, State Street, and Vanguard. There are other players, but people need to understand that they have a fundamental choice to make: Do they want to allocate their index fund on a cap-weighted or a fundamentally weighted basis?

Once people understand the benefits of fundamentally weighted indexes, they don't feel comfortable going 100 percent capitalization-weighted. That will be the division going forward: cap-weighted index funds versus fundamentally weighted index funds. If your choice is cap-weighted, you have Barclays, Vanguard, and State Street—three world-class asset managers. If you want fundamentally weighted, there is only one place to go—WisdomTree. WisdomTree has a full line that covers the world and can be used for broad asset allocation.

The RAFI [Research Associates Fundamental Index] products from Powershares are also fundamentally weighted, but they have been commercialized at very expensive price points. WisdomTree has a built-in expense ratio advantage—our products cost less.

Another thing that makes WisdomTree different is that, unlike other investment managers, we create our own indexes and launch funds to track those indexes. Originally, fund managers had to be unaffiliated from the index provider. WisdomTree received permission from the SEC to create our own indexes. We outsource administration of the index and management of the fund to a third party. This allows us to be both fund manager and index creator. That's one thing that makes WisdomTree different.

We are also going to actively pursue getting our ETFs into 401(k) platforms. That will be a watershed when it happens. Right now there is a moat around the 401(k) market. ETFs have not been able to get in there. Once they're in there, that will change the dynamics.

Who is your typical customer?

We sell through intermediaries, not to the individual users. About 80 percent of our business is registered investment advisors (RIAs), brokers, and wirehouses. Twenty percent of our market consists of family offices, institutions that use ETFs, consultants, endowments, and even hedge funds. Our sales effort is geared to RIAs, brokers, and wirehouses that have WRAP programs [where the fees are not based on actual transactions and may include portfolio management or other investment advice] or fee-based asset managers. We target managers who have discretion over client assets.

What is the tax situation with your funds?

What we try to do is keep the turnover low—we reconstitute once a year. The turnover at the index level is low—10 to 20 percent for the large/broad portfolio. Our turnover is very low compared to active management. In addition, our turnover is lower than an equal-weighted index and a lot of other indexes, but slightly higher than cap-weighted, but not in a meaningful way. Taxes can be ameliorated through the creation/redemption mechanism. Most ETFs have not distributed capital gains due to mechanisms in the creation/redemption process. iShares has gone five years with no capital gains distributions on any ETFs. Powershares has never paid capital gains; it hasn't distributed capital gains at the fund level. This doesn't mean that capital gains never happen. They can happen. However, they are usually zero or close to zero. Dividends, of course, are distributed. We disclose updated tax distribution and dividend distribution on our Web site, wisdomtree.com.

How do you see the change in the economy or economic outlook influencing sales?

There's a macro trend at work with the weakening of the dollar around the world, which causes foreign currencies to appreciate and has benefited our foreign funds. We are 65 percent international at this point. WisdomTree is principally an international ETF company. Of our 38 funds, 26 are international. These funds open large portions of international equity markets to American investors. With the growth of international equity markets and emerging markets, it is important for investors to have exposure there. Most American investors have been typically underallocated internationally.

Wherever people are comfortably using iShares internationally, it is our goal to have a fundamentally weighted fund to give them a choice.

We believe, over time, fundamentally weighted indexes have the potential to deliver higher returns with lower volatility than comparable cap-weighted indexes. Our research has shown that that happens, over time, if you have a long enough holding period, including market cycles that have some down years.

The debate between fundamentally weighted indexes and cap-weighted indexes is revolutionary because for a long time cap-weighted indexes were considered the outcome of a portfolio, and you couldn't go beyond that. In reality, capitalization-weighted indexes have too much risk, which investors are not compensated for. Cap-weighted indexes make you buy market at too high of a price/earnings ratio. WisdomTree gives you the market at a lower P/E, and higher dividend yield, than a cap-weighted index.

When you look back on your career, are you surprised you are doing what you are doing?

I surprise myself all the time. For me this is only the third act. I was fortunate to have a career in politics, financial journalism, and now finance. I never cease to surprise myself. People become experts by doing things.

XSHARES AND HEALTHSHARES

X Shares Group, LLC, is a registered investment advisor (RIA) that is authorized to launch ETFs. It has developed a platform to allow other investment managers to use its services to launch their own ETFs, without having to go to the SEC to seek an exemption under the 40 Act to become an ETF provider. At the moment, Jeffrey Feldman and XShares are best known for starting HealthShares—an ETF company that has launched 20 ETFs based on companies that are involved in treating various diseases and disorders.

Jeffrey L. Feldman is chairman and founder of XShares.

Given your long experience in financial markets, how do you think capital markets have changed in recent years, especially with the rise of ETFs and all these indexed products?

For your purposes there is a very long answer. Just so you know I'm an economist; I'm a macroeconomist. I am going to justify everything I have to say by first going back 50 years. If I can find a trend line that gets us to where we are today, then I feel pretty good about my analysis.

Let's go back to 1960—about 50 years ago. Four million Americans owned stock, and 85 percent of them owned the "Nifty 50." Everybody had a passbook. We were a nation of savers. Your parents had passbooks. Your grandparents had passbooks. I had a passbook. Passbooks paid an interest rate of 5¼ percent, which was great when inflation was 2 to 3 percent. We were one of the highest saving nations in the world, as a percent of GDP, and we were very content until the 1972–1973 period, when we started to enter into the first energy crisis and the resulting stagflation.

And for the first time, people said that 5¼ percent ain't that great when inflation is 6, 7, 8, 9, 10 percent. Harry Brown and Bruce Bent invented the first money market fund, the Reserve Fund, in 1971. As a result, people moved their money out of savings, for the first time, and into money market funds. We were still savers, however. Then we got to the late 1970s, and money had poured out of savings into a variety, at that time, of money market funds.

In 1974, while this was all going on, very quietly, ERISA (Employee Retirement Income Security Act) passed, which created the retirement accounts that we have today. In 1978, the "prudent man" rule came from the Department of Labor, which said that you could buy stocks in ERISA accounts. That was the launching of the mutual fund industry as we know it today.

The interest rates went to 9 percent in 1981, and people looked up and said, "Well I can go back to my passbook," but the mutual fund industry beckoned, just as the baby boomers were coming of age. The people in the generation born in 1946 were now getting into their mid-thirties. Baby boomers were coming of age. They went to college. They were smarter than their parents, and they said, "You know what? We're going to go with the mutual fund industry. We can invest." So in 1980 we had 20 million shareholders, and we became, over the next 20 years, a nation of investors. We moved from our savings mentality to a zero savings rate. In 1980 we had 20 million shareholders. In 2000 we had 100 million shareholders. We poured money into investing. Dow was 1000 in 1980. Dow was 11,000 in 2000.

What's an investor? An investor is somebody who wants to buy low and sell high. When you have all that liquidity coming in for 20 years, it's easy to buy low and sell high because someone's always there to take you out at a higher price. We get to 2000 and the question becomes, buy low and sell to whom? We all own stocks, and so for seven years the market moves sideways. A nation of savers became a nation of investors, and now it doesn't work anymore. We have to transition again. A nation of investors has to become a nation of owners, and that's what these current vehicles are about. The passbook was the tool of the saver. The mutual fund was the tool of the investor. The ETF is the tool of the owner. We have to own investments that will benefit us in our portfolio, regardless of whether we can find somebody to take us out at a higher price.

Now the ETF technology allows me to build portfolios exactly the way I want. So let me use a health-care example. I'm 60 years old, and I want to buy long-term care insurance. As a typical 60-year-old, I'm hopeful that I am going to pay for that insurance for 25 years and never use it. So, it's basically term insurance. But now I can buy an ETF of companies that operate nursing homes, assisted living facilities, and hospices, which are the very types of facilities that I may need 25 years from now. Now I can "equitize" some of those costs, because, alongside of the premium I pay every year, I can make an investment in those facilities. If I buy into the macro argument that there are 78 million baby boomers and only 10 million beds in all those industries put together, there's probably an overdemand for the supply, which is going to drive the price up. So my insurance premiums may go up, but I've got a way to mitigate it. I've got a way to use a portfolio to "equitize" some of my costs, and that's never been possible before.

ETFs can be defined very, very narrowly, and this is one of the battles we are having in the industry. The industry says define them broadly for risk mitigation. I say, risk mitigation doesn't take place at the level of the investment; risk mitigation takes place at the level of the portfolio. Define the portfolios narrowly, and then I'll build my own risk management profile, at the level of my portfolio. I will build into my portfolio things that I want to own for a long time. You want yield? Fine. You can own yield. You want to own commodities because you believe that you need to own commodities or you need to own precious metals? Great. ETFs are a cheap way of building a very, very customized portfolio.

We believe very, very strongly, and most of this hasn't happened yet, that ETFs will be a big part of risk management, not only at the level of the individual, but also at the level of businesses. The analogy that I like to use is agriculture. If a cereal manufacturer decides right now that next spring's wheat is going to be too expensive, it can go to the futures market and buy the wheat. On the other side of that trade will be a hedge fund. The agriculture industry has close ties to the capital markets because of the tools that are available, but I can't go to the capital markets and buy a futures contract on a basket of nursing home stocks. In agriculture you have perfect ties to the capital markets, and what do you have? A low-margin efficient business. In health care, there are no ties to the capital market, and you have a high-margin inefficient business. If agriculture can lay off its risk/reward equation onto the capital market, why can't health care?

Actuaries have been keeping insurance companies profitable for decades by analyzing disease-based populations, cost of treatment, etc. That's perfect investment analysis; we've never done it before, because once you did it, what were you going to do with it? Now there are tools that will allow you to manage risk. A hospital that is dealing with cancer should eventually be able to own an ETF of companies that are developing those expensive new devices and therapies the hospital is going to have to buy, and it should be able to start to engage in risk mitigation and cost management. That, to me, makes ETFs the most important capital market tool that's ever been invented, because they completely revolutionize the market. I think most people don't see that yet.

How did you create the idea for HealthShares?

I should say that I came to ETFs through the back door. I teach. In my academic work, in the late 1990s, I started to study health care. Being one of the older baby boomers, I am somewhat sensitized to what is going on in health care. Health care's percent of GDP was 8 in 1980 and 16 in 2007. The NIH says it will be 20 percent by 2015. Four trillion dollars by 2015. It's two trillion currently. There are a number of reasons as to why this has happened: the aging baby boomers, the Dole-Bayh Act that created the commercialization of expensive medicines after 1982, and the launch of the biotech industry.

But, we have a high-margin inefficient business that is patent-protected. So when I started to study the business, I started with the pharmaceutical industry, which is where you would naturally start. The pharmaceutical industry is an oligopoly, and its mission is to treat symptoms. The biggest selling class of drugs in the United States is statins, which are given to people who have high cholesterol. Over 45 million people take statins. The way statins work, basically, is to cause the liver to overexpress an enzyme that chews up cholesterol. So if you stop taking your statin, you're going to get back to the high cholesterol that you had very quickly. You're treating symptoms. In a world, in a country, where most people are young and healthy, you can treat people who have symptoms this way, and you can afford it. Now we have 120 million people with chronic illness. High blood pressure. High cholesterol. Twenty million people with diabetes. All the people who have cardio problems. Cancer. Metabolic and endocrine problems. The total is over 120 million people, and 78 million baby boomers are currently between 43 and 61 years of age. They're still basically young. So they're now aging into a system that everybody knows is broken. But one of the primary reasons it's broken is that we simply can't afford to treat symptoms anymore. We have to change the course of the underlying disease. We have to engage in preventative measures.

If I say the word *diagnosis* to you, in a medical context, then you get an image, in your mind, of a doctor in a white coat standing over a patient in his underwear sitting on a roll of saran wrap. The doctor has a stethoscope, a tongue depressor, and a blood pressure machine and does an analysis and says, "OK, I know what's wrong with you," and turns to his little pad and writes something. That's not what diagnosis means anymore. Diagnosis means taking a drop of somebody's blood, analyzing the proteins in the blood, looking at his DNA, and saying, "With your DNA and with these proteins in the blood, and with these bonding agents, those proteins are going to get together in 10 or 12 years, and they're going to create a malady. We need to stop that from happening now."

But when that diagnosis is done and the diagnostician turns to the pharmaceutical industry, the pharmaceutical industry says, "Come back when he's sick. We can take care of him. We ain't got anything for him now." The biotech industry does. The biotech industry is working on treatments to change the course of underlying disease. When I looked at this from the perspective of eight years ago, I said that there's a paradigm shift taking place here. In investing, which I know something about, it's always done on a legacy basis. We invest in the rearview mirror. It's as if we're driving a semi down the road at 70 miles per hour, but we're steering it by looking in the rearview mirror. As long as the road stays straight, it's OK. But when it hooks left, we don't know, and this is an industry that is hooking left. If you are looking at any mutual fund or ETF that calls itself health care, biotech, or pharma, it's mostly market cap-weighted, and it skews your investment two-thirds to three-quarters to the big-cap companies, mostly into the pharmaceutical industry. In contrast, we don't have any companies with over $15 billion in market capitalization in our funds.

So what we said was, the industry has to change. Look at Pfizer's annual report. Pfizer's got 10 drugs that represent two-thirds of its sales and profits. They tell you that on page five. All of those drugs, except Celebrex, come off patent by 2012. The company has to be completely redefined. There's an article in today's *Investor's Business Daily* with the head of PricewaterhouseCoopers's pharmaceutical practice who says the blockbuster business is over. It's now not pharmacology, the treatment of symptoms, but pharmacogenomics, customized medicine that will allow us to treat the underlying cause of the disease. There was a big brouhaha in March and April about a public company called Dendreon, which had a cancer vaccine for prostate cancer. An FDA advisory panel of outside experts recommended its approval. This is a vaccine. Two shots and it's over—if it works for you. It works for 15 percent of the population.

There's a company in California called Isis that has, in Phase II trials, a vaccine for the treatment of high cholesterol. So the vaccine reregulates the liver to produce a higher rate of the enzyme that chews up cholesterol. You don't take a pill every day. You're done. The pharmaceutical industry, not unlike times we've had strong oligopolies in this country, looks at that and says, "That's not part of our capital structure." The strongest oligopoly in the United States in the 1960s was steel. The import laws changed, and they all went bankrupt. In the 1970s we had a saying in this country, "As GM goes, so goes the nation." Energy crisis; the Japanese came in, GM said, "What do you want from us? Our plants make big gas-guzzling cars." In the early 1980s the only way you could make a long-distance telephone call was on AT&T. The wireless guys came to AT&T, and AT&T said, "Copper wire, copper wire. Got a trillion dollars of copper wire. Can't do this to us." If in the 1990s I said airlines to you, you would say United, TWA, Delta, Pan Am. The largest airline in the country now is Southwest. It's not long haul, big planes; it's short haul, little planes. Every time an oligopoly stands between the market and a better or cheaper product, it eventually loses. The pharmaceutical industry is saying symptoms, and the biotech industry is saying disease. The biotech industry is going to win. But we're still investing most of our money in the pharmaceutical industry, because it's the legacy.

When I came up with this idea of therapeutic area investments, I had never heard of ETFs. I went around the Street saying that I built these portfolios. I am an old guy. I am thinking UITs [unit investment trusts], but they're a little too static for me. Then, about four years ago, through a mutual friend, I met the president of this firm, Tony Dudzinski, who has been a market maker on the Street for over 25 years. I said to Tony, "What are these?" He said, "They're ETFs." I said, "Great, what's an ETF?" And so he taught me about ETFs, and then, and only then, in 2005, we formed HealthShares, and we then applied for the exemptive relief necessary to issue ETFs. Last year, in June about halfway through that labyrinthine process, I said assets are growing, investors are finding out about these things, there are only a few guys out there with exemptive orders. It's probably true that there are a lot of people out there who would like to issue ETFs, but can't. So, I formed XShares, with X being a blank. I formed it as a platform for others. We are doing one for TD Ameritrade. We have over 300 calls relating to this service, and we're talking to major firms all around the world that want to create an ETF in the United States.

A distinguishing feature of XShares products is the "vertical investing" concept. Could you elaborate on that and what it means for investors in your funds?

It's using ETFs to divide an industry. Most investment is horizontal. Say you're a portfolio manager, and someone gives you a bunch of money. You look at an industry, it used to be the whole economy, and you take out the best company in each sector. Then you get down to investing in a sector. In a sector that has stable demand and technology that is not changing very much, you want to buy the companies across the top of the industry, what some people call the best of breed. You want to buy the best companies. But in an industry that is undergoing rapid change in technology and rapid increase in demand, that is, health care, the companies across the top are established. The good stuff lies deeper down. It's hard to tell on an absolute or relative basis whether they're good or bad. I don't want the pharmaceutical industry, I want the stuff deeper down in the industry—there are some 360 biotech companies—but it's harder to understand. I put all the companies that are working in the same area in one vertical. That way I get exposure to innovation and mitigation of risk. It turns out that there's a critical mass of companies working in each of the therapeutic areas of medicine. At a time of great technological change and increasing demand, when you are moving away from the companies that are controlling the industry, this is the way to go. If we had this kind of structure in the Internet bubble, you wouldn't have had 250 pet food companies online because someone could have looked at the vertical of B to C companies and said, "Enough already."

Your fund chose equal weighting. What drove the decision?

We're dealing with companies with products in development. It would be hard to weight them any other way. I believe, when you are looking at these companies, that all the stocks are mispriced. Either the drug is going to work, in which case the stock is too cheap, or the drug doesn't work, in which case the stock is worthless. So you have these binary events coming, and you can't really handicap and say, "This drug has a better shot than that drug." Even if drugs are having good results in trials, side effects may not develop for two or three years, so you can't favor one over the other. So it just makes sense.

You can't get caught up with the whole indexing thing. It matters what you buy. It also matters what kind of market you are in. People always ask me, "What is the biggest risk for the ETF business?" My answer is always the same: "A roaring bull market." Because if there is a roaring bull market, people are just going to buy Yahoo! or whatever the next Yahoo! is. Any portfolio is going to lag the best performers in a bull market.

There are only two motivators for investors: fear and greed. We've been fearful for the past few years, but we're going to get greedy again. We always do.

One area of concern to our readers is taxes. Many of your funds are global funds that do not meet the IRS rules for the foreign tax credit. How did you make that decision?

We just wanted to make sure we included everybody that had something to offer in each therapeutic area. We did not consider taxes. We don't see this as a rate-of-return type of investment. We think that health care will be an explosive area of growth over the next 20 years, and it will outperform every other area. We wanted to make sure we had the best exposure to what's going on in each therapeutic area.

By and large, these companies don't have dividends, so there is little tax liability expected, and capital gains are not an issue in Europe.

One area where some ETFs have fallen short is in liquidity, especially on the short side. How is XShares doing here? Have you had difficulty getting market makers?

ETFs are hard to short. They're hard to short because they're hard to borrow. That continues to be an issue. We, as an industry, keep talking about how you can short them as a hedging tool, but we're not there yet. Only the big, big, most liquid ones are easily shorted. The rest of them are hard to short, and they're hard to short for two reasons. One is they're hard to find, and two, when you can find them, the spreads are very wide on the short side. We believe, as an industry, that's going to get better as we move away from the specialist model to the electronic platforms. Probably, by the time your book comes out, there will be few, if any, specialists in ETFs. On the electronic platforms they'll be easier to short.

One related issue is the seed capital issue. That's a very important issue. When the industry got started, the specialists put up huge amounts of seed capital. When the Qs [the Qs, known by the symbol QQQQ, is the ETF that tracks the Nasdaq-100 index] got started, Susquehanna put up a billion dollars of seed capital. It was very common for Goldman, Labranche, Susquehanna, and Bear Wagner to put up $25 million to $50 million per ETF. Now there is virtually no seed capital available to do creations of ETFs. The specialists were buying the order flow, and now that it has gone over the wall to the electronic side, there's nothing for the specialists. There are 350 ETFs in registration right now, and a lot of them are really hurting in terms of getting themselves launched because they can't get that initial seed capital, and they're being delayed. The whole industry is being delayed. [Specialists used that seed capital to create the ETFs by depositing baskets of stock.]

Many institutions and large brokerage firms will not look at certain ETFs if they do not have a minimum level of assets under management, and those ETFs won't be accessible through their trading platforms.

Who is your competition?

Well, it varies by ETF family. HealthShares, because they're the only ETFs currently available that provide investors with precise exposure to subsectors of the health-care market, don't have any competition. Where most other health-care ETFs overweight the well-known, large-cap names, HealthShares include primarily those small- and mid-cap innovative companies that hold the promise of long-term outperformance.

Adelante Shares, our family of narrowly sliced segments of the real estate market, do compete somewhat with other real estate ETFs in the market. However, our real estate ETFs have a slightly different way of slicing and dicing the market and they equal weight their constituents. The TDAX Independence ETFs are the only life-cycle ETFs in the market, and they are also the first ETFs to incorporate equities and bonds in a single security.

Who is your typical customer?

Registered investment advisors (RIAs) are our primary customers, and the secondary customers are wirehouse brokers. They usually make asset allocations based on a model such as Standard & Poor's that recommends 20 percent into health care. We are saying if you are putting 20 percent of your money into health care, all the other funds offer you the same stocks, and they offer you none of the stocks that are in our portfolio. So we are saying, "Why not put 20 percent of that 20 percent into HealthShares?"

We see it as a long-term investment for retail investors. These are investments for people in their 40s and 50s.

It is important to remember that what you buy matters. For those who are capital appreciation oriented, and some of us are, broad indexes are just going to provide a mediocre, unsatisfactory return. For people who want to own the broad market for the long term, go do that. There are people who want to try to do better. If we all own the same thing, there will be no one to sell it to down the road. That's what makes markets— differences of opinion.

When you look back on your career, are you surprised you're doing what you are doing?

Shocked. Shocked and amazed at what I am doing. I never could have anticipated it. I'm grateful to whatever forces put me here. I expected to be a full-time teacher. I never had a plan. Everything I've done in my life is an accident. I got a job at Goldman Sachs as a keypunch operator. We worked in the basement. I went up the elevator to the third floor to get my coffee at 55 Broad Street, and when I got on the elevator, I was carrying a library book about the mathematics of puts and calls by Burton Malkiel, from Princeton, and this guy on the elevator says to me, "Are you smart?" I replied, "I don't know." He said, "Do you understand that book?" I said, "Yes, I understand that book." He replied, "If you'd like to discuss that book, come see me." I said, "Great, who are you?" He said, "My name's Bob Rubin." When I went to my boss and I said Bob Rubin wants to see me, my boss's eyebrows went up, and he asked, "Why?" I answered, "He wants to talk with me." As a result of that talk, I got moved to the research department, and that's how I became a securities analyst at Goldman Sachs. Entirely an accident. When I worked at Goldman Sachs, in the late 1960s and early 1970s, it was a small company: it had 600 employees and 17 partners.

I learned a lot of things at Goldman Sachs. Gus Levy of Goldman Sachs once told me, "There's only one thing you need to know about this business. Everything you see you will see again." That's the best advice I have received about this business. Goldman constantly reinvents itself and goes where the opportunities are.

ETFs are looking at the mutual fund industry and developing themselves based on what they see in the mutual fund industry. ETFs must be relevant. Mutual funds were very relevant to the economy—the tool of the investor when people wanted to be investors. ETFs need to be relevant to what people want today, and what people want today is tools to mitigate, to hedge, and to engage in capital formulation. We need to be part of the capital formation process in this country, or we'll be an irrelevant industry. It's not about building broad-risk mitigated indexes. Who cares? We've got to take some chances. We've got to take some risks and develop relevant products that are going to restore this country to the acme of world finance, which certainly we can do.

Appendix A

U.S. ETFs AND TRADING VOLUME AS OF OCTOBER 1, 2007

The following information is accurate as of October 1, 2007. (An explanation of the column heads can be found on page 312.) For recent volume information check a Web site such as http://finance.yahoo.com.

Investment Manager	Fund Name	Ticker Symbol	20-Day Average Share Volume	Ranking of 20-Day Average Share Volume	20-Day Average $ Volume	Ranking of 20-Day Average $ Volume
Ameristock	Ameristock/Ryan 1 Year Treasury ETF	GKA	1,290	498	$33,127	499
Ameristock	Ameristock/Ryan 10 Year Treasury ETF	GKD	2,360	471	$61,502	481
Ameristock	Ameristock/Ryan 2 Year Treasury ETF	GKB	125	536	$3,195	536
Ameristock	Ameristock/Ryan 20 Year Treasury ETF	GKE	270	532	$7,304	531
Ameristock	Ameristock/Ryan 5 Year Treasury ETF	GKC	30	540	$785	540
BGI USA	iShares Cohen & Steers Realty Majors	ICF	676,483	59	$63,481,232	48
BGI USA	iShares COMEX Gold Trust	IAU	211,275	106	$15,575,193	100
BGI USA	iShares DJ Select Dividend Index Fund	DVY	562,365	65	$39,101,238	67
BGI USA	iShares DJ US Basic Materials	IYM	221,665	104	$16,548,401	97
BGI USA	iShares DJ US Consumer Services	IYC	89,070	164	$6,013,116	152
BGI USA	iShares DJ US Energy	IYE	114,255	139	$14,928,558	101
BGI USA	iShares DJ US Financial Sector	IYF	171,760	118	$18,850,660	89
BGI USA	iShares DJ US Financial Services	IYG	34,890	245	$4,253,091	176
BGI USA	iShares DJ US Healthcare	IYH	79,070	176	$5,622,660	157
BGI USA	iShares DJ US Industrial	IYJ	48,095	217	$3,656,663	187
BGI USA	iShares DJ US Consumer Goods	IYK	23,120	286	$1,473,671	257
BGI USA	iShares DJ US Real Estate	IYR	5,279,531	17	$405,890,343	15
BGI USA	iShares DJ US Technology	IYW	253,010	97	$15,990,232	99
BGI USA	iShares DJ US Telecommunications	IYZ	403,475	75	$13,710,081	104
BGI USA	iShares DJ US Index [Total Market]	IYY	108,285	147	$8,072,647	130
BGI USA	iShares DJ US Transportation Index Fund	IYT	618,922	62	$53,778,133	55
BGI USA	iShares DJ US Utilities	IDU	81,955	172	$8,000,447	132

BGI USA	iShares Dow Jones Aerospace & Defense	ITA	117,513	137	$8,234,136	127
BGI USA	iShares Dow Jones Broker-Dealers	IAI	1,809,135	41	$94,744,400	39
BGI USA	iShares Dow Jones Health Care Providers	IHF	40,230	232	$2,373,972	220
BGI USA	iShares Dow Jones Home Construction	ITB	562,762	64	$11,514,111	109
BGI USA	iShares Dow Jones Insurance	IAK	6,850	402	$367,982	388
BGI USA	iShares Dow Jones Medical Devices	IHI	84,895	168	$5,135,299	161
BGI USA	iShares Dow Jones Oil & Gas Exploration and Production	IEO	66,485	188	$3,949,867	180
BGI USA	iShares Dow Jones Oil Equipment & Services	IEZ	88,567	165	$5,657,669	156
BGI USA	iShares Dow Jones Pharmaceuticals	IHE	16,165	326	$878,244	305
BGI USA	iShares Dow Jones Regional Banks	IAT	17,540	317	$804,209	319
BGI USA	iShares EPAC Select Dividend	IDV	11,530	359	$582,380	347
BGI USA	iShares FTSE NAREIT Industrial/Office Index Fund	FIO	22,040	292	$980,780	290
BGI USA	iShares FTSE NAREIT Mortgage REITs Index Fund	REM	14,275	340	$442,525	374
BGI USA	iShares FTSE NAREIT Real Estate 50 Index Fund	FTY	6,060	409	$274,518	417
BGI USA	iShares FTSE NAREIT Residential Index Fund	REZ	1,405	492	$67,075	480
BGI USA	iShares FTSE NAREIT Retail Index Fund	RTL	21,545	296	$967,371	293
BGI USA	iShares FTSE/Xinhua China 25 Index	FXI	3,376,427	23	$618,820,736	13
BGI USA	iShares Global Materials	MXI	95,935	157	$7,679,405	137
BGI USA	iShares Goldman Sachs Natural Resources	IGE	71,200	181	$9,182,664	119
BGI USA	iShares Goldman Sachs Networking Index	IGN	148,910	126	$5,459,041	159
BGI USA	iShares Goldman Sachs Semiconductor Index	IGW	149,950	125	$10,228,090	114
BGI USA	iShares Goldman Sachs Software Index	IGV	101,120	154	$5,059,034	162
BGI USA	iShares Goldman Sachs Technology Index	IGM	320,985	86	$19,387,494	87
BGI USA	iShares GSCI Commodity Trust	GSG	92,265	162	$4,330,919	175

(Continues)

Investment Manager	Fund Name	Ticker Symbol	20-Day Average Share Volume	Ranking of 20-Day Average Share Volume	20-Day Average $ Volume	Ranking of 20-Day Average $ Volume
BGI USA	iShares iBoxx $ High Yield Corporate Bond Fund	HYG	60,215	198	$6,290,661	148
BGI USA	iShares iBoxx $ Investment Grade Corporate Bond Fund	LQD	108,475	146	$11,385,536	110
BGI USA	iShares KLD 400 Social Index Fund	DSI	6,790	403	$366,660	389
BGI USA	iShares KLD Select Social Index	KLD	6,945	398	$444,480	372
BGI USA	iShares Lehman 20+ Year Treasury Bond Fund	TLT	2,519,862	32	$222,856,595	20
BGI USA	iShares Lehman 1–3 Year Credit Bond Fund	CSJ	21,210	297	$2,130,332	231
BGI USA	iShares Lehman 1–3 Year Treasury Bond Fund	SHY	755,711	56	$61,197,477	50
BGI USA	iShares Lehman 10–20 Year Treasury Bond Fund	TLH	7,965	389	$802,713	321
BGI USA	iShares Lehman 3–7 Year Treasury Bond	IEI	35,875	241	$3,662,838	186
BGI USA	iShares Lehman 7–10 Year Treasury Bond Fund	IEF	350,540	82	$29,301,639	78
BGI USA	iShares Lehman Aggregate Bond Fund	AGG	516,806	70	$51,422,197	57
BGI USA	iShares Lehman Credit Bond Fund	CFT	2,840	461	$282,750	413
BGI USA	iShares Lehman Government/Credit Bond Fund	GBF	16,560	324	$1,666,764	248
BGI USA	iShares Lehman Intermediate Credit Bond Fund	CIU	4,525	432	$451,414	369
BGI USA	iShares Lehman Intermediate Government/ Credit Bond Fund	GVI	9,135	378	$922,361	298
BGI USA	iShares Lehman MBS Fixed Rate Bond Fund	MBB	17,125	320	$1,719,350	246
BGI USA	iShares Lehman Short Treasury Bond Fund	SHV	78,019	177	$8,537,619	123
BGI USA	iShares Lehman TIPS Bond Fund	TIP	173,413	117	$17,620,495	95
BGI USA	iShares Morningstar Large Core Index Fund	JKD	12,160	354	$996,512	287
BGI USA	iShares Morningstar Large Growth Index Fund	JKE	29,305	260	$2,127,543	232
BGI USA	iShares Morningstar Large Value Index Fund	JKF	49,810	214	$4,394,238	174
BGI USA	iShares Morningstar Mid Core Index Fund	JKG	9,365	374	$824,963	314

BGI USA	iShares Morningstar Mid Growth Index Fund	JKH	22,855	289	$2,305,612	223
BGI USA	iShares Morningstar Mid Value Index Fund	JKI	9,220	375	$789,416	322
BGI USA	iShares Morningstar Small Core Index Fund	JKJ	14,965	335	$1,303,900	270
BGI USA	iShares Morningstar Small Growth Index Fund	JKK	7,825	391	$656,361	339
BGI USA	iShares Morningstar Small Value Index Fund	JKL	10,215	365	$805,248	318
BGI USA	iShares MSCI EAFE	EFA	6,769,449	15	$560,848,850	14
BGI USA	iShares MSCI EAFE Growth	EFG	66,665	187	$5,309,334	160
BGI USA	iShares MSCI EAFE Value	EFV	107,736	148	$8,441,676	124
BGI USA	iShares MSCI EM	EEM	11,850,255	9	$1,788,321,982	5
BGI USA	iShares MSCI-Australia	EWA	1,466,336	45	$46,981,405	64
BGI USA	iShares MSCI-Austria	EWO	100,706	155	$3,812,739	184
BGI USA	iShares MSCI-Belgium	EWK	105,175	152	$2,768,374	207
BGI USA	iShares MSCI-Brazil	EWZ	10,713,533	11	$803,514,975	10
BGI USA	iShares MSCI-Canada	EWC	1,211,218	49	$39,885,409	66
BGI USA	iShares MSCI-EMU	EZU	200,806	110	$24,251,341	80
BGI USA	iShares MSCI-France	EWQ	227,670	103	$8,763,018	122
BGI USA	iShares MSCI-Germany	EWG	873,445	55	$30,256,135	77
BGI USA	iShares MSCI-Hong Kong	EWH	5,436,060	16	$115,298,833	35
BGI USA	iShares MSCI-Italy	EWI	126,353	133	$4,427,409	173
BGI USA	iShares MSCI-Japan	EWJ	18,779,866	6	$269,866,674	19
BGI USA	iShares MSCI-Malaysia	EWM	1,805,040	42	$21,610,841	83
BGI USA	iShares MSCI-Mexico	EWW	2,876,771	28	$168,492,477	28
BGI USA	iShares MSCI-Netherlands	EWN	70,615	182	$2,268,860	225
BGI USA	iShares MSCI-Pacific ex-Japan	EPP	217,191	105	$36,431,618	69
BGI USA	iShares MSCI-Singapore	EWS	2,818,474	29	$42,840,805	65
BGI USA	iShares MSCI-South Africa	EZA	106,058	150	$14,171,470	102
BGI USA	iShares MSCI-South Korea	EWY	2,178,934	37	$151,152,869	29
BGI USA	iShares MSCI-Spain	EWP	291,551	91	$17,635,920	94
BGI USA	iShares MSCI-Sweden	EWD	210,340	107	$7,759,443	136
BGI USA	iShares MSCI-Switzerland	EWL	106,288	149	$2,866,587	205

(Continues)

Investment Manager	Fund Name	Ticker Symbol	20-Day Average Share Volume	Ranking of 20-Day Average Share Volume	20-Day Average $ Volume	Ranking of 20-Day Average $ Volume
BGI USA	iShares MSCI-Taiwan	EWT	8,240,626	13	$140,585,080	31
BGI USA	iShares MSCI-U.K.	EWU	672,624	60	$17,407,509	96
BGI USA	iShares Nasdaq Biotech	IBB	1,239,909	48	$103,470,406	37
BGI USA	iShares NYSE 100 Index Fund	NY	10,310	364	$825,831	313
BGI USA	iShares NYSE Composite Index Fund	NYC	15,310	332	$1,408,520	259
BGI USA	iShares Russell 1000	IWB	659,001	61	$54,831,915	54
BGI USA	iShares Russell 1000 Growth	IWF	2,879,295	27	$177,940,431	26
BGI USA	iShares Russell 1000 Value	IWD	1,499,676	44	$129,422,039	33
BGI USA	iShares Russell 2000	IWM	79,210,192	3	$6,392,262,494	2
BGI USA	iShares Russell 2000 Growth	IWO	3,345,435	24	$288,309,588	18
BGI USA	iShares Russell 2000 Value	IWN	2,512,804	33	$194,440,774	22
BGI USA	iShares Russell 3000	IWV	562,150	66	$49,598,495	59
BGI USA	iShares Russell 3000 Growth	IWZ	81,325	174	$4,076,009	178
BGI USA	iShares Russell 3000 Value	IWW	59,950	201	$6,691,619	144
BGI USA	iShares Russell MicroCap Index	IWC	137,835	129	$7,966,863	133
BGI USA	iShares Russell MidCap Growth	IWP	308,850	89	$36,055,149	70
BGI USA	iShares Russell MidCap Index	IWR	239,150	101	$26,036,261	79
BGI USA	iShares Russell MidCap Value	IWS	341,090	84	$51,890,022	56
BGI USA	iShares S&P 100 Index Fund	OEF	1,259,314	47	$90,393,559	41
BGI USA	iShares S&P 1500	ISI	19,960	305	$2,705,778	210
BGI USA	iShares S&P 500	IVV	2,368,712	35	$363,123,550	16
BGI USA	iShares S&P 500 Growth	IVW	474,630	72	$33,841,119	71
BGI USA	iShares S&P 500 Value	IVE	381,415	77	$31,218,818	73
BGI USA	iShares S&P Europe 350 Index	IEV	267,757	94	$31,887,181	72

	Fund Name	Ticker				
BGI USA	iShares S&P Global 100 Index Fund	IOO	67,610	185	$5,622,285	158
BGI USA	iShares S&P Global Consumer Discretionary	RXI	2,130	474	$127,672	456
BGI USA	iShares S&P Global Consumer Staples	KXI	12,817	349	$772,481	324
BGI USA	iShares S&P Global Energy Index Fund	IXC	44,620	226	$6,166,038	150
BGI USA	iShares S&P Global Financials Index Fund	IXG	33,242	248	$2,983,470	200
BGI USA	iShares S&P Global Healthcare Index Fund	IXJ	37,692	237	$2,261,520	226
BGI USA	iShares S&P Global Industrials	EXI	30,960	255	$2,072,772	235
BGI USA	iShares S&P Global Technology Index Fund	IXN	69,825	183	$4,704,110	168
BGI USA	iShares S&P Global Telecomm. Index Fund	IXP	105,570	151	$8,240,784	126
BGI USA	iShares S&P Global Utilities	JXI	12,300	352	$803,560	320
BGI USA	iShares S&P Latin America 40	ILF	376,293	78	$91,371,466	40
BGI USA	iShares S&P MidCap 400	IJH	693,980	58	$61,500,508	49
BGI USA	iShares S&P MidCap 400/Citigroup Growth	IJK	178,160	114	$16,176,928	98
BGI USA	iShares S&P MidCap 400/Citigroup Value	IJJ	93,305	160	$7,888,938	135
BGI USA	iShares S&P National Municipal Bond Fund	MUB	0	543	$0	543
BGI USA	iShares S&P SmallCap 600	IJR	1,929,368	39	$135,345,165	32
BGI USA	iShares S&P SmallCap 600/Citigroup Growth	IJT	95,575	158	$13,745,597	103
BGI USA	iShares S&P SmallCap 600/Citigroup Value	IJS	119,806	136	$9,094,473	120
BGI USA	iShares S&P US Preferred Listed Stock Index Fund	PFF	20,535	300	$967,404	292
BGI USA	iShares S&P World ex-US Property	WPS	21,095	298	$1,145,880	276
BGI USA	iShares S&P/TOPIX 150	ITF	20,169	304	$2,539,075	213
BGI USA	iShares Silver Trust	SLV	424,435	74	$57,778,337	52
Claymore	Claymore/Clear Global Vaccine	JNR	885	511	$22,169	513
Claymore	Claymore BIR Leaders Small-Cap Core ETF	BES	3,285	454	$80,450	474
Claymore	Claymore MacroShares Oil Down	DCR	15,130	334	$695,980	332
Claymore	Claymore MacroShares Oil Up	UCR	3,530	446	$262,703	420
Claymore	Claymore S&P Global Water ETF	CGW	112,642	142	$2,939,956	202
Claymore	Claymore/BBD High Income	LVL	420	526	$9,559	527

(*Continues*)

Investment Manager	Fund Name	Ticker Symbol	20-Day Average Share Volume	Ranking of 20-Day Average Share Volume	20-Day Average $ Volume	Ranking of 20-Day Average $ Volume
Claymore	Claymore/BIR Leaders 50 ETF	BST	915	508	$24,028	508
Claymore	Claymore/BIR Leaders Mid-Cap Value ETF	BMV	915	508	$22,719	512
Claymore	Claymore/BNY BRIC	EEB	373,545	79	$18,116,933	92
Claymore	Claymore/Clear Global Exchanges, Brokers and Asset Mangers	EXB	615	517	$15,997	521
Claymore	Claymore/Clear Mid-Cap Growth ETF	MCG	770	515	$19,751	515
Claymore	Claymore/Clear Spin-Off	CSD	23,060	287	$672,891	336
Claymore	Claymore/Great Companies Large-Cap Growth ETF	XGC	1,295	497	$33,359	498
Claymore	Claymore/IndexIQ Small-Cap Value ETF	SCV	555	518	$12,993	522
Claymore	Claymore/KLD Sudan-Free large Cap Core ETF	KSF	40	539	$971	539
Claymore	Claymore/LGA Green	GRN	1,465	490	$39,423	491
Claymore	Claymore/Morningstar Information Super Sector Index ETF	MZN	60	538	$1,561	538
Claymore	Claymore/Morningstar Manufacturing Super Sector Index ETF	MZG	140	535	$3,794	535
Claymore	Claymore/Morningstar Services Super Sector Index ETF	MZO	195	534	$5,017	534
Claymore	Claymore/Ocean Tomo Growth ETF	OTR	555	518	$16,123	520
Claymore	Claymore/Ocean Tomo Patent	OTP	2,485	468	$73,158	477
Claymore	Claymore/Robb Report Global Luxury ETF	ROB	3,365	451	$86,952	470
Claymore	Claymore/Robeco Boston Partners Large-Cap Value	CLV	30	540	$743	541
Claymore	Claymore/Robeco Developed International Equity ETF	EEN	1,395	493	$36,912	495

Claymore	Claymore/Robeco Developed World Equity ETF	EEW	475	523	$12,773	523
Claymore	Claymore/Sabrient Defender	DEF	17,635	316	$481,612	365
Claymore	Claymore/Sabrient Insider	NFO	29,980	256	$919,187	299
Claymore	Claymore/Sabrient Stealth	STH	5,880	412	$156,114	448
Claymore	Claymore/SWM Canadian Energy Income ETF	ENY	16,745	323	$437,212	376
Claymore	Claymore/Zacks Country Rotation ETF	CRO	1,475	488	$37,992	493
Claymore	Claymore/Zacks Growth & Income ETF	CZG	360	528	$9,481	528
Claymore	Claymore/Zacks International Yield Hog ETF	HGI	1,940	475	$46,948	488
Claymore	Claymore/Zacks Mid-Cap Core ETF	CZA	730	516	$19,279	516
Claymore	Claymore/Zacks Sector Rotation	XRO	18,440	311	$572,746	350
Claymore	Claymore/Zacks Yield Hog	CVY	146,750	127	$3,843,089	183
Fidelity	Nasdaq Comp. Index Tracking Stock	ONEQ	14,045	343	$1,495,933	255
First Trust Advisors	First Trust Amex Biotechnology	FBT	99,435	156	$2,565,423	212
First Trust Advisors	First Trust Consumer Discretionary AlphaDEX Fund	FXD	400	527	$7,404	530
First Trust Advisors	First Trust Consumer Staples AlphaDEX	FXG	1,785	481	$35,414	497
First Trust Advisors	First Trust DB Strategic Value Index	FDV	15,135	333	$368,991	386
First Trust Advisors	First Trust DJ Internet	FDN	36,725	238	$964,031	294
First Trust Advisors	First Trust DJ Stoxx DVD 30	FDD	0	543	$0	543
First Trust Advisors	First Trust Dow Jones Select Microcap Index	FDM	4,760	430	$115,430	461
First Trust Advisors	First Trust Energy AlphaDEX Fund	FXN	2,795	462	$60,875	482
First Trust Advisors	First Trust EPRA/NAREIT Global Real Estate	FFR	0	543	$0	543

(*Continues*)

Investment Manager	Fund Name	Ticker Symbol	20-Day Average Share Volume	Ranking of 20-Day Average Share Volume	20-Day Average $ Volume	Ranking of 20-Day Average $ Volume
First Trust Advisors	First Trust Financials AlphaDEX Fund	FXO	1,730	483	$31,157	501
First Trust Advisors	First Trust Health Care AlphaDEX Fund	FXH	1,310	496	$26,790	504
First Trust Advisors	First Trust Industrials/Producer Durables AlphaDEX Fund	FXR	3,240	456	$60,718	483
First Trust Advisors	First Trust IPOX-100 Fund	FPX	9,100	379	$223,770	429
First Trust Advisors	First Trust ISE-Revere Natural Gas Index Fund	FCG	8,265	388	$172,160	444
First Trust Advisors	First Trust ISE Chindia Index Fund	FNI	51,550	211	$1,391,850	262
First Trust Advisors	First Trust ISE Water Index Fund	FIW	8,750	384	$196,788	436
First Trust Advisors	First Trust Large Cap Core AlphaDEX Fund	FEX	3,080	457	$90,644	469
First Trust Advisors	First Trust Large Cap Growth Opportunities AlphaDEX	FTC	2,400	470	$74,136	476
First Trust Advisors	First Trust Large Cap Value Opportunities AlphaDEX Fund	FTA	1,915	479	$54,501	485
First Trust Advisors	First Trust Materials AlphaDEX Fund	FXZ	555	518	$11,992	525
First Trust Advisors	First Trust Mid Cap Core AlphaDEX Fund	FNX	4,305	434	$125,878	458

First Trust Advisors	First Trust Morningstar Dividend Leaders	FDL	19,490	306	$448,855	371
First Trust Advisors	First Trust Multi-Cap Value AlphaDEX Fund	FAB	1,140	502	$31,931	500
First Trust Advisors	First Trust Multi-Cap Growth AlphaDEX Fund	FAD	3,360	452	$103,925	462
First Trust Advisors	First Trust Nasdaq Clean Edge US Liquid Series Index Fund	QCLN	12,094	355	$308,397	406
First Trust Advisors	First Trust Nasdaq-100 Equal Weighted Fund	QQEW	12,694	350	$292,978	411
First Trust Advisors	First Trust Nasdaq-100 Ex-Technology Sector Index Fund	QQXT	551	521	$12,232	524
First Trust Advisors	First Trust Nasdaq-100 Technology Sector Fund	QTEC	11,790	358	$267,987	418
First Trust Advisors	First Trust S&P REIT Index Fund	FRI	1,930	477	$36,033	496
First Trust Advisors	First Trust Small Cap Core AlphaDEX Fund	FYX	1,600	484	$46,240	489
First Trust Advisors	First Trust Technology AlphaDEX Fund	FXL	1,745	482	$38,198	492
First Trust Advisors	First Trust Utilities AlphaDEX Fund	FXU	545	522	$10,475	526
First Trust Advisors	First Trust Value Line 100	FVL	49,183	216	$859,227	307
First Trust Advisors	First Trust Value Line Dividend Index	FVD	37,905	236	$633,393	342
First Trust Advisors	First Trust Value Line Equity Allocation Index	FVI	6,100	408	$128,710	454
Powershares	BLDRs Asia 50 ADR Fund	ADRA	67,411	186	$2,427,470	218

(*Continues*)

Investment Manager	Fund Name	Ticker Symbol	20-Day Average Share Volume	Ranking of 20-Day Average Share Volume	20-Day Average $ Volume	Ranking of 20-Day Average $ Volume
Powershares	BLDRs Developed Markets 100 ADR Fund	ADRD	84,840	169	$2,757,300	208
Powershares	BLDRs Emerging Markets 50 ADR Fund	ADRE	244,900	99	$13,119,293	106
Powershares	BLDRs Europe 100 ADR Fund	ADRU	14,304	339	$487,051	362
Powershares	Buyback Achievers	PKW	35,320	242	$895,009	302
Powershares	DB US Dollar Index Bearish	UDN	60,230	197	$1,647,899	250
Powershares	DB US Dollar Index Bullish	UUP	23,825	283	$574,421	349
Powershares	DWA Technical Leaders Portfolio	PDP	81,690	173	$2,195,010	229
Powershares	Dynamic Aggressive Growth	PGZ	24,685	277	$714,631	330
Powershares	Dynamic Deep Value	PVM	2,755	464	$69,867	479
Powershares	Dynamic Large Cap	PJF	4,215	435	$117,809	460
Powershares	Dynamic Market Portfolio	PWC	76,175	178	$3,945,865	181
Powershares	Dynamic Mid Cap	PJG	11,850	356	$330,023	399
Powershares	Dynamic OTC Portfolio	PWO	13,525	346	$759,158	326
Powershares	Dynamic Small Cap	PJM	7,110	395	$182,585	441
Powershares	Financial Preferred	PGF	43,931	228	$982,736	289
Powershares	FTSE RAFI Basic Materials	PRFM	5,383	420	$360,661	390
Powershares	FTSE RAFI Consumer Goods	PRFG	1,937	476	$103,513	463
Powershares	FTSE RAFI Consumer Services	PRFS	3,513	448	$186,400	438
Powershares	FTSE RAFI Energy	PRFE	8,267	387	$589,024	346
Powershares	FTSE RAFI Financials	PRFF	5,584	419	$278,865	414
Powershares	FTSE RAFI Health Care	PRFH	5,243	423	$275,730	416
Powershares	FTSE RAFI Industrials	PRFN	24,175	281	$1,511,907	253
Powershares	FTSE RAFI Telecom & Technology	PRFQ	8,432	386	$514,436	357
Powershares	FTSE RAFI US 1500 Small-Mid	PRFZ	15,738	329	$892,974	303
Powershares	FTSE RAFI Utilities	PRFU	2,267	472	$129,174	453

Powershares	Golden Dragon Halter USX China	PGJ	931,618	52	$31,050,828	74
Powershares	High Yield Equity Dividend Achievers	PEY	116,994	138	$1,737,361	245
Powershares	Nasdaq-100 Index Tracking Stock	QQQQ	103,768,512	2	$5,354,455,219	3
Powershares	Aerospace and Defense Fund	PPA	202,760	109	$4,835,826	166
Powershares	Cleantech	PZD	24,430	279	$775,408	323
Powershares	DB G10 Currency Harvest	DBV	156,185	122	$4,464,486	172
Powershares	Dividend Achievers Portfolio	PFM	54,385	207	$967,509	291
Powershares	Dynamic Asia Pacific	PUA	13,370	347	$405,646	378
Powershares	Dynamic Banking	PJB	140,945	128	$3,076,829	199
Powershares	Dynamic Basic Materials	PYZ	24,205	280	$853,226	308
Powershares	Dynamic Biotechnology and Genome	PBE	120,654	135	$2,317,763	221
Powershares	Dynamic Building and Construction Portfolio	PKB	57,810	205	$1,145,216	277
Powershares	Dynamic Consumer Discretionary	PEZ	3,690	444	$97,748	466
Powershares	Dynamic Consumer Staples	PSL	8,855	380	$244,575	425
Powershares	Dynamic Developed Intl. Opportunities	PFA	20,525	301	$531,187	354
Powershares	Dynamic Energy	PXI	11,445	360	$391,535	380
Powershares	Dynamic Energy and Exploration Portfolio	PXE	46,485	221	$1,055,674	284
Powershares	Dynamic Europe	PEH	3,475	449	$86,145	471
Powershares	Dynamic Financial	PFI	5,160	425	$130,909	452
Powershares	Dynamic Food and Beverage	PBJ	40,140	233	$685,663	333
Powershares	Dynamic Hardware and Consumer Electronics Portfolio	PHW	29,140	261	$574,932	348
Powershares	Dynamic Healthcare	PTH	22,845	290	$670,960	337
Powershares	Dynamic Healthcare Services	PTJ	10,655	362	$303,347	408
Powershares	Dynamic Industrials	PRN	158,225	121	$5,039,466	163
Powershares	Dynamic Large Cap Growth	PWB	133,731	130	$2,516,817	214

(*Continues*)

Investment Manager	Fund Name	Ticker Symbol	20-Day Average Share Volume	Ranking of 20-Day Average Share Volume	20-Day Average $ Volume	Ranking of 20-Day Average $ Volume
Powershares	Powershares Dynamic Large Cap Value	PWV	63,153	192	$1,313,582	267
Powershares	Powershares Dynamic Leisure & Entertainment	PEJ	35,145	243	$639,639	341
Powershares	Powershares Dynamic Media	PBS	209,900	108	$3,341,608	192
Powershares	Powershares Dynamic Mid Cap Growth	PWJ	169,119	119	$4,019,959	179
Powershares	Powershares Dynamic Mid Cap Value	PWP	42,293	229	$839,093	310
Powershares	Powershares Dynamic Networking	PXQ	12,890	348	$257,283	421
Powershares	Powershares Dynamic Oil and Gas Services Portfolio	PXJ	231,002	102	$6,405,685	145
Powershares	Powershares Dynamic Pharmaceuticals	PJP	128,820	132	$2,392,200	219
Powershares	Powershares Dynamic Retail Portfolio	PMR	21,860	293	$390,201	381
Powershares	Powershares Dynamic Semiconductors	PSI	61,135	195	$1,158,508	275
Powershares	Powershares Dynamic Small Cap Growth	PWT	25,945	273	$473,756	366
Powershares	Powershares Dynamic Small Cap Value	PWY	45,525	225	$814,898	317
Powershares	Powershares Dynamic Software	PSJ	46,395	223	$929,292	297
Powershares	Powershares Dynamic Technology	PTF	10,380	363	$286,914	412
Powershares	Powershares Dynamic Telecommunications and Wireless Portfolio	PTE	15,895	328	$340,948	396
Powershares	Powershares Dynamic Utilities Portfolio	PUI	9,680	371	$183,155	440
Powershares	Powershares FTSE RAFI Asia Pacific Ex-Japan	PAF	3,905	442	$226,217	428
Powershares	Powershares FTSE RAFI Asia Pacific Ex-Japan Small-Mid	PDQ	0	543	$0	543
Powershares	Powershares FTSE RAFI Developed Mkts Ex-US	PXF	6,870	401	$350,233	392
Powershares	Powershares FTSE RAFI Developed Mkts Ex-US Small-Mid Portfolio	PDN	0	543	$0	543
Powershares	Powershares FTSE RAFI Emerging Mkts	PXH	0	543	$0	543

Company	Fund	Ticker				
Powershares	Powershares FTSE RAFI Europe	PEF	990	504	$51,262	486
Powershares	Powershares FTSE RAFI Europe Small-Mid	PWD	0	543	$0	543
Powershares	Powershares FTSE RAFI Japan	PJO	1,430	491	$73,030	478
Powershares	Powershares FTSE RAFI US 1000	PRF	122,005	134	$7,547,229	140
Powershares	Powershares Global Clean Energy	PBD	25,515	275	$736,108	328
Powershares	Powershares Global Water Resources	PHO	540,608	69	$11,671,727	107
Powershares	Powershares Global Water Portfolio	PIO	111,370	143	$2,895,620	204
Powershares	Powershares High Growth Rate Dividend Achievers	PHJ	7,870	390	$130,957	451
Powershares	Powershares Insurance Portfolio	PIC	14,835	336	$267,030	419
Powershares	Powershares International Dividend Achievers	PID	472,950	73	$10,070,997	116
Powershares	Powershares International Listed Private Equity	PFP	0	543	$0	543
Powershares	Powershares Listed Private Equity	PSP	36,395	239	$932,804	296
Powershares	Powershares Lux Nanotech Portfolio	PXN	47,760	218	$833,890	311
Powershares	Powershares Magniquant	PIQ	40,690	231	$1,119,382	278
Powershares	Powershares Wilderhill Progressive Energy	PUW	17,490	318	$510,708	359
Powershares	Value Line Industry Rotation	PYH	22,585	291	$665,783	338
Powershares	Wilderhill Clean Energy	PBW	345,805	83	$7,932,767	134
Powershares	Zacks Micro Cap	PZI	61,800	194	$1,063,578	282
Powershares	Zacks Small Cap Portfolio	PZJ	23,250	284	$648,210	340
Powershares/DB Commodity Svcs.	DB Agriculture Fund	DBA	369,715	80	$10,932,473	112
Powershares/DB Commodity Svcs.	DB Base Metals	DBB	31,310	252	$826,271	312
Powershares/DB Commodity Svcs.	DB Energy Fund	DBE	27,700	266	$839,310	309
Powershares/DB Commodity Svcs.	DB Gold Fund	DGL	20,640	299	$601,491	344
Powershares/DB Commodity Svcs.	DB Oil Fund	DBO	15,640	330	$459,347	368

(Continues)

Investment Manager	Fund Name	Ticker Symbol	20-Day Average Share Volume	Ranking of 20-Day Average Share Volume	20-Day Average $ Volume	Ranking of 20-Day Average $ Volume
Powershares/DB Commodity Svcs.	DB Precious Metals	DBP	23,875	282	$682,109	335
Powershares/DB Commodity Svcs.	DB Silver Fund	DBS	13,855	345	$372,700	385
Powershares/DB Commodity Svcs.	Powershares DB Commodity Index Tracking Fund	DBC	240,935	100	$6,705,197	143
ProShares	Short Dow30 ProShares	DOG	198,212	111	$11,240,603	111
ProShares	Short Midcap400 ProShares	MYY	50,870	212	$2,939,269	203
ProShares	Short QQQ ProShares	PSQ	60,055	200	$3,209,339	197
ProShares	Short Russell 2000 ProShares	RWM	26,872	267	$1,838,179	240
ProShares	Short S&P 500 ProShares	SH	167,425	120	$9,775,946	117
ProShares	Short Small Cap 600 ProShares	SBB	3,001	459	$199,356	434
ProShares	Ultra Basic Materials ProShares	UYM	15,540	331	$1,505,671	254
ProShares	Ultra Consumer Goods ProShares	UGE	1,215	501	$91,769	468
ProShares	Ultra Consumer Services ProShares	UCC	1,545	486	$97,891	464
ProShares	Ultra Dow30 ProShares	DDM	313,232	88	$30,894,072	75
ProShares	Ultra Financials ProShares	UYG	86,175	167	$4,944,722	164
ProShares	Ultra Health Care ProShares	RXL	4,600	431	$338,560	397
ProShares	Ultra Industrials ProShares	UXI	5,805	416	$512,175	358
ProShares	Ultra Midcap400 ProShares	MVV	81,295	175	$7,384,025	141
ProShares	Ultra Oil & Gas ProShares	DIG	60,135	199	$6,709,713	142
ProShares	Ultra QQQ ProShares	QLD	1,892,131	40	$205,636,797	21
ProShares	Ultra Real Estate ProShares	URE	25,975	271	$1,244,203	272
ProShares	Ultra Russell 1000 Growth ProShares	UKF	9,540	373	$734,580	329
ProShares	Ultra Russell 1000 Value ProShares	UVG	2,250	473	$155,295	449

ProShares	Ultra Russell 2000 Growth ProShares	UKK	6,315	405	$450,891	370
ProShares	Ultra Russell 2000 ProShares	UWM	256,112	96	$18,035,407	93
ProShares	Ultra Russell 2000 Value ProShares	UVT	6,135	407	$351,105	391
ProShares	Ultra Russell MidCap Growth ProShares	UKW	4,055	439	$301,165	409
ProShares	Ultra Russell MidCap Value ProShares	UVU	4,000	440	$251,560	422
ProShares	Ultra S&P500 ProShares	SSO	929,540	53	$89,273,022	42
ProShares	Ultra Semiconductor ProShares	USD	36,115	240	$3,239,516	196
ProShares	Ultra Small Cap 600 ProShares	SAA	9,606	372	$707,290	331
ProShares	Ultra Technology ProShares	ROM	26,010	270	$2,236,860	227
ProShares	Ultra Utilities ProShares	UPW	5,840	415	$468,777	367
ProShares	UltraShort Basic Materials ProShares	SMN	49,215	215	$2,273,733	224
ProShares	UltraShort Consumer Goods ProShares	SZK	9,880	368	$624,810	343
ProShares	UltraShort Consumer Services ProShares	SCC	14,480	338	$1,074,887	280
ProShares	UltraShort Dow 30 ProShares	DXD	2,521,980	31	$116,616,355	34
ProShares	UltraShort Financials ProShares	SKF	614,022	63	$48,022,661	63
ProShares	UltraShort Health Care ProShares	RXD	2,440	469	$159,088	447
ProShares	UltraShort Industrials ProShares	SIJ	9,160	377	$483,556	364
ProShares	UltraShort MidCap 400 ProShares	MZZ	402,741	76	$20,712,970	85
ProShares	UltraShort Oil & Gas ProShares	DUG	250,251	98	$10,162,693	115
ProShares	UltraShort QQQ ProShares	QID	24,058,188	5	$928,679,738	8
ProShares	UltraShort Real Estate ProShares	SRS	551,566	67	$48,626,059	62
ProShares	UltraShort Russell 1000 Growth ProShares	SFK	5,325	421	$327,168	401
ProShares	UltraShort Russell 1000 Value ProShares	SJF	2,610	465	$174,922	443
ProShares	UltraShort Russell 2000 Growth ProShares	SKK	20,245	303	$1,307,827	269
ProShares	UltraShort Russell 2000 ProShares	TWM	2,993,002	26	$194,126,110	23
ProShares	UltraShort Russell 2000 Value ProShares	SJH	31,500	251	$2,488,500	216
ProShares	UltraShort Russell MidCap Growth ProShares	SDK	1,920	478	$118,944	459
ProShares	UltraShort Russell MidCap Value ProShares	SJL	7,220	394	$542,439	352
ProShares	UltraShort S&P 500 ProShares	SDS	13,085,978	8	$658,355,553	11

(Continues)

Investment Manager	Fund Name	Ticker Symbol	20-Day Average Share Volume	Ranking of 20-Day Average Share Volume	20-Day Average $ Volume	Ranking of 20-Day Average $ Volume
ProShares	UltraShort Semiconductor ProShares	SSG	8,765	383	$440,003	375
ProShares	UltraShort Small Cap 600 ProShares	SDD	32,970	249	$2,064,911	236
ProShares	UltraShort Technology ProShares	REW	4,110	437	$221,899	430
ProShares	UltraShort Utilities ProShares	SDP	6,885	399	$388,176	382
Rydex	CurrencyShares Australian Dollar	FXA	69,425	184	$6,189,933	149
Rydex	CurrencyShares British Pound	FXB	39,285	235	$8,031,425	131
Rydex	CurrencyShares Canadian Dollar	FXC	59,335	203	$5,969,694	153
Rydex	CurrencyShares Japanese Yen Trust	FXY	353,880	81	$30,539,844	76
Rydex	CurrencyShares Mexican Peso	FXM	4,820	428	$442,977	373
Rydex	CurrencyShares Swedish Krona	FXS	5,300	422	$824,945	315
Rydex	CurrencyShares Swiss Franc	FXF	74,065	180	$6,372,553	146
Rydex	Rydex Euro Currency	FXE	152,030	124	$21,668,836	82
Rydex	Rydex Russell Top 50 ETF	XLG	39,430	234	$4,527,353	171
Rydex	Rydex S&P 400 Pure Growth ETF	RFG	4,400	433	$251,108	423
Rydex	Rydex S&P 400 Pure Value ETF	RFV	8,625	385	$300,668	410
Rydex	Rydex S&P 500 Pure Growth ETF	RPG	5,595	418	$215,911	432
Rydex	Rydex S&P 500 Pure Value ETF	RPV	10,025	367	$343,056	395
Rydex	Rydex S&P 600 Pure Growth ETF	RZG	435	524	$19,097	517
Rydex	Rydex S&P 600 Pure Value ETF	RZV	9,190	376	$347,382	394
Rydex	Rydex S&P Equal Weight Consumer Discretionary	RCD	50,060	213	$2,218,159	228
Rydex	Rydex S&P Equal Weight Consumer Staples	RHS	1,520	487	$78,402	475
Rydex	Rydex S&P Equal Weight Energy	RYE	2,790	463	$178,281	442
Rydex	Rydex S&P Equal Weight Financials	RYF	345	529	$16,477	519
Rydex	Rydex S&P Equal Weight Healthcare	RYH	21,665	294	$1,230,789	273
Rydex	Rydex S&P Equal Weight Industrial	RGI	2,520	467	$149,083	450

	Fund	Ticker				
Rydex	Rydex S&P Equal Weight Materials	RTM	1,570	485	$92,269	467
Rydex	Rydex S&P Equal Weight Technology	RYT	1,835	480	$97,750	465
Rydex	Rydex S&P Equal Weight Utilities	RYU	435	524	$26,626	505
Rydex	Rydex S&P Equal Weight ETF	RSP	728,500	57	$36,628,980	68
State Street	Consumer Discretionary Select Sector SPDR	XLY	3,933,776	22	$145,431,699	30
State Street	Consumer Staples Select Sector SPDR	XLP	2,425,687	34	$67,506,869	47
State Street	DJ Euro STOXX 50	FEZ	95,230	159	$5,901,403	154
State Street	DJ STOXX 50	FEU	46,440	222	$2,489,184	215
State Street	DJ Wilshire REIT	RWR	286,040	92	$23,303,679	81
State Street	Dow Diamonds—DJIA	DIA	11,362,039	10	$1,582,277,551	6
State Street	Energy Select Sector SPDR	XLE	18,047,104	7	$1,352,449,974	7
State Street	Financial Select Sector SPDR	XLF	52,535,136	4	$1,807,208,678	4
State Street	Health Care Select Sector SPDR	XLV	1,369,386	46	$48,709,060	61
State Street	Industrial Select Sector SPDR	XLI	4,616,905	21	$189,800,965	24
State Street	KBW Bank	KBE	946,325	51	$49,492,798	60
State Street	KBW Capital Markets	KCE	892,240	54	$59,262,581	51
State Street	KBW Insurance	KIE	318,685	87	$18,251,090	91
State Street	KBW Regional Banks	KRE	1,156,815	50	$51,119,655	58
State Street	Materials Select Sector SPDR	XLB	7,845,861	14	$331,879,920	17
State Street	Morgan Stanley Technology	MTK	54,370	208	$3,631,916	188
State Street	S&P 400 MidCap SPDR	MDY	5,279,246	18	$854,393,172	9
State Street	S&P 500 SPDR	SPY	157,632,336	1	$24,128,781,672	1
State Street	SPDR Lehman Aggregate Bond ETF	LAG	5,795	417	$307,019	407
State Street	SPDR Barclays Capital TIPS ETF	IPE	3,455	450	$169,468	445
State Street	SPDR DJ Global Titans	DGT	16,865	322	$1,372,811	263
State Street	SPDR DJ Wilshire Intl. Real Estate	RWX	132,724	131	$8,434,610	125
State Street	SPDR DJ Wilshire Large Cap ETF	ELR	3,260	455	$228,070	427
State Street	SPDR DJ Wilshire Large Cap Growth ETF	ELG	18,030	314	$1,070,982	281
State Street	SPDR DJ Wilshire Large Cap Value ETF	ELV	7,785	392	$685,002	334
State Street	SPDR DJ Wilshire Mid Cap ETF	EMM	6,325	404	$387,849	383

(Continues)

Investment Manager	Fund Name	Ticker Symbol	20-Day Average Share Volume	Ranking of 20-Day Average Share Volume	20-Day Average $ Volume	Ranking of 20-Day Average $ Volume
State Street	SPDR DJ Wilshire Mid Cap Growth ETF	EMG	3,975	441	$276,183	415
State Street	SPDR DJ Wilshire Mid Cap Value ETF	EMV	950	507	$56,582	484
State Street	SPDR DJ Wilshire Small Cap ETF	DSC	4,790	429	$309,913	405
State Street	SPDR DJ Wilshire Small Cap Growth ETF	DSG	5,180	424	$536,648	353
State Street	SPDR DJ Wilshire Small Cap Value ETF	DSV	4,880	427	$347,846	393
State Street	SPDR DJ Wilshire Total Market	TMW	7,045	397	$771,005	325
State Street	SPDR FTSE/Macquarie Global Infrastructure 100 ETF	GII	3,815	443	$221,270	431
State Street	SPDR Lehman 1–3 Month T-Bill ETF	BIL	83,295	171	$3,811,579	185
State Street	SPDR Lehman Intermediate Term Treasury ETF	ITE	3,530	446	$189,879	437
State Street	SPDR Lehman Long Term Treasury ETF	TLO	6,230	406	$320,720	402
State Street	SPDR Lehman Municipal Bond ETF	TFI	0	543	$0	543
State Street	SPDR MSCI ACWI ex-US	CWI	31,305	253	$1,337,976	266
State Street	SPDR Russell/Nomura Prime Japan	JPP	16,510	325	$918,451	300
State Street	SPDR Russell/Nomura Small Cap Japan	JSC	59,514	202	$2,834,652	206
State Street	SPDR S&P Biotech	XBI	155,825	123	$9,073,690	121
State Street	SPDR S&P BRIC 40 ETF	BIK	191,950	113	$5,835,280	155
State Street	SPDR S&P China	GXC	114,105	140	$10,902,733	113
State Street	SPDR S&P Dividend ETF	SDY	16,880	321	$1,021,713	286
State Street	SPDR S&P Emerging Asia Pacific	GMF	25,962	272	$2,308,801	222
State Street	SPDR S&P Emerging Europe	GUR	17,190	319	$1,112,709	279
State Street	SPDR S&P Emerging Latin America	GML	24,630	278	$1,927,765	239
State Street	SPDR S&P Emerging Markets	GMM	15,940	327	$1,212,556	274
State Street	SPDR S&P Emerging Middle East & Africa	GAF	11,835	357	$815,432	316

Provider	Fund	Ticker				
State Street	SPDR S&P Homebuilders	XHB	4,990,391	19	$108,890,332	36
State Street	SPDR S&P International Small Cap ETF	GWX	57,960	204	$2,146,838	230
State Street	SPDR S&P Metals & Mining	XME	300,425	90	$19,227,200	88
State Street	SPDR S&P Oil & Gas Equipment and Services	XES	74,635	179	$2,971,966	201
State Street	SPDR S&P Oil & Gas Exploration and Production	XOP	174,815	115	$8,221,549	128
State Street	SPDR S&P Pharmaceuticals	XPH	5,860	413	$198,537	435
State Street	SPDR S&P Retail	XRT	1,766,675	43	$69,288,994	46
State Street	SPDR S&P Semiconductor	XSD	5,895	411	$327,173	400
State Street	SPDR S&P World Ex-US ETF	GWL	1,390	494	$47,399	487
State Street	streetTRACKS Gold Trust	GLD	8,875,800	12	$653,258,880	12
State Street	Technology Select Sector SPDR	XLK	3,116,834	25	$84,684,380	43
State Street	Utilities Select Sector SPDR	XLU	4,676,487	20	$188,135,072	25
Vanguard	Vanguard Consumer Discretionary Index Fund	VCR	51,795	210	$3,114,433	198
Vanguard	Vanguard Consumer Staples Index Fund	VDC	12,500	351	$875,625	306
Vanguard	Vanguard Dividend Appreciation Index Fund	VIG	18,090	313	$1,046,868	285
Vanguard	Vanguard Emerging Markets	VWO	542,279	68	$56,971,832	53
Vanguard	Vanguard Energy Fund	VDE	44,395	227	$4,839,055	165
Vanguard	Vanguard European	VGK	173,635	116	$13,540,057	105
Vanguard	Vanguard Extended Market	VXF	19,000	309	$2,111,470	234
Vanguard	Vanguard Financials Index Fund	VFH	54,840	206	$3,338,659	194
Vanguard	Vanguard FTSE All-World Ex-US Index Fund	VEU	192,685	112	$11,561,100	108
Vanguard	Vanguard Growth Index Fund	VUG	325,780	85	$21,172,442	84
Vanguard	Vanguard Health Care Index Fund	VHT	27,975	265	$1,718,504	247
Vanguard	Vanguard Industrial Fund	VIS	19,180	308	$1,483,381	256
Vanguard	Vanguard Information Technology Index Fund	VGT	64,470	191	$3,906,882	182
Vanguard	Vanguard Intermediate-Term Bond ETF	BIV	17,780	315	$1,339,367	265
Vanguard	Vanguard Large-Cap Index Fund	VV	88,195	166	$6,033,420	151
Vanguard	Vanguard Long-Term Bond ETF	BLV	12,185	353	$910,951	301
Vanguard	Vanguard Materials Index Fund	VAW	29,910	257	$2,646,437	211

(Continues)

Investment Manager	Fund Name	Ticker Symbol	20-Day Average Share Volume	Ranking of 20-Day Average Share Volume	20-Day Average $ Volume	Ranking of 20-Day Average $ Volume
Vanguard	Vanguard Mid Cap Growth Index Fund	VOT	51,860	209	$3,378,612	191
Vanguard	Vanguard Mid Cap Value Index Fund	VOE	31,120	254	$1,828,922	242
Vanguard	Vanguard Mid-Cap Index Fund	VO	60,490	196	$4,817,424	167
Vanguard	Vanguard Pacific Stock	VPL	104,690	153	$7,639,229	139
Vanguard	Vanguard REIT Fund	VNQ	273,645	93	$19,554,672	86
Vanguard	Vanguard Short-Term Bond ETF	BSV	45,900	224	$3,489,772	189
Vanguard	Vanguard Small-Cap Growth Index Fund	VBK	62,265	193	$4,621,931	170
Vanguard	Vanguard Small-Cap Index Fund	VB	110,790	144	$8,087,670	129
Vanguard	Vanguard Small-Cap Value Index Fund	VBR	65,205	190	$4,651,073	169
Vanguard	Vanguard Telecom Services Fund	VOX	41,770	230	$3,476,521	190
Vanguard	Vanguard Total Bond Market ETF	BND	83,950	170	$6,324,793	147
Vanguard	Vanguard Total Stock Market	VTI	485,789	71	$73,708,765	45
Vanguard	Vanguard Utilities Index Fund	VPU	25,555	274	$2,121,321	233
Vanguard	Vanguard Value Index Fund	VTV	258,235	95	$18,489,626	90
Vanguard	Vanguard Europe Pacific ETF	VEA	0	543	$0	543
Vanguard	Vanguard High Dividend Yield ETF	VYM	10,165	366	$555,517	351
Van Eck	Market Vectors Agribusiness	MOO	0	543	$0	543
Van Eck	Market Vectors Environment Services ETF	EVX	5,855	414	$313,945	404
Van Eck	Market Vectors Global Alternative Energy ETF	GEX	28,840	263	$1,407,248	260
Van Eck	Market Vectors Gold Miners ETF	GDX	2,204,377	36	$99,632,109	38
Van Eck	Market Vectors Nuclear Energy ETF	NLR	66,255	189	$2,749,583	209
Van Eck	Market Vectors Russia ETF	RSX	92,886	161	$4,206,807	177
Van Eck	Market Vectors Steel Index ETF	SLX	113,740	141	$9,214,077	118

Sponsor	Fund	Ticker				
Victoria Bay Asset Management	United States Natural Gas Fund	UNG	2,095,704	38	$80,200,496	44
Victoria Bay Asset Management	United States Oil Fund	USO	2,746,685	30	$170,859,188	27
WisdomTree	DEFA Dividend	DWM	46,880	219	$3,338,794	193
WisdomTree	DEFA High-Yielding Equity	DTH	20,525	301	$1,421,767	258
WisdomTree	Dividend Top 100	DTN	28,570	264	$1,737,630	244
WisdomTree	Europe Total Dividend	DEB	3,310	453	$230,211	426
WisdomTree	Europe High-Yielding Equity	DEW	7,550	393	$514,910	356
WisdomTree	Europe SmallCap Dividend	DFE	18,205	312	$1,261,607	271
WisdomTree	High-Yielding Equity	DHS	23,195	285	$1,368,505	264
WisdomTree	International Dividend Top 100	DOO	33,535	247	$2,455,433	217
WisdomTree	International LargeCap Dividend	DOL	14,175	341	$992,817	288
WisdomTree	International MidCap Dividend	DIM	22,920	288	$1,656,887	249
WisdomTree	International SmallCap Dividend	DLS	46,640	220	$3,264,800	195
WisdomTree	Japan Total Dividend	DXJ	8,855	380	$484,280	363
WisdomTree	Japan High Yielding Equity	DNL	5,985	410	$332,168	398
WisdomTree	Japan Small Cap	DFJ	19,235	307	$952,133	295
WisdomTree	LargeCap Dividend	DLN	29,695	258	$1,820,600	243
WisdomTree	MidCap Dividend	DON	28,885	262	$1,629,692	251
WisdomTree	Pacific Ex-Japan Dividend	DND	90,195	163	$7,659,359	138
WisdomTree	Pacific Ex-Japan High Yielding Equity	DNH	26,265	269	$2,030,022	237
WisdomTree	SmallCap Dividend	DES	33,900	246	$1,837,719	241
WisdomTree	Total Dividend	DTD	9,760	369	$589,797	345
WisdomTree	WisdomTree Earnings 500	EPS	7,060	396	$368,250	387
WisdomTree	WisdomTree Earnings Top 100	EEZ	3,055	458	$159,532	446
WisdomTree	WisdomTree International Basic Materials Sector	DBN	34,995	244	$1,393,676	261

(Continues)

Investment Manager	Fund Name	Ticker Symbol	20-Day Average Share Volume	Ranking of 20-Day Average Share Volume	20-Day Average $ Volume	Ranking of 20-Day Average $ Volume
WisdomTree	WisdomTree International Communications Sector	DGG	10,805	361	$380,444	384
WisdomTree	WisdomTree International Consumer Cyclical Sector	DPC	2,590	466	$81,999	473
WisdomTree	WisdomTree International Consumer Non-Cyclical Sector	DPN	14,115	342	$424,156	377
WisdomTree	WisdomTree International Energy Sector	DKA	21,640	295	$742,685	327
WisdomTree	WisdomTree International Financial Sector	DRF	13,870	344	$403,617	379
WisdomTree	WisdomTree International Health Care Sector	DBR	8,840	382	$248,934	424
WisdomTree	WisdomTree International Industrial Sector	DDI	14,805	337	$507,219	360
WisdomTree	WisdomTree International Technology Sector	DBT	18,765	310	$522,981	355
WisdomTree	WisdomTree International Utilities Sector	DBU	26,870	268	$888,054	304
WisdomTree	WisdomTree Intl. Real Estate	DRW	24,735	276	$1,313,426	268
WisdomTree	WisdomTree Low P/E	EZY	9,690	370	$498,066	361
WisdomTree	WisdomTree MidCap Earnings	EZM	4,085	438	$201,699	433
WisdomTree	WisdomTree SmallCap Earnings	EES	6,875	400	$315,700	403
WisdomTree	WisdomTree Total Earnings	EXT	3,560	445	$184,408	439
WisdomTree	WisdomTree Emerging Markets High-Yielding Equity ETF	DEM	29,470	259	$1,559,552	252
XShares	HealthShares Autoimmune-Inflation ETF	HHA	790	514	$18,336	518
XShares	HealthShares Cancer ETF	HHK	4,175	436	$126,043	457
XShares	HealthShares Cardiology Devices ETF	HHE	850	513	$22,789	511
XShares	HealthShares Composite ETF	HHQ	2,985	460	$84,446	472

XShares	HealthShares Dermatology and Wound Care ETF	HRW	955	506	$22,895	510
XShares	HealthShares Diagnostics ETF	HHD	31,700	250	$1,057,829	283
XShares	HealthShares Emerging Cancer ETF	HHJ	1,475	488	$31,019	502
XShares	HealthShares Enabling Technologies ETF	HHV	1,260	499	$39,564	490
XShares	HealthShares European Medical Products and Devices	HHT	115	537	$2,709	537
XShares	HealthShares European Drugs ETF	HRJ	895	510	$23,565	509
XShares	HealthShares GI/Gender Health ETF	HHU	240	533	$5,957	533
XShares	HealthShares Infectious Disease ETF	HHG	345	529	$7,662	529
XShares	HealthShares Metabolic-Endocrine Disorders ETF	HHM	870	512	$20,924	514
XShares	HealthShares Neuroscience ETF	HHN	1,115	503	$24,262	507
XShares	HealthShares Ophthalmology ETF	HHZ	1,245	500	$29,855	503
XShares	HealthShares Orthopedic Repair ETF	HHP	0	543	$0	543
XShares	HealthShares Patient Care Services ETF	HHB	4,970	426	$128,425	455
XShares	HealthShares Respiratory/Pulmonary ETF	HHR	970	505	$25,375	506
XShares	HealthShares Cardiology ETF	HRD	295	531	$6,921	532
XShares/ Adelante	Adelante RE Classics	ACK	0	543	$0	543
XShares/ Adelante	Adelante RE Composite	ACB	0	543	$0	543
XShares/ Adelante	Adelante RE Growth	AGV	0	543	$0	543
XShares/ Adelante	Adelante RE Shelter	AQS	0	543	$0	543
XShares/ Adelante	Adelante RE Value	AVU	20	542	$493	542
XShares/ Adelante	Adelante Shares RE Kings	AKB	0	543	$0	543

(*Continues*)

Investment Manager	Fund Name	Ticker Symbol	20-Day Average Share Volume	Ranking of 20-Day Average Share Volume	20-Day Average $ Volume	Ranking of 20-Day Average $ Volume
XShares/ Adelante	Adelante RE Yield Plus	ATY	0	543	$0	543
Ziegler Capital Mgt.	NYSE Arca Tech 100 ETF	NXT	1,355	495	$37,263	494

Explanation of columns:

Investment Manager: Company that manages the exchange-traded fund (ETF).

Fund Name: ETF.

Ticker Symbol: Symbol used to look up quotes from a broker or on http://finance.yahoo.com or other Web sites.

20-Day Average Share Volume: Average trading volume over the past 20 days.

Ranking of 20-Day Average Share Volume: Rank of ETF in trading volume with 1 for the highest volume and 543 for the lowest volume.

20-Day Average $ Volume: Average dollar trading volume (share price × volume) over the past 20 days.

Ranking of 20-Day Average $ Volume: Rank of ETF in dollar trading volume with 1 for the highest volume and 543 for the lowest volume.

Source: State Street Global Advisors.

Appendix B

SPDR STRATEGIES

S PDRs (Standard & Poor's depository receipts) are unique ETFs. We are all familiar with the S&P 500. There is a way to divide the S&P into nine sections. The market has leaders and laggards. You can load up on the leaders or simply choose those ETFs that meet your investment objectives.

Are you a savvy individual investor, financial advisor, or institutional investor? Then the following six strategies demonstrate how you can use Select Sector SPDRs to meet your investment objectives. These are the most common strategies, and they will allow you to "slice and dice" the S&P 500 for maximum return.[1]

Strategy 1: Building a Customized and Diversified Equity Portfolio That Matches Your Specific Objective

Select Sector SPDRs allow you to purchase the S&P 500 in pieces, enabling you to customize your portfolio. You can purchase the nine Select Sector SPDRs in weightings consistent with the S&P 500 or use your own weightings to meet specific investment goals.

Example

Your investment objective is to maximize yield within the large-cap equity portion of your portfolio. The utilities, materials, and energy sectors have historically been higher-yielding sectors of the S&P 500 Index. However, as shown in Figure B-1, their collective weight is only 16 percent of the index. By comparison, the lower-yielding, higher-volatility technology and consumer discretionary stocks represent approximately 28 percent of the S&P 500. The flexibility of Select Sector SPDRs allows you to create a customized portfolio that reduces exposures to the technology and

Select Sector SPDR	Trading Symbol	S&P Weighting as of 6/30/06	Your Portfolio Place Your Allocation Here)
Consumer Discretionary	XLY	10%	%
Consumer Staples	XLP	10%	%
Energy	XLE	10%	%
Financial	XLF	22%	%
Health Care	XLV	12%	%
Industrial	XLI	12%	%
Materials	XLB	3%	%
Technology	XLK	18%	%
Utilities	XLU	3%	%
		100%	%

Figure B-1   S&P Asset Allocation Recommendations as of June 30, 2006

consumer discretionary sectors while overweighting allocations to the higher-yielding utility, energy, and materials sectors. If you think energy will go up, simply increase that portion.

Strategy 2: Manage Risk through Asset Allocation by Sector

Asset allocation is the centerpiece of any long-term investment program. However, an asset allocation program that is too broad may not account properly for the level of risk that is embedded within each asset class. Incorporating sector diversification within your asset allocation strategy can help you create a portfolio that is more consistent with your risk and return objectives. Select Sector SPDRs and Ibbotson, a financial research firm, have created a risk profile questionnaire to assist in the portfolio construction process. (This questionnaire can be found at www.sectorspdr.com. Based on the questionnaire, investors are grouped into one of five investor profiles that matches their investment time horizon and ability to withstand losses in a portfolio.)

Example

You are a conservative investor whose investment time horizon and ability to withstand portfolio losses are limited. (See Figure B-2.) Because of your risk profile, your investments are primarily allocated toward fixed income and cash, with a smaller percentage devoted to equity. To complete the equity portion of your portfolio, you have

	Conservative	Moderate Conservative	Moderate	Moderate Aggressive	Aggressive
Domestic Equity	15%	30%	42%	53%	63%
Non-U.S. Equity	5%	11%	16%	22%	28%
Fixed Income	65%	49%	37%	25%	9%
Cash Equivalents	15%	10%	5%	0%	0%
Total	100%	100%	100%	100%	100%

Domestic Equity Breakdown	S&P 500	Conservative	Moderate Conservative	Moderate	Moderate Aggressive	Aggressive
Consumer Discretionary	10%	5%	8%	10%	13%	15%
Consumer Staples	10%	16%	13%	11%	9%	8%
Energy	10%	14%	11%	9%	7%	6%
Financial	22%	15%	17%	19%	20%	23%
Health Care	12%	10%	11%	13%	15%	16%
Industrial	12%	15%	13%	11%	10%	9%
Materials	3%	10%	8%	7%	6%	5%
Technology	18%	0%	11%	15%	17%	18%
Utilities	3%	15%	8%	5%	3%	0%
Total	100%	100%	100%	100%	100%	100%

Note: Underweight—underlined percentages; overweight—gray boxed percentages.

Figure B-2   Asset Allocation Models

a number of choices. Broad-based mutual funds may or may not be constructed with sectors and are consistent with your risk and return profile. In addition, you may not feel comfortable with the volatility of investing in individual stocks.

By incorporating this strategy, your risk profile is not only reflected in your allocation between stocks and bonds, but also by your equity sector allocation. You can periodically rebalance sector weightings so that your portfolio consistently matches your preferred level of risk.

Strategy 3: Rebalance Portfolio Based on Current Sector Weightings

As a prudent investor, you must make periodic appraisals of your portfolio. Investment positions may need to be adjusted in order for you to remain consistent with your investment objectives.

Example

A market rally in one sector can leave you exposed to a downturn in the next business cycle, and one is just around the corner. The run-up in technology stocks between 1998 and 2000 resulted in portfolios that no longer matched their original asset allocation guidelines. Figure B-3 shows the percentage of the S&P 500 that was represented by the technology sector at several intervals during the last few years.

Investors who bought the S&P 500 Index in 1998 were expecting approximately 17 percent exposure to technology stocks. However, by March 2000, technology stocks accounted for almost 40 percent of the market capitalization of the index. Within

Sector	Date	Percentage of S&P 500 (By Market Cap)
Technology (XLK)	12/31/98	17%
Technology (XLK)	03/31/00	39%
Technology (XLK)	06/30/01	24%
Technology (XLK)	09/30/02	16%

Figure B-3   Technology Sector (S&P 500)
Source: State Street Global Advisors (SSgA)

15 months from its peak, the technology index had already lost nearly half its value.

By owning the S&P 500 in pieces, you can use the individual Select Sector SPDRs to periodically rebalance your portfolio and ensure that you are not overly exposed to one segment of the market.

Strategy 4: Gain Diversified Access to Attractive Investment Themes

Business and economic cycles tend to move in stages, during which certain sectors are more likely to outperform than are other sectors. In addition, changes in interest rates, inflation, and tax laws can also create unique investment opportunities. Sector SPDRs low cost and flexibility make it easier to take advantage of these opportunities as they occur.

Examples

Utilities

The Jobs & Growth Tax Relief Reconciliation Act of 2003 (JGTRRA) that was signed into law in May 2003 increased the attractiveness of cash dividends. (However, there is no guarantee that the next administration will retain these tax breaks.) Coupled with low yields on fixed-income securities, the change in tax law focused a lot of attention on utility stocks, which have been historically the highest-yielding sector of the market. The utility

Select Sector SPDR provides a low-cost way to gain diversified access to utility stocks and offers yield-oriented investors an alternative to fixed-income investments.

Materials and Energy

Geopolitical events and changes in supply and demand can have profound effects on the prices of raw materials and commodities. Whether you are bullish or bearish on future price movements, you can use Select Sector SPDRs to gain concentrated access to specific market segments. Each Select Sector SPDR is composed of a basket of securities within the same market sector and therefore allows you to take advantage of an attractive investment theme in a way that may offer less volatility than do individual stocks.

Strategy 5: Enhance After-Tax Returns with Tax Swaps

Select Sector SPDRs can help you manage a more tax-efficient investment portfolio.

Examples

Taking individual stock losses while maintaining sector exposure

You are holding a large position in Wal-Mart, and your portfolio is dangerously out of balance. Furthermore, the Wal-Mart shares you purchased happen to be trading below your purchase price. Since Wal-Mart is one of the largest components of the consumer staples SPDR, you can: (1) sell your Wal-Mart stock, (2) realize the loss, and (3) buy the Wal-Mart-heavy ETF to maintain your exposure to Wal-Mart and to that sector in general. Then, after 30 days, you can choose to buy back some or all of your Wal-Mart position and sell the ETF, or maintain your position in the consumer staples SPDR for more diversified access to the sector.

Swapping one ETF for another ETF or mutual fund

Sell an ETF, a closed-end fund, or a mutual fund currently trading below purchase price, realize the loss and maintain similar market exposure by purchasing the appropriate Select Sector SPDR. For example, you currently own a technology mutual fund that is trading below its original purchase price. You can sell the fund, realize the loss, and buy the technology Select Sector SPDR to maintain similar exposure.

Strategy 6: Use ETF Flexibility to Hedge Concentrated Positions

The use of incentive stock options as a form of compensation has created a growing segment of investors with a large percentage of their portfolios tied up in an individual stock. Furthermore, restrictions may be in place that prohibit or limit transactions on the stock itself to reduce its exposure.

The transparency and concentration of Select Sector SPDRs make them excellent hedging vehicles. Each Select Sector SPDR can be borrowed and sold short to minimize the industry risk of a particular stock. Options are also available on each Select Sector SPDR and can be used to lock in gains or minimize downside risk.

Appendix C

WEB SITES

For additional ETF information, try the following Web sites.

www.finance.yahoo.com

Most major trading firms have their own in-house research departments. If you could peek over the shoulders of their traders to see what they actually look at, you'd see a lot of them scrolling through Yahoo's finance pages. Yahoo! was one of the early big drivers of the Nasdaq phenomenon of the late 1990s, and though the name may have seemed silly, its commitment to research and hard useful information was very serious. That's still true today. The Yahoo! Finance Web site exhibits an intuitive understanding of exactly what the trader needs. The most important information is easiest to find. This is an excellent resource for traders of any experience level and should be your first stop every morning. (See Figures C-1, C-2, and C-3.)

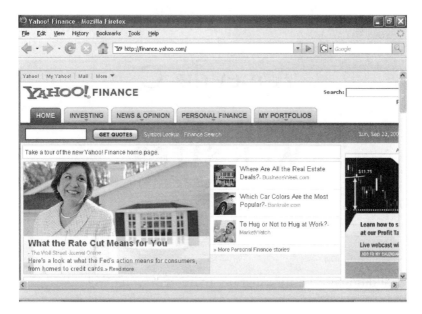

Figure C-1   Yahoo! Finance Home Page

Figure C-2   Yahoo! Finance Investing Categories

Figure C-3   Yahoo! Finance ETF Center Opening Page

www.etfguide.com

One way to describe ETFGuide is that it's one big advertisement for itself although it is couched as a general information Web site about ETFs. Many of the links take the reader back to various ways to subscribe to an array of services offered by ETFGuide. To be fair, links are also provided to many of the other producers of ETF content on the Web. The tabbed pages along the top of the site take the reader to information of only the most cursory kind. (See Figure C-4.) For example, the News & Commentary tab contained only one story that was less than a month old on the day we visited.

Figure C-4 ETFGuide Home Page

www.etfconnect.com

ETFConnect is a subsite of Nuveen Investments. As such, it is a brokerage-owned Web site. Yes, it's packed with (very conservatively presented) information. But remember, when you come here, you are browsing to buy. The reader can navigate to ETFConnect directly, or link to it from the regular Nuveen site. Nuveen, a lovely old-line investment company, was established in Chicago in 1898. It went public in 1992.

The ETFConnect Web site provides useful charting and portfolio-tracking tools for following your ETFs. Education tabs link the reader to detailed explanations about the various types of ETFs (including Treasury note exchange-traded notes [ETNs]), as

Figure C-5 ETFConnect Home Page

well as the tax consequences of each. (See Figure C-5.) Overall, this is a very useful site.

www.indexuniverse.com

IndexUniverse was originally intended to be a data and information complement to *Active Index Investing* by Steven A. Schoenfeld (Wiley, 2004). The site has expanded considerably in the intervening years. It now hosts an international cast of regular contributors on a wide variety of index-related subjects, including a fine array of ETF-specific information. The blogs offer links to literate and

Figure C-6 IndexUniverse Home Page

fairly in-depth discussions of timely investment and market-related topics. The Advanced/Power Search (from the home page click on ETFs and then click the "Advanced Index/ETF Data Search" box) tool permits the investor to specify hundreds of category combinations to pinpoint his or her research target. The site is well put together and easy to use. Overall, this is a very professional site that even a novice can put to effective use. (See Figure C-6.)

www.finra.org

The Securities Exchange Act of 1934 mandated a self-regulatory organization to provide oversight of all securities firms doing business with the public. As of July 26, 2007, that organization is FINRA (Financial Industry Regulatory Authority). FINRA is the successor to the NASD (National Association of Securities Dealers). It was formed from the consolidation of the enforcement branches of the New York Stock Exchange and NASD. (See Figure C-7.)

Its mandate, according to SEC chairman Chris Cox (SEC Press Release 2007-151): "The consolidation of NASD's and NYSE's member firm regulatory functions is an important step toward making our self-regulatory system not only more efficient, but more effective in protecting investors. The Commission will work closely with FINRA to eliminate unnecessary duplicative regulation, including consolidating and strengthening what until now have

Figure C-7   Financial Industry Regulatory Authority (FINRA) Home Page

been two different member rulebooks and two different enforcement systems."

www.amex.com/etf/EtMain.jsp

The American Stock Exchange likes to remind us that ETFs were
born, raised, and spend most of their quality time at the Amex.
While we are not sure about quality time, we do know that this
exchange has been a pioneer in developing ETFs. Just about any
question the public has concerning ETFs can be answered. Plus
from time to time Amex offers a hotline where you can call in and
have questions immediately answered. If you want to teach yourself about ETFs, this is the place to start. (See Figure C-8.)

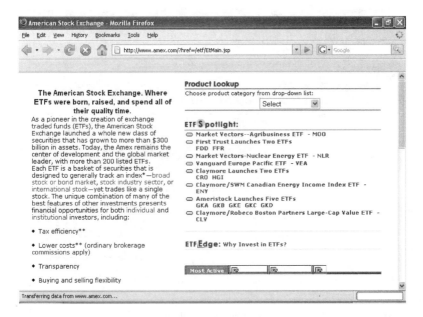

Figure C-8   American Stock Exchange Home Page

www.fidelity.com

While not known as an educational site, Fidelity brokerage's ETF section offers a way to construct an ETF portfolio using Fidelity's "lens method," which breaks the market down into different groupings. The ETF section is accessed through the Mutual Funds link under Our Products on the home page. Traders should understand the basics of ETFs before tackling this site. (See Figures C-9, C-10, and C-11.)

Most brokerage firms offer full service. And though the commissions may be higher, initial orders should be placed with the assistance of a broker.

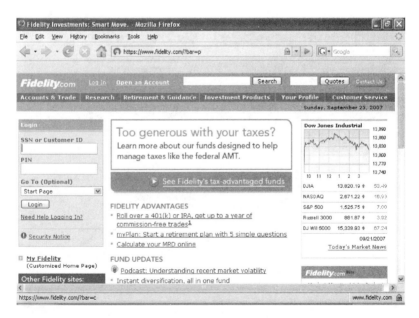

Figure C-9   Fidelity.com Home Page

Figure C-10   Fidelity.com Mutual Funds Product Opening Page

Figure C-11   Fidelity.com ETF Opening Page

Figure C-12 Gecko Software Home Page

www.geckosoftware.com

Gecko Software is located in Logan, Utah, and offers a unique end-of-day charting program for ETFs. As the number of ETFs keeps growing, the firm updates the database every evening. The charting program allows the novice trader to easily identify support and resistance points. This is a perfect site for the first-time stock and ETF trader. However, this is only an end-of-day program and not meant for day trading. (See Figure C-12.)

www.investors.com/etf

Yes, *Investor's Business Daily* has a Web site. (See Figure C-13.) The daily column on ETFs is a great read. The newspaper's coverage of

Figure C-13 *Investor's Business Daily* Web Site Home Page

all the markets assists traders in choosing an ETF portfolio that matches their investment objectives. If you are new to investing, a subscription to *Investor's Business Daily* will give you a perspective and the basics of a trading system.

www.lrosenberg.com

LRosenberg Consulting offers mentoring, training, and seminars dealing with ETF strategies and investments, including customized newsletters and podcasts.

www.seekingalpha.com

Seeking Alpha's Web site offers a forum for traders and investors to communicate. After readers qualify for postings, they can choose the type of financial information they want. About 10 percent of the postings relate to ETFs. This site was one of the first to tell readers to short ETFs dealing with home builders. "Alpha" is a term used to describe a means of trading where traders attempt to beat the market return. (See Figure C-14.)

With Seeking Alpha you can receive e-mails directly on investment issues. Be prepared to have your mailbox socked daily. Once people meet the site's requirements, they can post on Alpha. There is a plethora of sharp, intelligent investors out there. They may not

Figure C-14   Seeking Alpha Home Page

Figure C-15 Cheat the Street Home Page

be celebrities on CNBC, but their track records are enviable. One word of caution: watch out for the occasional scam.

www.cheatthestreet.com

The world of ETF options is still evolving. Cheat the Street is a site that has a continuing education program where you can learn the basics of options. From there traders can learn how to construct sophisticated strategies with ETF options. (See Figure C-15.)

www.vanguard.com

This site is a favorite of the authors and a good place to start your ETF search. Particularly attractive are its low expenses.

www.optionsxpress.com

ETF trading at optionsXpress is robust both in terms of the number of funds available to trade and the range of free analytical tools on hand to evaluate them. The optionsXpress site boasts its own "ETF hub" where investors can categorize ETFs based on sector, size, or geographical location. (See Figure C-16.) This hub also allows investors to access technical charts and view Morningstar information, including past fund performance, expenses, and fees.

Figure C-16 optionsXpress ETF Hub

The unique optionsXpress Screener tool enables investors to scan the market for ETFs based on specific parameters such as style, sector, or region. The site even offers a free on-demand webinar— "ETFs vs. Mutual Funds"—designed specifically to help investors decide if ETFs are a good fit for their investment portfolios.

ENDNOTES

Chapter 1

1. The Investment Company Act of 1940 describes the types of Investment Companies.

CLASSIFICATION OF INVESTMENT COMPANIES
SEC. 4. 80a–4 For the purposes of this title, investment companies are divided into three principal classes, defined as follows: (1) "Face-amount certificate company" means an investment company which is engaged or proposes to engage in the business of issuing face-amount certificates of the installment type, or which has been engaged in such business and has any such certificate outstanding. (2) "Unit investment trust" means an investment company which (A) is organized under a trust indenture, contract of custodianship or agency, or similar instrument, (B) does not have a board of directors, and (C) issues only redeemable securities, each of which represents an undivided interest in a unit of specified securities; but does not include a voting trust. (3) "Management company" means any investment company other than a face-amount certificate company or a unit investment trust.

SUBCLASSIFICATION OF MANAGEMENT COMPANIES

SEC. 5. 80a–5 (A) For the purposes of this title, management companies are divided into open-end and closed-end companies, defined as follows: (1) "Open-end company" means a management company which is offering for sale or has outstanding any redeemable security of which it is the issuer. (2) "Closed-end company" means any management company other than an open-end company.

(B) Management companies are further divided into diversified companies and non-diversified companies, defined as follows: (1) "Diversified company" means a management company which meets the following requirements: At least 75 per centum of the value of its total assets is represented by cash and cash items (including receivables), Government securities, securities of other investment companies, and other securities for the purposes of this calculation limited in respect of any one issuer to an amount not greater in value than 5 per centum of the value of the total assets of such management company and to not more than 10 per centum of the outstanding voting securities of such issuer. (2) "Non-diversified company" means any management company other than a diversified company.

2. "(2) 'Unit investment trust' means an investment company which (A) is organized under a trust indenture, contract of custodianship or agency, or similar instrument, (B) does not have a board of directors, and (C) issues only redeemable securities, each of which represents an undivided interest in a unit of specified securities; but does not include a voting trust." — Investment Company Act of 1940 SEC. 4 80a–4.

3. NYSE Regulation. "NYSE Informed Investor: What You Should Know about Exchange-Traded Funds," 2006; State Street Global Advisors, "SSGA ETF Data Spreadsheet," www.etfconnect.com/documents/ ssga.xls, October 1, 2007.

4. Cliff Weber, senior vice president for the ETF Marketplace at the American Stock Exchange, in "Experts Talk Strategy on ETFs," Exchange Traded

Report: Featuring News and Analysis on Global Exchanges and ETFs [sic],
A Supplement to *Wall Street Letter* (an online newsletter of *Institutional
Investor*), November 2006, p. 21.

5. Indexes that are weighted by market capitalization tend to overweight the
overvalued issues and underweight the undervalued issues, which reduces
the possibility for performance in the long run, according to Robert
Arnott. Source: Kathleen McBride, "Fundamental Indexing Goes Main
Street: Breaking the Link between Market Cap and Index Weighting,"
Investment Advisor, November 2006, p. 86.

6. Admittedly, investors could also short various stock indexes on futures
markets, but those contracts may be too large or unsuitable for many
investors.

7. Investment Company Act of 1940, Section 12(a)(3).

Chapter 2

1. Note that futures and commodities are considered securities.

2. A regulated investment company (RIC) needs to meet the following
diversification requirements (among other requirements) to prevent
taxation of its earnings at the corporate level:

    A. At the end of each quarter of the RIC's tax year, at least 50% of the value
of its assets must be invested in the following items.
- Cash and cash items (including receivables),
- Government securities,
- Securities of other RICs, and
- Securities of other issuers, except that the investment in a single issuer
of securities may not exceed 5% of the value of the RIC's assets or 10%
of the outstanding voting securities of the issuer (except as provided in
section 851(e)). See sections 851(b)(3) and 851(c).

B. At the end of each quarter of the RIC's tax year, no more than 25% of the value of the RIC's assets may be invested in the securities of:

- A single issuer (excluding government securities or securities of other RICs),
- Two or more issuers controlled by the RIC and engaged in the same or related trades or businesses, or
- One or more qualified publicly traded partnerships as defined in section 851(h). See sections 851(b)(3) and 851(c) for further details.

Source: IRS Instructions for form 1120.

Chapter 3

1. SPDR stands for Standard & Poor's depository receipts—the first ETF. It is a unit investment trust that tracks the S&P 500 Index and trades on the American Stock Exchange. It was launched in 1993.

2. According to the streetTRACKS Gold Trust prospectus, "Baskets may be created or redeemed only by Authorized Participants. Each Authorized Participant must (1) be a registered broker-dealer or other securities market participant such as a bank or other financial institution which is not required to register as a broker-dealer to engage in securities transactions, (2) be a participant in the Depository Trust Company or DTC Participant, (3) have entered into an agreement with the Trustee and the Sponsor, or the Participant Agreement, and (4) have established an unallocated gold account with the Custodian, or the Authorized Participant Unallocated Account. The Participant Agreement provides the procedures for the creation and redemption of Baskets and for the delivery of gold and any cash required for such creations or redemptions." Source: streetTRACKS Gold Trust, *Form S-3 Registration Statement under the Securities Act of 1933*, filed November 30, 2006, p. 5.

Chapter 4

1. Securities and Exchange Commission, "SEC Concept Release: Actively Managed Exchange-Traded Funds," Section I.B. 17 CFR Part 270. (Release NO. IC-25258; File No. S7-20-01) RIN 3235-AI-35, www.sec.gov/rules/concept/ic-25258.htm, November 8, 2001.

2. Investment Company Act of 1940, Section Ib. The complete list of conditions follows:

   (1) when investors purchase, pay for, exchange, receive dividends upon, vote, refrain from voting, sell, or surrender securities issued by investment companies without adequate, accurate, and explicit information, fairly presented, concerning the character of such securities and the circumstances, policies, and financial responsibility of such companies and their management;

   (2) when investment companies are organized, operated, managed, or their portfolio securities are selected, in the interest of directors, officers, investment advisers, depositors, or other affiliated persons thereof, in the interest of underwriters, brokers, or dealers, in the interest of special classes of their security holders, or in the interest of other investment companies or persons engaged in other lines of business, rather than in the interest of all classes of such companies' security holders;

   (3) when investment companies issue securities containing inequitable or discriminatory provisions, or fail to protect the preferences and privileges of the holders of their outstanding securities;

   (4) when the control of investment companies is unduly concentrated through pyramiding or inequitable methods of control, or is inequitably distributed, or when investment companies are managed by irresponsible persons;

   (5) when investment companies, in keeping their accounts, in maintaining reserves, and in computing their earnings and the asset value of their outstanding securities, employ unsound or misleading methods, or are not subjected to adequate independent scrutiny;

(6)   when investment companies are reorganized, become inactive, or change the character of their business, or when the control or management thereof is transferred, without the consent of their security holders;

(7)   when investment companies by excessive borrowing and the issuance of excessive amounts of senior securities increase unduly the speculative character of their junior securities; or

(8)   when investment companies operate without adequate assets or reserves.

3.   "As a specific benchmark, the General Partner will endeavor to place USOF's trades in Oil Futures Contracts and other Oil Interests and otherwise manage USOF's investments so that A will be within plus/minus 10 percent of B, where:

- A is the average daily change in USOF's NAV for any period of 30 successive Valuation Days, and

- B is the average daily change in the price of the Benchmark Oil Futures Contract over the same period."

Source: United States Oil Fund, LP, *Prospectus*, February 2, 2007, p. 1.

4.   United States Oil Fund, LP, *Prospectus*, February 2, 2007, p. 6.

5.   United States Oil Fund, LP, *Prospectus*, February 2, 2007, p. 17.

6.   United States Oil Fund, LP, *Prospectus*, February 2, 2007, p. 16.

7.   United States Oil Fund, LP, *Prospectus*, February 2, 2007, p. 16.

8.   United States Oil Fund, LP, *Prospectus*, February 2, 2007, p. 17.

9.   United States Oil Fund, LP, *Prospectus*, February 2, 2007, p. 24.

10. United States Oil Fund, LP, *Prospectus*, February 2, 2007, p. 18.

11. IRS Instructions for form 1120, p. 12.

Eligibility. To qualify to make the election, the RIC must meet the following requirements:

- More than 50% of the value of the RIC's total assets at the end of the tax year must consist of stock or securities in foreign corporations.

- The RIC must meet the holding period requirements of section 901(k) with respect to its common and preferred stock. If the RIC fails to meet these holding period requirements, the election that allows an RIC to pass through to its shareholders the foreign tax credits for foreign taxes paid by the RIC is disallowed. Although the foreign taxes paid may not be taken as a credit by either the RIC or the shareholder, they are still deductible at the fund level."

Chapter 5

1. A simple average of two stocks is calculated in the following manner: Let

$$x_1 = \text{Price of Stock 1}$$
$$x_2 = \text{Price of Stock 2}$$
$$\bar{x} = \text{Average}$$
$$\bar{x} = \frac{x_1 + x_2}{2}$$

2. Shares in float are those available to investors, as opposed to all of the company's shares. This excludes shares that are held by shareholders who are interested in maintaining control of the company (such as board members or corporate founders) as well as government agencies or other publicly traded companies. (*Source:* Standard & Poor's: *S&P U.S. Indices Methodology,* January 2007, p. 16.)

A weighted average of two stocks is calculated in the following manner: Let

$$x_1 = \text{Price of Stock 1}$$
$$w_1 = \text{Weight of Stock 1}$$
$$x_2 = \text{Price of Stock 2}$$
$$w_2 = \text{Weight of Stock 2}$$
$$\bar{x}_w = \text{Weighted Average}$$
$$\bar{x}_w = \frac{(w_1 x_1) + (w_2 x_2)}{w_1 + w_2}$$

Chapter 6

1. *New Oxford American Dictionary*, 2nd ed., definition for "growth stock."
2. *New Oxford American Dictionary*, 2nd ed., definition for "value stock."
3. As of April 30, 2007, there were five U.S. core funds and one in Japan in the worldwide totals. (*Source:* State Street Global Advisors ETF Data Spreadsheet, which is available at www.etfconnect.com/industry/industrylink.asp.)
4. Barclays Global Investors, *Prospectus: iShares Bond Funds*, July 1, 2006, p. 6.

Chapter 7

1. Whipsaw definition from Investopedia, www.investopedia.com/terms/w/whipsaw.asp, accessed on December 14, 2007.
2. Special thanks to Bob Hunt from The Pattern Trapper for his assistance. Free material is available at www.patterntrapper.com.

Chapter 15

1. Cyprus and Malta will join the eurozone on January 1, 2008.

Appendix B

1. Much of the information contained in this appendix was distributed to the attendees at the June 14–15, 2007, Institutional Advisors Exchange-Traded Fund Product Summit Conference held in New York City and sponsored by Financial Research Associates, LLC. In addition, special permission was received from Select Sector SPDRs (www.sectorspdr.com) for use of the specific strategies identified in this section.

BIBLIOGRAPHY

Abramowitz, Pam, "ETFs Still Going Strong—Thanks to the Little Guy," *Exchange Traded Report*, a sponsored supplement to *Wall Street Letter*, a publication of *Institutional Investor News*, November 2006, pp. 12–17.

Amenc, Noël, Felix Goltz, and Véronique Le Sourd, *Assessing the Quality of Stock Market Indices: Requirements for Asset Allocation and Performance Measurement*, EDHEC Risk and Asset Management Research Centre, September 2006.

Bodie, Zvi, Alex Kane, and Alan J. Marcus, *Investments*, 5th ed. (New York: McGraw-Hill Irwin, 2002).

Bogle, John C., *Common Sense on Mutual Funds: New Imperatives for the Intelligent Investor* (New York: John Wiley & Sons, 1999).

Currier, Chet, "Index Fund Pioneer Sees Trouble on Horizon," *The Journal News*, December 10, 2006, p. 5D.

Delegge, Ronald, "ETF Reporter," *Research*, March 2007, p. 27.

Dieckmann, Raimar, "Retail Certificates: A German Success Story," Deutsche Bank Research. Frankfurt Am Main, Germany, March 19, 2007, www.dbresearch.de/PROD/DBR_INTERNET_DE-PROD/PROD0000000000208184.pdf.

"Experts Talk Strategy on ETFs," *Exchange Traded Report*, a sponsored supplement to *Wall Street Letter*, a publication of *Institutional Investor News*, November 2006, pp. 20–25.

Gardner, Grant, Andra Kondra, and Mahesh Pritamani, "Russell Indexes: Examining the Frequency of U.S. Reconstitution,"

Investment Policy & Research, Frank Russell Company, July 6, 2001.

Gastineau, Gary L., *The Exchange Traded Funds Manual* (New York: John L. Wiley & Sons, 2002).

Gastineau, Gary L., "Re: Actively-Managed Exchange-Traded Funds. File No. S7-20-01." Letter from Gary L. Gastineau of Nuveen Investments to Jonathan Katz, Secretary of the Securities and Exchange Commission, in response to the commission's request for comment on issues relating to actively managed exchange-traded funds (ETFs) ["SEC Concept Release: Actively Managed Exchange-Traded Funds." SEC Release Number IC-25258; File S7-20-01 (November 8, 2001), 66 Fed. Reg. 575614 (Nov. 15, 2001)]. January 14, 2002.

Internal Revenue Service, *Instructions for Form 1120-RIC: U.S. Income Tax Return for Regulated Investment Companies*, Internal Revenue Service, 2005.

International Organization of Securities Commissions, "IOSCO Membership and Committees Lists," International Organization of Securities Commissions, www.iosco.org, accessed on April 2, 2007.

Investment Company Act of 1940, August 22, 1940, ch. 686, title I, 54 Stat. 789 (15 U.S.C. 80a–1 et seq.) Short title, see 15 U.S.C. 80a–51.

Investment Company Institute, *A Guide to Understanding Mutual Funds*. Investment Company Institute, 2006, available online at www.ici.org.

iShares, *iShares Bond Funds Prospectus*, July 1, 2006.

iShares, *iShares Cohen & Steers Realty Majors Index Fund Prospectus*, August 1, 2006.

iShares, *iShares Dow Jones Series Prospectus*, August 1, 2006.

iShares, *iShares MSCI Series Prospectus*, January 1, 2007.

iShares, *iShares Morningstar Series Prospectus*, August 1, 2006.

iShares, *iShares Russell Series Prospectus*, August 1, 2006.

iShares, *iShares S&P Series Prospectus*, August 1, 2006 (revised September 12, 2006).

Jain, Siddharth, *Introduction of KBW Regional Banking Index and KBW Mortgage Finance Index*, Report published by Keefe, Bruyette, and Woods, Inc., July 22, 2005, http://media.corporate-ir.net/media_files/irol/20/202535/news/KBWIndices_072505.pdf.

McBride, Kathleen, "Fundamental Indexing Goes Main Street: Breaking the Link between Market Cap and Index Weighting," *Investment Advisor*, November 2006, pp. 86–87.

Morningstar, *Morningstar Indexes Methodology Overview*, 2004, http://corporate.morningstar.com/us/documents/MethodologyDocuments/FactSheets/MorningstarIndex_FactSheet.pdf.

The New Oxford American Dictionary, 2nd ed., Erin McKean, editor (New York: Oxford University Press, 2005).

NYSE Regulation, "NYSE Informed Investor: What You Should Know About Exchange Traded Funds," New York Stock Exchange, 2006, www.nyse.com.

PDR Services, *Standard & Poor's Depository Receipts Prospectus*, January 26, 2007.

Standard & Poor's, "S&P U.S. Indices Methodology," report, January 2007, www.indices.standardandpoors.com.

State Street Global Advisors, *Select Sector SPDRs Prospectus*, January 31, 2007.

State Street Global Advisors, "SSGA ETF Data Spreadsheet," www.etfconnect.com/documents/ssga.xls.

streetTRACKS Gold Trust, *Form S-3 Registration Statement under the Securities Act of 1933*, November 30, 2006.

Swensen, David F., *Pioneering Portfolio Management: An Unconventional Approach to Institutional Investment* (New York: The Free Press, 2000).

Swensen, David F., *Unconventional Success: A Fundamental Approach to Personal Investment* (New York: The Free Press, 2006).

United States Oil Fund, LP, *Prospectus*, February 2, 2007.

U.S. Securities and Exchange Commission, "Concept Release: Actively Managed Exchange-Traded Funds; Release No. IC-25258," U.S. Securities and Exchange Commission, www.sec.gov/rules/concept/ic-25258.htm.

U.S. Securities and Exchange Commission, "Invest Wisely: An Introduction to Mutual Funds," brochure published by the U.S. Securities and Exchange Commission, www.sec.gov/investor/pubs/inwsmf.htm.

Van Eck Global, *Market Vectors Prospectus*, April 9, 2007.

INDEX

ABOUT THE AUTHORS

Laurence M. Rosenberg began his career in the financial services industry in 1961 at the Chicago Board of Trade. In 1965 Mr. Rosenberg became a member of the Chicago Mercantile Exchange (CME).

His commitment to active membership at the Chicago Mercantile Exchange brought him to the chair of many committees that are integral to the exchange and its relationships with both the public and government. Mr. Rosenberg served on the CME board of directors for 24 years and, during this period, served the maximum allowable three terms as chairman.

He also served as first vice chairman of the board for 6 years and was a member of the executive committee for 20 years, during which time he held the chair for three terms. Mr. Rosenberg also served as chief legislative liaison and as chairman of the international steering and strategic planning committees. He was also elected senior policy advisor to the board. Mr. Rosenberg has held several senior financial services management positions over the past 35 years. Currently Mr. Rosenberg runs LRosenberg Consulting, a financial services consulting company based in Chicago.

He is a graduate of Lake Forest College with a degree in economics, and he served in the U.S. Army Counter Intelligence Corps.

Neal T. Weintraub is a former floor trader who now trades securities and futures through Fidelity and World Wide Chicago. He currently teaches fundamental analysis, fed policy, and spread trading at the Chicago Mercantile Exchange and gives ETF seminars for investors in Chicago and Singapore.

Mr. Weintraub's corporate experience includes MTV, The Disney Channel, Nickelodeon, and The Chicago Board of Trade, where he directed marketing and sales activities. He is the author of *Tricks of the Floor Trader*, *Trading Chicago Style*, and *The Weintraub Day Trader*.

Mr. Weintraub received a direct commission as an officer in the U.S. Naval Reserve.

Andrew S. Hyman is marketing director at Fiske Walter Capital Management, a commodity trading advisor. Before that, he worked at the Global Energy, Utilities, and Mining Group at PricewaterhouseCoopers, where he served as a consultant and knowledge manager. He also does institutional and public seminars on exchange-traded funds.

Mr. Hyman recently served as the cochairman of the Chicago steering committee of the Professional Risk Managers International Association (PRMIA). He has been a member of the steering committee since its inception. He was the lead author of *Energy Risk Management: A Primer for the Utility Industry* and coauthored *America's Electric Utilities: Past, Present and Future* and *The Water Business: Understanding the Water and Wastewater Industry*, all published by Public Utilities Reports. He also contributed to

Weather Derivatives: An Introduction published by the ICFAI University Press in India.

Mr. Hyman has a B.S. degree in applied physics from Tufts University, a master of public policy degree from Vanderbilt University, and a master of arts in geography degree from the University of Illinois at Urbana-Champaign. He lives in Chicago with his wife, Adiel, and his daughter, Julia.